REA: THE TEST PREP AP® TEACHERS RECOMMEND

AP® U.S. HISTORY CRASH COURSE®

By Larry Krieger, M.A., M.A.T.

Research & Education Association
www.rea.com

Research & Education Association
258 Prospect Plains Road
Cranbury, New Jersey 08512
Email: info@rea.com

AP® U.S. HISTORY CRASH COURSE®, 5th Edition

Printed in the United States of America

Library of Congress Control Number 2019948986

ISBN-13: 978-0-7386-1269-0
ISBN-10: 0-7386-1269-3

A20

AP® U.S. HISTORY CRASH COURSE TABLE OF CONTENTS

About Our Book v
A Letter from Our Author vi
About Our Author viii

INTRODUCTION

Chapter 1 Seven Keys for Success on the AP® U.S. History Exam 1
Chapter 2 Key Terms 9

CONTENT REVIEW

UNIT 1 | PERIOD 1: 1491–1607 18
Chapter 3 A New World 19

UNIT 2 | PERIOD 2: 1607–1754 25
Chapter 4 English North America 27
Chapter 5 Key Trends in Colonial Life and Thought 35

UNIT 3 | PERIOD 3: 1754–1800 40
Chapter 6 Severing Ties with Great Britain 41
Chapter 7 Creating a New National Government 49
Chapter 8 The Federalist Era 59

UNIT 4 | PERIOD 4: 1800–1848 65
Chapter 9 The Early Republic 67
Chapter 10 The Age of Jackson 75
Chapter 11 The Old South 83
Chapter 12 A Burst of Change 89
Chapter 13 Religion, Reform, and Romanticism 97

UNIT 5 | PERIOD 5: 1844–1877 105
Chapter 14 Territorial Expansion 107
Chapter 15 The Road to Disunion 113
Chapter 16 The Civil War 121
Chapter 17 Reconstruction and the New South 129

UNIT 6 | PERIOD 6: 1865–1898 141
Chapter 18 The New West 143
Chapter 19 Industry and Labor 151
Chapter 20 Urban America 161

UNIT 7 | PERIOD 7: 1890–1945 169
Chapter 21 Populists and Progressives 171
Chapter 22 Becoming a World Power 183
Chapter 23 The New Era 195
Chapter 24 The Great Depression and the New Deal 205
Chapter 25 The United States and the World 217

UNIT 8 | PERIOD 8: 1945–1980 229
Chapter 26 Truman, the Cold War, and the Second Red Scare 231
Chapter 27 The Eisenhower Era 243
Chapter 28 The 1960s 255
Chapter 29 The 1970s 269

UNIT 9 | PERIOD 9: 1980–PRESENT 281
Chapter 30 The Reagan–Bush Era 283
Chapter 31 Key Events and Trends in Post–Cold War America 291

TEST-TAKING STRATEGIES AND PRACTICE QUESTIONS
Chapter 32 Strategies for the Multiple-Choice Questions 299
Chapter 33 Practice Multiple-Choice Questions 307
Chapter 34 Strategies for the Short-Answer Questions 323
Chapter 35 Strategies for the Document-Based Essay Question 329
Chapter 36 Strategies for the Long-Essay Question 339

PRACTICE TEST .... ***www.rea.com/studycenter***

ABOUT OUR BOOK

REA's ***AP® U.S. History Crash Course*** is designed for the last-minute studier or any student who wants a quick refresher on the AP® course. The ***Crash Course*** is based on the 2019–2020 AP® U.S. History course and exam and focuses only on the topics tested, so you can make the most of your study time.

Written by a nationally recognized APUSH test expert, our ***Crash Course*** gives you a concise review of the major concepts and important topics tested on the AP® U.S. History exam.

- **Chapters 1 and 2** offer you our **Keys for Success**, so you can tackle the exam with confidence and include a glossary of **Key Terms** that you absolutely must know.
- **Chapters 3 through 31** cover **Key Content Review** in chronological order that focus on all of the periods and topical themes found in the AP® U.S. History course framework.
- **Chapters 32 through 36** give you specific **Test-Taking Strategies** to help you conquer the multiple-choice and free-response questions, along with AP®-style practice questions to prepare you for what you'll see on test day.

ABOUT OUR ONLINE PRACTICE EXAM

How ready are you for the AP® U.S. History exam? Find out by taking **REA's online practice exam** available at *www.rea.com/studycenter*. This test features automatic scoring, detailed explanations of all answers, and diagnostic score reporting that will help you identify your strengths and weaknesses so you'll be ready on exam day.

Whether you use this book throughout the school year or as a refresher in the final weeks before the exam, REA's ***Crash Course*** will show you how to study efficiently and strategically, so you can boost your score.

Good luck on your AP® U.S. History exam!

A LETTER FROM OUR AUTHOR

The first four editions of *AP® U.S. History Crash Course* blazed a new trail in AP® test prep. As an experienced APUSH teacher, I chose not to write a book containing an endless catalog of names, dates, places, people, and events. Instead, I focused on a predictable set of topics that generated most of the exam questions. This strategy worked, as readers achieved high exam scores.

A REVISED FRAMEWORK AND EXAM

After a lengthy process of evaluation and review, the College Board released a new APUSH Framework along with a redesigned APUSH exam that debuted in 2016. The new Framework includes a detailed 25-page "Concept Outline" covering 9 periods from 1491 to the present. With the release of the *2019–2020 Course and Exam Description*, the College Board further refined and clarified the scope of the course and exam.

Today's APUSH course is more than just a chronological sequence of required topics. A careful analysis of all the released exam questions reveals that the test-taker should no longer rely on knowing only isolated facts. Instead, questions now test a specific and predictable set of historical thinking skills. These skills include the ability to make meaningful connections between different historical developments and to evaluate the impact and importance of key turning point events and movements.

THE UNIQUE CRASH COURSE APPROACH

The College Board's shift from a fact-driven exam based upon a brief topical outline to a skill-driven exam based upon a detailed concept outline required a new *Crash Course* approach. As always, my mission is to help you excel on the APUSH exam. I am very proud to tell you that this new 5th edition includes the following unique features:

1. Selective Content

The 5th edition is carefully aligned with the Framework's Concept Outline. If a topic is in the Concept Outline, I cover it; if it isn't in the Concept Outline, I omit it. As a result, you will find detailed coverage of expected topics such as the Chesapeake and New England colonies as well as unexpected topics such as the British West Indian colonies. But you will not find a discussion of the Great Recession of 2009 or the 2016 presidential election.

2. Native American, African American, and Women's History

The history of Native Americans, African Americans, and American women continues to generate a significant number of exam questions. Chapters 3 through 31 devote special attention to the key leaders and milestone events in the history of these groups. For example, you will find detailed sections that describe Native American cultural regions (Chapter 3), compare the goals of Dr. King and Malcolm X (Chapter 28), and evaluate the role of women in the Progressive movement (Chapter 21).

3. Important Historic Connections

This edition also includes 48 special "Making Connections" features designed to help you answer multiple-choice comparison questions and earn the complexity point on the DBQ and Long-Essay questions. For example, the Making Connections feature in Chapter 6 connects the Stamp Act Boycott with the Montgomery Bus Boycott.

4. Key Turning Points

The majority of Long-Essay questions have used turning points in American history to test the skill of causation. This edition includes 12 detailed sections on key turning points in American history. You will find predictable turning points such as the Missouri Compromise (Chapter 9) and *Brown v. Board of Education* (Chapter 27), and unexpected ones such as the transcontinental railroads (Chapter 18) and the 1960s counterculture (Chapter 28).

5. Test Tips

Each of the 29 content chapters contains 2 new Test Tips. This popular feature alerts you to topics that have the potential to generate exam questions. For example, a Test Tip in Chapter 26 points out that the First and Second Red Scares have generated more exam questions than any other specific topic.

On the first day of my APUSH class, I always tell my students that I have two primary goals. First, I strive to present an enjoyable and stimulating course. And second, I strive to teach the content and skills that will help everyone excel on the APUSH exam. This book is inspired by these same two goals!

—*Larry Krieger*

ABOUT OUR AUTHOR

Larry Krieger has been recognized by the College Board as one of the nation's foremost AP® teachers.

In a career spanning more than 40 years, Mr. Krieger has taught in urban, rural, and suburban public high schools in North Carolina and New Jersey. His teaching repertoire spans a variety of AP® subjects including United States History, World History, European History, United States Government and Politics, and Art History. He is renowned for his energetic presentation, commitment to scholarship, and dedication to helping students achieve high AP® scores.

Mr. Krieger's success has extended far beyond the classroom. He is the author of several widely used American History and World History textbooks, along with REA's Crash Course books for AP® U.S. Government and Politics (1st Edition), European History, and Psychology. In addition, he has spoken at numerous Social Studies conferences and continues to hopscotch across America to conduct SAT® and AP® workshops for students and teachers.

This 5th edition of the AP® U.S. History Crash Course is based upon Mr. Krieger's intensive study of the current APUSH Framework and released materials. He field-tested the materials in this book with students taking his APUSH prep courses. During the past five years, 90 percent of these students scored a 5, with the rest scoring 4s.

Mr. Krieger earned his B.A. and M.A.T. from the University of North Carolina at Chapel Hill and his M.A. from Wake Forest University.

ABOUT REA

Founded in 1959, Research & Education Association (REA) is dedicated to publishing the finest and most effective educational materials—including study guides and test preps—for students of all ages.

Today, REA's wide-ranging catalog is a leading resource for students, teachers, and other professionals. Visit *www.rea.com* to see a complete listing of all our titles.

ACKNOWLEDGMENTS

We would like to thank Pam Weston, Publisher, for setting the quality standards for production integrity and managing the publication to completion; John Paul Cording, Technology Director, for coordinating the design and development of the REA Study Center; Larry B. Kling, Editorial Director, for his overall direction; Kathy Caratozzolo of Caragraphics for typesetting; Bernard Yanelli for technically reviewing the manuscript; and Diane Goldschmidt for proofreading.

Chapter 1

SEVEN KEYS FOR SUCCESS ON THE AP® U.S. HISTORY EXAM

AP® American History textbooks are very thick and contain thousands of names, dates, places, and events. If all of these facts had an equal chance of appearing on your Advanced Placement® United States History (APUSH) exam, studying would be a nightmare. Where would you begin? What would you emphasize? Is there any information you can safely omit? Or must you study everything?

Fortunately, preparing for the APUSH exam does not have to be a nightmare. By studying efficiently and strategically, you can score a 4 or a 5 on the exam. This book will help you understand and use the following seven keys for success:

1. Understanding the APUSH Scale

Many students believe they must make close to a perfect score to receive a 5. Nothing could be further from the truth. Each APUSH exam contains a total of 140 points—55 from the multiple-choice and 85 from the free-response questions. Here is the score range for the 2018 APUSH exam:

Score Range	AP® Grade	Minimum Percent Right
109–140	5	77%
91–108	4	65%
73–90	3	52%
55–72	2	39%
0–54	1	0%–38%

This chart is not a misprint. As is clearly shown, you can achieve a 5 by correctly answering just 77 percent of the questions, a 4 by correctly answering just 65 percent of the questions, and a 3 by correctly answering just 52 percent of the questions!

2. Understanding the Division of AP® U.S. History into Nine Chronological Periods

APUSH test writers follow a detailed Course and Exam Description (CED) that divides American history into the following nine distinct periods of time:

PERIOD	EXAM WEIGHT
Unit 1: Period 1: 1491–1607	4%–6%
Unit 2: Period 2: 1607–1754	6%–8%
Unit 3: Period 3: 1754–1800	10%–17%
Unit 4: Period 4: 1800–1848	10%–17%
Unit 5: Period 5: 1844–1877	10%–17%
Unit 6: Period 6: 1865–1898	10%–17%
Unit 7: Period 7: 1890–1945	10%–17%
Unit 8: Period 8: 1945–1980	10%–17%
Unit 9: Period 9: 1980–Present	4%–6%

3. Understanding the APUSH Topical Themes

Many students believe that members of the APUSH exam development committee have the freedom to write any question they wish. This wide-spread belief is not true. APUSH test writers follow the Course and Exam Description based upon the following 8 themes or broad ideas that run throughout the course:

THEME 1: American and National Identity

THEME 2: Work, Exchange, and Technology

THEME 3: Geography and the Environment

THEME 4: Migration and Settlement

THEME 5: Politics and Power

THEME 6: America in the World

THEME 7: American and Regional Culture

THEME 8: Social Structures

These eight themes explain why there are so many questions on immigration trends, economic policies, cultural movements, and the influence of geographic conditions.

4. Understanding the APUSH Exam Format

Your APUSH exam will include four very different question formats. Here are the key facts about each of these formats:

A. MULTIPLE-CHOICE QUESTIONS

1. You will be asked to answer 55 multiple-choice questions.
2. The 55 questions will be grouped into sets containing between 2 and 4 questions. Each set of questions will be based upon a stimulus prompt. The prompts will be a brief source that could be a reading passage, a chart or graph, an illustration, or a map.
3. Each of the 55 questions will be worth 1 point for a total of 55 points. The multiple-choice questions will count for 40 percent of your total score.
4. You will be given 55 minutes to complete the multiple-choice questions.
5. See Chapter 32 for detailed strategies for answering multiple-choice questions.
6. See Chapter 33 to sample realistic multiple-choice questions.

B. SHORT-ANSWER QUESTIONS

1. You will be asked to answer 3 short-answer questions.
2. The first short-answer question will feature dueling opinions of two historians or contemporary writers. The second short-answer question will ask you to analyze a political cartoon or a historic image. The final two short-answer questions will ask you to compare important historical trends, patterns, and movements. You will only have to answer one of these two questions.
3. Each short-answer question will include three very specific sub-points. Your answers to these sub-points do not require a thesis. Concentrate on writing concise statements that include specific historic examples. Use complete sentences—an outline or list of bulleted points is not acceptable.

4. Each sub-point is worth 3.1 exam points. As a result, a full short-answer question is worth 9.3 exam points. Taken together, the three short-answer questions are worth a total of 28 points, or 20 percent of your total exam score.
5. You will be given 40 minutes to complete the three short-answer questions.
6. See Chapter 34 for detailed strategies for answering short-answer questions.

C. DOCUMENT-BASED QUESTION (DBQ)

1. The DBQ is an essay question that requires you to interpret and analyze 7 brief primary source documents. The documents typically include excerpts from diaries, speeches, letters, reports, and official decrees. In addition, DBQs often include at least one graph, chart, map, or political cartoon.
2. The College Board recommends that you devote 60 minutes to planning and writing your DBQ.
3. Your DBQ will be scored on a rubric that includes 7 specific points. Each rubric point is worth 5 exam points. Taken together, the DBQ is worth a maximum of 35 points, or 25 percent of your exam score.
4. See Chapter 35 for detailed strategies for answering the DBQ question.

D. LONG-ESSAY QUESTION

1. You will be given three long-essay questions. Although the three questions will be taken from different time periods, they will be related by a common theme and historical thinking skill. You will be asked to select and write about just ***one*** of the three long-essay questions.
2. You will be given 40 minutes to write your essay.
3. Your essay will be scored on a rubric that includes six specific points. Each rubric point is worth 3.5 exam points. Taken together the long-essay question is worth 21 points, or 15 percent of your total exam score.
4. See Chapter 36 for detailed strategies for answering the long-essay question.

5. Understanding the Meaning and Uses of Seven Historical Thinking Skills

The APUSH course stresses the understanding and use of seven key historical thinking skills. It is very important that you understand the meaning of each skill and the role it plays on the exam.

A. HISTORICAL CAUSATION

1. This skill involves the ability to identify and evaluate the long and short-term causes and consequences of a historical event, development or process.
2. This skill plays a significant role in the multiple-choice, short-answer, and long-essay questions.

B. PATTERNS OF CONTINUITY AND CHANGE OVER TIME

1. This skill involves the ability to recognize, analyze, and evaluate the dynamics of historical continuity and change over periods of time of varying length. It also involves the ability to connect these patterns to larger historical processes or themes.
2. This skill plays a significant role in the DBQ and long-essay questions.

C. COMPARISON

1. This skill involves the ability to identify, compare, and evaluate multiple perspectives on a given historical event, development, or process.
2. This skill plays a significant role in the DBQ and long-essay questions.

D. CONTEXTUALIZATION

1. This skill involves the ability to connect historical events and processes to specific circumstances of time and place as well as to broader regional, national, and global processes occurring at the same time.
2. This skill plays a significant role in the multiple-choice questions. It also generates a specific point in both the DBQ and long-essay rubrics.

E. **HISTORICAL ARGUMENTATION**

1. This skill involves the ability to create an argument and support it using relevant historical ideas.
2. This skill plays a significant role in both the DBQ and the long-essay questions. The rubrics in both of these questions award points for developing and supporting a defensible thesis.

F. **ANALYZING EVIDENCE**

1. This skill involves the ability to analyze features of historical evidence such as audience, purpose, point of view, and historical context. It also involves the ability to demonstrate a complex understanding of a historical development by using evidence to corroborate or qualify an argument.
2. This skill plays a particularly significant role in both the DBQ and the long-essay questions. The DBQ rubric awards up to 5 points for using and analyzing evidence while the long-essay rubric awards up to 4 points for these skills.

G. **INTERPRETATION**

1. This skill involves the ability to describe, analyze, and evaluate the different ways historians interpret the past.
2. This skill plays a significant role in the short-answer questions and DBQ.

6. Understanding How to Use Your *Crash Course* to Build a Winning Coalition of Points

This *Crash Course* book is based on a careful analysis of the 2019–2020 *AP® United States History Course and Exam Description* and the released exam questions. Chapter 2 contains key terms that you have to know. Chapters 3–31 provide you with a detailed chronological review of American history. And Chapters 32–35 provide you with examples of each of the four major question types that appear on the APUSH exam: multiple-choice, short-answer, document-based, and the long essay.

If you have the time, review the entire book. This is desirable, but not mandatory. The chapters can be studied in any order. Each chapter provides you with a digest of key information that is repeatedly tested. Battles, inventions, rulers, and political events that have never been asked about on the APUSH exam have been omitted. Unlike most review books, the digests are not meant to be exhaustive. Instead, they are meant to focus your attention on the vital material you must study.

Many of the chapters in this book have a special feature called "Making Comparisons." This feature is designed to provide you with in-depth discussions of key topics. The Making Comparison feature will help you develop the historical thinking skills of making comparisons and interpreting events.

In addition, many of the chapters contain sections devoted to "Turning Points in American History." This material is designed to help you prepare for DBQ and long-essay questions devoted to causation. All of the chapters contain at least one "Making Connections" section. The topics in these sections are designed to provide you with an inventory of examples you can use to demonstrate complexity in your DBQ and long-essay answers.

7. Using College Board Materials to Supplement Your *Crash Course*

This *Crash Course* contains everything you need to know to score a 4 or a 5 on your exam. You should, however, supplement it with other materials designed specifically for studying AP® U.S. History. Visit the College Board's AP® Central website for the full text of the *AP® United States History Course and Exam Description* and sample questions.

KEY TERMS

UNIT 1 | PERIOD 1: 1491–1607

1. **COLUMBIAN EXCHANGE**—The Columbian Exchange refers to the exchange of plants, animals, and germs between the New World and Europe following the discovery of America in 1492.

   New World crops such as maize (corn), tomatoes, and potatoes had a dramatic effect on the European diet, life span, and population growth. At the same time, Old World domesticated animals such as horses, cows, and pigs had a dramatic impact on the environment in the New World.

   European diseases, such as smallpox, decimated the Native America population. The demographic collapse enabled the Spanish to more easily gain control over Native American lands.

2. **THE *ENCOMIENDA* SYSTEM**—An *encomienda* was a license granted by the Spanish crown to royal officials to extract labor and tribute from native peoples in specified areas. The *encomienda* system began in the Caribbean and spread to Mexico.

UNIT 2 | PERIOD 2: 1607–1754

3. **AMERICAN EXCEPTIONALISM**—The belief that America has a special mission to be a beacon of democracy and liberty. First expressed in John Winthrop's "City Upon A Hill" sermon and now an important part of America's national identity.

4. **MERCANTILISM**—Economic philosophy guiding Great Britain and other European powers during the seventeenth and eighteenth centuries. Intended to enable Britain to achieve a favorable balance of trade by exporting more than it imported. Britain expected to achieve this goal by purchasing raw materials from its North American colonies and then selling more expensive manufactured goods back to the colonies. A series of Navigation Acts attempted to enforce this policy.

5. **FIRST GREAT AWAKENING**—A wave of religious revivals that began in New England in the mid-1730s and then spread across all the colonies during the 1740s.

6. **ENLIGHTENMENT**—An eighteenth-century philosophy stressing that reason could be used to improve the human condition by eradicating superstition, bigotry, and intolerance. Inspired by John Locke, Enlightenment thinkers such as Thomas Jefferson stressed the idea of natural rights. The second paragraph of the Declaration of Independence provides a timeless expression of Enlightened thought:

> *"We hold these truths to be self-evident, that all men are created equal, that they are endowed by their Creator with certain unalienable rights, that among these are life, liberty and the pursuit of happiness."*

UNIT 3 | PERIOD 3: 1754–1800

7. **VIRTUAL REPRESENTATION**—British belief that each member of Parliament represented the interests of all Englishmen, including the colonists. Rejected by colonists who argued that as Englishmen they could only be taxed by their own elected representatives.

8. **REPUBLICAN GOVERNMENT/REPUBLICANISM**—Refers to the belief that government should be based on the consent of the people. Defended by Thomas Paine in *Common Sense*. Republicanism inspired the eighteenth century American revolutionaries.

9. **SEPARATION OF POWERS**—The division of power among the legislative, judicial, and executive branches of government. Alexander Hamilton defended the principle of separation of powers when he wrote: "There is no liberty if the power of judging be not separated from the legislative and executive powers."

10. **CHECKS AND BALANCES**—System in which each branch of government can check the power of the other branches. For example, the President can veto a bill passed by Congress but Congress can override the president's veto.

11. **REPUBLICAN MOTHERHOOD**—Belief that the new American republic offered women the important role of raising their children to be virtuous and responsible citizens. Women would thus play a key role in shaping America's moral and political character.

12. **ANTIFEDERALISTS**—Opponents of the American Constitution at the time when the states were debating its adoption. They argued that the Constitution lacked a Bill of Rights and would create a powerful central government dominated by the rich.

13. **HAMILTON'S FINANCIAL PROGRAM**—Hamilton sought to create a sound financial foundation for the new republic by funding the federal debt, assuming state debts, creating a national bank, and imposing tariffs to protect home industries.

14. **STATES' RIGHTS**—Doctrine asserting that the Constitution arose as a compact among sovereign states. The states therefore retained the power to challenge and, if necessary, nullify federal laws. First formulated by Jefferson and Madison in the Kentucky and Virginia Resolutions.

UNIT 4 | PERIOD 4: 1800–1848

15. **JUDICIAL REVIEW**—The power of the Supreme Court to strike down an act of Congress by declaring it unconstitutional. This principle was established by the Marshall Court in the 1803 case of *Marbury v. Madison.*

16. **AMERICAN SYSTEM/INTERNAL IMPROVEMENTS**—The American System was a set of proposals sponsored by Henry Clay to unify the nation and strengthen the economy by means of protective tariffs, a national bank, and internal improvements or transportation projects such as canals and new roads.

17. **JACKSONIAN DEMOCRACY**—A set of political beliefs associated with Andrew Jackson and his followers. Jacksonian democracy included respect for the common man, expansion of white male suffrage, appointment of political supporters to government positions, and opposition to privileged Eastern elites.

18. **NULLIFICATION**—A legal theory that a state in the United States has the right to nullify or invalidate any federal law that the state deems unconstitutional. John C. Calhoun was the foremost proponent of the doctrine of nullification. Inspired by his leadership, a convention in South Carolina declared the tariffs of both 1828 and 1832 unenforceable in that state.

19. **MARKET REVOLUTION**—The dramatic increase between 1820 and 1850 in the exchange of goods among regional and national markets. The market revolution reflected the increased output of farms and factories, the entrepreneurial activities of traders and merchants, and the creation of a transportation network of canals, roads, steamship lines, and railroads.

20. **NATIVISM**—Anti-foreign sentiment favoring the interests of native-born people over the interests of immigrants. Nativism directed against Irish and German immigrants in the 1840s and 1850s fueled the rise of the Know-Nothing Party. Nativism reappeared as a reaction to the mass immigration from Eastern and Southern Europe between 1890 and 1920.

21. **THE SECOND GREAT AWAKENING**—Refers to a wave of religious enthusiasm that spread across America between 1800 and 1830. Middle-class women played an especially important role in the Second Great Awakening by making Americans aware of the moral issues posed by slavery. The religious fervor also led to reformist zeal for causes such as temperance, better care for the mentally ill, and higher standards for public schools.

22. **PERFECTIONISM**—Belief that humans can use conscious acts of will to create communities based upon cooperation and mutual respect. Utopian communities such as Brook Farm, New Harmony, and Oneida reflected the blossoming of perfectionist aspirations.

23. **CULT OF DOMESTICITY**—Idealized women in their roles as wives and mothers. As a nurturing mother and faithful spouse, the wife would create a home that was a "haven in a heartless world."

24. **TRANSCENDENTALISM**—An antebellum philosophical and literary movement that emphasized living a simple life and celebrating the truth found in nature and in personal emotion and imagination. Ralph Waldo Emerson, Henry David Thoreau, and Margaret Fuller were the foremost transcendentalist writers.

UNIT 5 | PERIOD 5: 1844–1877

25. **MANIFEST DESTINY**—Nineteenth-century belief that the United States was destined by Providence to spread democratic institutions and liberty from the Atlantic to the Pacific. The ideology of manifest destiny helped justify Polk's expansionist program.

26. **WILMOT PROVISO**—The 1846 proposal by Representative David Wilmot of Pennsylvania to ban slavery in territory acquired from the Mexican War. The proviso triggered a divisive and increasingly ominous dispute between the North and the South. It passed twice in the House but was defeated in the Senate.

27. **SLAVE POWER**—Antebellum term referring to the disproportionate power that Northerners believed wealthy slaveholders wielded over national political decisions.

28. **POPULAR SOVEREIGNTY**—Principle advocated by Stephen A. Douglas that the settlers of a given territory have the sole right to decide whether slavery will be permitted there. Popular sovereignty led to a divisive debate over the expansion of slavery into the western territories. The first great test of popular sovereignty occurred in Kansas following passage of the Kansas-Nebraska Act, which led to "Bleeding Kansas" and increased sectionalism.

29. **BLACK CODES**—Laws passed by Southern states after the Civil War denying ex-slaves the civil rights enjoyed by whites and punishing "crimes" such as failing to have a labor contract or travelling outside a plantation without a written pass.

30. **SHARECROPPING**—A labor system in the South after the Civil War. Tenants worked the land in return for a share of the crops produced instead of paying cash rent. The system perpetuated a seemingly endless cycle of debt and poverty.

31. **CARPETBAGGERS AND SCALAWAGS**—*Carpetbagger* is the derisive name given by ex-Confederates to Northerners who moved to the South during Reconstruction. *Scalawag* is the derisive name given to Southern whites who supported Republican Reconstruction.

32. **REDEEMERS**—White Southern political leaders who claimed to "redeem" or save the South from Republican domination. Redeemers supported diversified economic growth and white supremacy.

33. **JIM CROW**—A system of racial segregation in the South lasting from the end of Reconstruction until the 1960s.

UNIT 6 | PERIOD 6: 1865–1898

34. **FRONTIER THESIS**—Argument by historian Frederick Jackson Turner that the frontier experience helped make American society more democratic. Turner especially emphasized the importance of cheap, unsettled land and the absence of a landed aristocracy. Here is an illustrative quote:

    "From the beginning of the settlement of America, the frontier regions have exercised a steady influence toward democracy...American democracy is fundamentally the outcome of the experience of the American people in dealing with the West...."

35. **VERTICAL AND HORIZONTAL INTEGRATION**—*Vertical integration* is a business model in which a corporation controls all aspects of production from raw materials to packaged products. For example, Andrew Carnegie used vertical integration to gain control over the U.S. steel industry.

    Horizontal integration is a business model in which one company gains control over other companies that produce the same product. For example, John D. Rockefeller used horizontal integration to gain control over the U.S. oil industry.

36. **SOCIAL DARWINISM**—Refers to the belief that there is a natural evolutionary process by which the fittest will survive and prosper. During the Gilded Age, wealthy business and industrial leaders used Social Darwinism to justify their success.

37. **GOSPEL OF WEALTH**—View advanced by Andrew Carnegie that the wealthy were the guardians of society. Carnegie believed that the rich could best serve society by funding institutions such as colleges and public libraries that created "ladders of success."

38. **SOCIAL GOSPEL**—Late nineteenth-century reform movement based on the belief that Christians have a responsibility to actively confront social problems such as poverty. Led by Christian ministers, advocates of the Social Gospel argued that real social change would result from dedication to both religious practice and social reform.

39. **NEW IMMIGRANTS**—Refers to the massive wave of immigrants from Southern and Eastern Europe who came to America between 1890 and 1924.

40. **REALISM**—A late nineteenth and early twentieth-century movement calling for writers, artists, and photographers to portray daily life as precisely and truly as possible. Realists avoided idealized landscapes favored by the Hudson River School and instead painted raucous urban scenes favored by the Ashcan School of artists.

UNIT 7 | PERIOD 7: 1890–1945

41. **POPULISM**—The term refers to the mainly agrarian movement developed in the 1890s that supported the unlimited coinage of silver, government regulation of the railroads, and other policies favoring farmers and the working class.

42. **PROGRESSIVISM**—Progressivism sought to use government to help create a more just society. Progressives fought against impure foods, child labor, corruption, and trusts. Theodore Roosevelt and Woodrow Wilson were prominent Progressive presidents.

43. **MUCKRAKERS**—These were early twentieth century journalists who exposed illegal business practices, social injustices, and corrupt urban political bosses. Leading muckrakers included Upton Sinclair, Jacob Riis, and Ida Tarbell.

44. **RED SCARE**—A term for anticommunist hysteria that swept the United States after World War I and led to a series of government raids on alleged subversives and a suppression of civil liberties.

45. **GREAT MIGRATION**—A massive movement of blacks leaving the South for cities in the North that began slowly in 1910 and accelerated between World War I and the Great Crash.

46. **HARLEM RENAISSANCE**—The term refers to a flowering of African American artists, writers, and intellectuals during the 1920s. Harlem Renaissance writers used the term "New Negro" as a proud assertion of African American culture.

47. **ISOLATIONISM**—A U.S. foreign policy calling for Americans to avoid entangling political alliances following World War I. During the 1930s, isolationists drew support from ideas expressed in Washington's Farewell Address. The Neutrality Acts of the 1930s were expressions of a commitment to isolationism.

UNIT 8 | PERIOD 8: 1945–1980

48. **CONTAINMENT**—Advocated by George Kennan and adopted as the Truman Doctrine, containment was the name given to America's Cold War policy of blocking the expansion of Soviet influence.

49. **McCARTHYISM**—The term is associated with Senator Joseph McCarthy's anti-Communist crusade during the early 1950s. McCarthy's unsubstantiated accusations that communists had infiltrated the U.S. State Department and other federal agencies helped create a climate of fear and paranoia often called the Second Red Scare.

50. **BEATS**—A small but influential group of literary figures based in New York City and San Francisco in the 1950s. Led by Jack Kerouac and Allen Ginsberg, Beats rejected mainstream America's carefree consumption and mindless conformity.

51. **DOMINO THEORY**—This geopolitical theory refers to the belief that, if one country falls to communism, its neighbors will also be infected and fall to communism. For example, American Cold War hawks predicted that the fall of South Vietnam would lead to the loss of all of Southeast Asia.

52. **THE FEMININE MYSTIQUE**—The title of an influential book written in 1963 by Betty Friedan critiquing the prevailing cult of domesticity whereby women were to devote themselves to the roles of housewife and mother. Historians believe that Friedan's book helped spark a period known as second-wave feminism that focused on workplace inequalities, reproductive rights, and passage of the Equal Rights Amendment.

53. **BLACK POWER**—The Black Power movement of the 1960s advocated that African Americans establish control of their political and economic lives. Key advocates of Black Power included Malcolm X, Stokely Carmichael, and Huey Newton.

54. **COUNTERCULTURE**—A cultural movement during the late 1960s associated with hippies who advocated an alternative lifestyle based upon peace, love, and "doing your own thing."

55. **SILENT MAJORITY**—Term used by President Nixon in a 1969 speech to describe those who supported his foreign and domestic policies but did not participate in public protests.

56. **DÉTENTE**—The term refers to the policy advocated by President Nixon and his Secretary of State Henry Kissinger to relax tensions between the United States and the Soviet Union. Examples of détente include the Strategic Arms Limitation Talks (SALT), expanded trade with the Soviet Union, and President Nixon's trips to China and Russia.

57. **STAGFLATION**—An economic term to describe the unusual combination of high unemployment and inflation during the 1970s.

UNIT 9 | PERIOD 9: 1980–PRESENT

58. **REAGANOMICS**—Term used to describe President Reagan's supply-side economic policies that attempted to promote growth and investment by deregulating business, reducing corporate tax rates, and lowering federal tax rates for upper- and middle-income Americans.

59. **SUN BELT**—Name given to the states in the Southwest and South that experienced a rapid growth in population and political power during the past half century.

60. **MULTICULTURALISM**—The promotion of diversity in gender, race, ethnicity, religion, and sexual preferences. This political and social policy became increasingly influential and controversial during the period from 1980 to the present.

UNIT 1

PERIOD 1
1491–1607

KEY CONCEPTS

KEY CONCEPT 1.1
As native populations migrated and settled across the vast expanse of North America over time, they developed distinct and increasingly complex societies by adapting to and transforming their diverse environments.

KEY CONCEPT 1.2
Contact among Europeans, Native Americans, and Africans resulted in the Columbian Exchange and significant social, cultural, and political changes on both sides of the Atlantic Ocean.

A NEW WORLD

I. THE FIRST AMERICANS

A. ARRIVAL AND DISPERSAL

1. The earliest North American residents crossed a land bridge between Siberia and Alaska between 15,000 and 30,000 years ago.
2. Following large game animals, these Asian immigrants gradually spread through North and South America, reaching the tip of South America by 9000 BCE.

B. NORTH AMERICAN CULTURAL REGIONS

1. Pacific Northwest
   a. The abundant natural resources of the Pacific Northwest supported a relatively dense population. Rivers teemed with salmon and other fish providing an easily available source of nutritious food. The thick forests provided wood for housing and boats.
   b. Tribes such as the Haida collected shellfish from the beaches and hunted the ocean for whales, sea otters, and seals.
   c. The Kwakiutl celebrated their abundance by carving magnificent totems that included symbols of ancestral spirits.
2. Desert Southwest
   a. The Southwest challenged Native Americans with a much drier climate than that of the Pacific Northwest.
   b. The Pueblo built settlements near the Rio Grande and its tributaries. The Hopi lived near cliffs that could be easily defended. They collected rainwater in rock cisterns and carefully parceled it out to their fields and to families living in clusters of houses called pueblos.
   c. People throughout the region lived in multi-story houses made of adobe. They coaxed crops of maize (corn), beans, melons, and squash from sun-parched, but fertile, soil.

3. The Great Plains

   a. The Great Plains are flat open grasslands extending from the Rockies to the Mississippi River. Hot, dry summers followed cold, snowy winters. Huge buffalo herds roamed across the vast grasslands.

   b. The Pawnee planted corn, squash, and beans. Once the plants were strong enough to survive, the entire tribe packed up for the spring buffalo hunt. While on the hunt, the Pawnee lived in portable houses made of buffalo skin called tepees.

4. Eastern Woodlands

   a. Hardwood forests dominated the land stretching from the Great Lakes and St. Lawrence River in the north to the Gulf of Mexico in the south. It was said that a squirrel could travel from Tennessee to New York without ever touching the ground.

   b. Tribes such as the Creek, Choctaw, and Powhatan cleared the forest and built villages. They blended hunting and gathering with agriculture based upon the cultivation of maize, squash, and beans.

   c. John White created a detailed engraving of Secotan, an Algonquian village on the Pamlico River in present-day North Carolina. White depicted a complex society living in a permanent agricultural settlement. The villagers devoted two fields to tobacco but saw no need to construct a defensive fence.

5. Common Characteristics

   a. The early peoples of North America lived in families that were part of larger clans. They lived in village communities, divided labor by gender, and shared a strong sense of spirituality.

   b. The early peoples did not develop wheeled vehicles, waterwheels, or a tradition of private property rights. Native Americans viewed land and water as communal possessions that could not be owned or traded.

Don't neglect to study these cultural regions. They can be used to generate a short-answer question asking you to describe how geographic conditions influenced the culture of Native Americans prior to the arrival of European explorers.

II. THE SPANISH CONQUEST

A. CHRISTOPHER COLUMBUS

1. Columbus hoped to discover a new trade route to Asia.
2. He saw no reason to respect or learn about the customs of the Native Americans he encountered. Instead, Columbus proposed to Christianize the indigenous peoples, seize their mineral wealth, and exploit their labor.

B. THE CONQUISTADORES

1. Hernán Cortés conquered the Aztec Empire in 1521.
2. Francisco Pizarro conquered the Inca Empire in 1533.
3. Both Cortés and Pizarro overthrew rulers who led centralized governments.
4. Advanced metal weapons, horses, ruthless tactics, and diseases such as smallpox, influenza, and measles enabled the Spanish conquistadores to topple the Aztec and Inca empires.

III. THE COLUMBIAN EXCHANGE

A. INTRODUCTION

1. The Columbian Exchange refers to the exchange of plants, animals, and germs between the New World and Europe following the discovery of America in 1492.
2. New World crops included maize (corn), tomatoes, and potatoes. In addition, New World mines provided a steady supply of gold and silver. For example, the fabulously rich Potosi mines (in modern-day Bolivia) produced 200 tons of silver a year for two centuries.
3. Old World crops included wheat, sugar, rice, and coffee. In addition, Europeans introduced horses, cows, chickens, and pigs into the New World.

B. IMPACT ON EUROPE

1. New World foods transformed European society by increasing agricultural yields and improving diets, thus stimulating population growth.

2. The Columbian Exchange generated a profitable trans-Atlantic trade that helped spark European economic development by facilitating the shift from feudalism to capitalism.

C. IMPACT ON NATIVE AMERICANS

1. Old World diseases decimated the Native American population. Demographers estimate that the Native American population plummeted by 90 percent or more in the first century of contact with Europe.

2. This demographic collapse enabled the Spanish to more easily gain control over Native American lands.

IV. CHARACTERISTICS OF NEW SPAIN

A. INTRODUCTION

1. The Spanish established a New World empire in order to spread their Roman Catholic faith and extend the king's wealth and power.

2. Spain created a rigid and highly centralized New World government controlled by the crown in Madrid.

B. THE *ENCOMIENDA* SYSTEM

1. An *encomienda* was a license granted by the Spanish crown to royal officials to extract labor and tribute from native peoples living in specified areas. For example, Cortés appropriated tribute from 23,000 families in the fertile Oaxaca Valley.

2. The *encomienda* system began in the Caribbean and then spread to Mexico. It enabled Spanish colonial administrators to marshal native labor to support plantation-based agriculture and extract precious metals. In exchange, the *encomenderos* were responsible for Christianizing the native peoples under their protection.

3. Although the native peoples were legally not slaves, ruthless *encomenderos* nevertheless created an often brutal system of forced labor that led to many abuses.

4. The inhumanity of the system appalled Dominican priest Bartolomé de las Casas. He renounced his *encomienda* and became an eloquent critic of how the Spanish mistreated the native peoples.

C. A NEW SOCIETY

1. As disease and warfare reduced their numbers, the native population could not meet the Spaniards' growing demand for a large body of captive laborers. By the early 1500s, the Spanish began to import enslaved Africans to labor on sugar plantations and in the silver mines.
2. About 300,000 enslaved Africans arrived in New Spain between 1500 and 1650. At the same time, at least 350,000 Spaniards migrated to the Caribbean, Mexico, and the Andes.
3. Males comprised the majority of Spanish migrants. As a result, intermarriage produced a diverse mixture of Europeans, Africans, and Native Americans. Those who ruled in New Spain often followed the advice of Machiavelli, who insisted that successful rulers must be ruthless and pragmatic, always remembering that the end justifies the means.
4. The Spanish attempted to enforce an elaborate racial hierarchy with themselves at the top and natives on the bottom. Mestizos (Spaniard-Indian) and Mulattos (Spaniard-African) fell in between. The Spanish justified this stratified society as proof of the higher level of civilization among Europeans. Juan Ginés de Sepúlveda, a Spanish nobleman, used this same justification when he engaged in a famous debate with Bartolomé de las Casas in the 1550s over the proper treatment of Native Americans.

V. THE PUEBLO REVOLT

A. CAUSES

1. During the seventeenth century the Spanish gradually gained control over the Pueblo people living in what is today New Mexico.
2. The Spanish disrupted the Pueblos' traditional culture by forcing them to labor on *encomiendas* and worship in Catholic missions.

B. POPÉ

1. Popé was a determined and dynamic Pueblo leader who deeply resented the Spanish. His message was simple—expel the Spanish and return to the old ways of life that had given the Pueblo peace, prosperity, and independence.
2. Led by Popé, the Pueblo rose in revolt in 1680. They soon killed hundreds of Spaniards while destroying their buildings and burning their fields.

C. CONSEQUENCES

1. The uprising did not bring peace and prosperity to the Pueblo. Following Popé's death in 1688, the Spanish launched a successful reconquest of the Pueblo.
2. When the Spanish returned, they adopted a policy of greater cultural accommodation. They no longer tried to eradicate the Pueblo culture. Over the next century, New Mexico became a blend of Spanish and Pueblo cultures.

Period 1 generates a predictable set of multiple-choice questions focusing on the impact of the Columbian Exchange, the characteristics of the* encomienda *system, and the Pueblo Revolt.

UNIT 2

PERIOD 2
1607–1754

KEY CONCEPTS

KEY CONCEPT 2.1

Europeans developed a variety of colonization and migration patterns, influenced by different imperial goals, cultures, and the varied North American environments where they settled, and they competed with each other and American Indians for resources.

KEY CONCEPT 2.2

The British colonies participated in political, social, cultural, and economic exchanges with Great Britain that encouraged both stronger bonds with Britain and resistance to Britain's control.

Chapter 4

ENGLISH NORTH AMERICA

I. NORTH AMERICA

A. CONTEXT

1. The Spanish carved out a vast New World empire that stretched from what is today New Mexico to Peru. They built impressive cathedrals in Mexico City and Lima and even opened universities in both of these cities.
2. As the seventeenth century opened, France and England had yet to establish permanent colonies in the rest of North America.
3. Influenced by different economic and imperial goals, the French and English founded very contrasting colonies in North America.

B. CHARACTERISTICS OF FRENCH NORTH AMERICA

1. Explored by sea captains looking for a northwest passage to Asia.
2. Settled by traders and trappers who developed a lucrative fur trade with the Indian tribes.
3. Included Canada, the entire Mississippi River Valley, and Louisiana.
4. Christianized by Jesuit priests who did not require Native American converts to move to missions. The French enjoyed generally cooperative relations with Native American tribes.
5. Populated primarily by male trappers who lived and worked in widely scattered trading posts.

C. CHARACTERISTICS OF BRITISH NORTH AMERICA

1. Settled by a variety of migrants who sought social mobility, economic prosperity, and religious freedom. Religious motives played a dominant role in the New England colonies, while economic motives played a dominant role in the Chesapeake colonies.
2. Included a long but narrow line of settlements stretching along the Atlantic coast from Massachusetts to Georgia.
3. Exhibited initial tolerance for the Native American tribes. However, peaceful relations quickly deteriorated as wars broke out due to conflicts over land and culture.

4. Populated by families living in compact communities in New England and widely scattered plantations and farms in the Chesapeake region. Young single males initially played a greater role in the Chesapeake colonies. English colonists rarely intermarried with Native Americans.

D. IMPACT ON NATIVE AMERICANS

1. Old World diseases and warfare decimated the Native American tribes.
2. British conflicts with Native American Indians over land, resources, and political boundaries led to military confrontations such as the Powhatan War in Virginia and King Philip's War in New England.
3. Native American tribes attempted to survive by utilizing European material goods and forming temporary alliances with the French and English.

The Spanish, French, and English established very different colonial empires. Be prepared for short-answer questions asking you to compare and contrast the characteristic features of two of these New World empires.

II. THE CHESAPEAKE COLONIES

A. KEY FACTS

1. Jamestown was founded in 1607 by a joint-stock company to make a profit.
2. Religion played a minor role in the founding of Jamestown.
3. The scarcity of women and the high rate of men's mortality strengthened the socio-economic status of women in the Chesapeake colonies.
4. Virginia's House of Burgesses was the first representative legislative assembly in British North America.
5. Lord Baltimore founded Maryland as a refuge for his fellow Roman Catholics. The Act of Religious Toleration (1649) was intended to protect the minority rights of Catholics in Maryland from religious persecution by Protestants. The Act was repealed after the Glorious Revolution.

B. TOBACCO

1. Jamestown tottered on the brink of collapse as about 80 percent of its first colonists died from diseases and malnutrition.
2. Tobacco enabled the Chesapeake colonies to become economically viable.
3. The profitable cultivation of tobacco created a demand for a large and inexpensive labor force.
4. Chesapeake Bay planters initially used indentured servants from England.
5. Between 1607 and 1676, indentured servants comprised the chief source of agricultural labor in the Chesapeake colonies.

C. BACON'S REBELLION, 1676

1. Bacon's Rebellion exposed tensions between the former indentured servants, who were poor, and the gentry (the genteel class of planters), who were rich.
2. As planters became more wary of their former indentured servants, they turned to enslaved Africans as a more reliable and cost-effective source of labor.

III. UNDERSTANDING CAUSATION: WHAT CAUSED THE GROWTH OF SLAVERY?

A. GEOGRAPHIC FACTORS

1. Fertile land, a warm climate, abundant rainfall, and a long growing season enabled ambitious planters to grow tobacco, rice, and indigo as cash crops.
2. Numerous navigable rivers provided convenient and inexpensive routes to transport goods to Atlantic ports such as Norfolk, Charleston, and Savannah.

B. ECONOMIC FACTORS

1. Tobacco saved the Chesapeake colonies. As demand in England increased, tobacco production soared from 4 barrels in 1614 to 10 million pounds in 1670.
2. Tobacco required a large supply of inexpensive labor. The spread of tobacco cultivation beyond the Chesapeake colonies created additional demand for slave labor.

3. Indentured servants proved to be both unreliable and rebellious.
4. In 1662, Virginia changed its laws regarding slavery; from that point, slavery became a lifelong, inheritable status. As such, the value of slaves increased over time.
5. Following Bacon's Rebellion (1676), planters began to replace indentured servants with imported African slaves. The number of enslaved Africans in Virginia rose from 300 in 1650 to 150,000 or 40 percent of the colony's 1750 population.

C. SOCIAL FACTORS

1. A small but powerful group of wealthy planters dominated Southern society.
2. Although the majority of white families in the South did not own slaves, they did aspire to become slave owners.
3. Impoverished whites felt superior to black slaves, thus providing support for the slave system.
4. Few seventeenth- and eighteenth-century white colonists questioned human bondage as morally unacceptable.
5. Resistance to slavery proved to be futile. Following the Stono Rebellion (1739), the South Carolina legislature enacted strict laws prohibiting slaves from assembling in groups, earning money, and learning to read. Other southern states followed South Carolina's example as laws defined the descendants of African American mothers as black and therefore enslaved for perpetuity.

The causes of slavery have generated a significant number of essay and DBQ questions. Be sure that you have a solid knowledge of how geographic, economic, and social factors combined to support the growth of slavery in the American South.

IV. THE PURITANS

A. CONTEXT

1. The Puritans were Protestants who wanted to reform or "purify" the Church of England. They renounced elaborate rituals and argued that a hierarchy of religious leaders was unnecessary.
2. The Puritans left England to escape political repression, religious restrictions, and an economic recession.

B. "CITY UPON A HILL"

1. The Puritans had a powerful sense of mission—to build an ideal Christian society.
2. John Winthrop's famous "City Upon a Hill" sermon expressed the Puritan belief that they had a special pact with God to build a model Christian society:

   "For we must consider that we shall be a city upon a hill, the eyes of all people are upon us. So that if we shall deal falsely with our God in this work we shall have undertaken, and so cause Him to withdraw His present help from us, we shall be made a story and a by-word throughout the world."

3. Making Connections
   a. Winthrop's sermon is often cited as the first example of American exceptionalism, the belief that America has a mission to be a beacon of democratic reform.
   b. President Reagan often used the image of a "shining city" to express his ideal of an America "God-blessed and teeming with peoples of all kinds living in harmony and peace."

C. RELIGIOUS DISSENTERS

1. Religion occupied a central position in Puritan society. Convinced that they were doing God's work, the Puritans emphasized religious conformity. Although the Puritans came to America for religious freedom, they did not tolerate outspoken religious dissenters.
2. The Puritans banished Anne Hutchinson because of her unorthodox religious views. Hutchinson challenged the subordinate role of women in Puritan society and boldly challenged the clergy's sole ability to interpret the Bible, insisting that "The power of the Holy Spirit dwelleth perfectly in every believer."
3. Making Connections
   a. Hutchinson's willingness to publicly proclaim her views can be compared with abolitionist women in the 1840s who also asserted their right to speak on behalf of a cause.
   b. Hutchinson's emphasis upon personal salvation was later echoed in the Second Great Awakening of the 1830s.
4. The Puritans banished Roger Williams for his unorthodox religious and political views. Williams championed the cause of religious toleration and freedom of thought. He advocated the separation of church and state, arguing that the state was an inappropriate

organization to interfere in matters of faith. Williams founded the Rhode Island colony based upon freedom of religion.

5. The Puritans were unable to stamp out religious dissent. Ironically, religious intolerance in Massachusetts Bay promoted religious tolerance in Rhode Island.

D. PURITAN SOCIETY

1. Puritans typically migrated to New England in family groups rather than as single individuals.
2. Puritans typically lived in compact villages clustered around a community meeting house where they met to worship and discuss local issues. These town meetings provided important experience in self-government.
3. Puritans established a patriarchal society in which women and children played a subordinate role.
4. Puritans valued education as a means to read and understand the Bible. They required each community of 50 or more families to provide a teacher of reading and writing. They founded Harvard College to ensure an adequate supply of trained ministers.
5. Puritan communities strove for a close relationship between civil and religious authorities. Puritan ministers and magistrates enforced a strict code of moral conduct.

E. RELATIONS WITH NATIVE AMERICANS

1. The Puritans did not settle in an uninhabited wilderness. As many as 100,000 Indians lived in New England.
2. In the beginning, the coastal Indians taught the newcomers how to plant corn. The native people welcomed the opportunity to exchange furs and food for manufactured goods.
3. As the Puritans grew in number and strength, they expanded their settlements and began to see the native peoples as a "savage people, who are cruel, barbarous, and most treacherous." Given this new hostile attitude, conflict soon erupted in 1636 when the New Englanders destroyed a Pequot village slaughtering almost 400 people.
4. Smallpox epidemics soon decimated the Indian population. By 1675 the population of southern New England tribes fell to below 20,000 people.
5. Surviving Indian leaders realized that the English settlers intended to "deprive us of the privileges of our land and drive us to utter

ruin." In 1675, led by Chief Metacom (also known as King Philip), Indians attacked and burned settlements across Massachusetts.

6. King Philip's War caused great destruction. The war claimed the lives of about 1,000 settlers or one-tenth of the colony's male population. In addition, Metacom's followers destroyed 12 villages and heavily damaged 52 others.
7. King Philip's War had an even greater destructive impact upon the native people, leaving at least 3,000 dead. The survivors were a broken people, living on the social margins of a land that had irrevocably changed.

V. THE MIDDLE ATLANTIC COLONIES

A. GEOGRAPHIC CHARACTERISTICS

1. The Middle Atlantic colonies enjoyed moderate winters, fertile soil, fine harbors, and a longer growing season than the New England colonies.
2. The Hudson, Delaware, and Susquehanna rivers enabled early settlers to tap into the lucrative interior fur trade. They also enabled merchants to develop thriving commercial ports in Philadelphia and New York City.

B. PENNSYLVANIA

1. William Penn founded Pennsylvania as a "Holy Experiment" that would serve as a refuge for Quakers.
2. Penn created an unusually liberal colony that included a representative assembly elected by the landowners.
3. Pennsylvania granted freedom of religion and, similar to the colony of Rhode Island, did not have a state-supported church.
4. Penn launched an aggressive advertising campaign that attracted a diverse mix of ethnic and religious groups. By 1700, only Virginia and Massachusetts had larger populations.

C. QUAKERS

1. Quakers were pacifists who refused to bear arms.
2. Quakers advocated freedom of worship and accepted a greater role for women in church services.
3. Quakers opposed slavery and were among America's first abolitionists.

VI. MAKING COMPARISONS: VIRGINIA AND MASSACHUSETTS

A. GEOGRAPHIC CONDITIONS

1. Virginia's fertile soil, warm weather, and wide navigable rivers all promoted the cultivation of tobacco as a cash crop.
2. Massachusetts' rocky soil, cold winters, and short, fast-moving rivers all precluded the growth of plantation agriculture. Instead, small farms grew a healthy mix of crops. The cold weather checked the spread of contagious diseases, thus prolonging life expectancy. A Massachusetts colonist who survived childhood could expect to live to 70, about 25 years longer than a comparable colonist in Virginia.

B. IMPORTANCE OF RELIGION

1. Virginia was founded by a joint-stock company to make a profit.
2. Massachusetts was founded by Pilgrims and Puritans committed to building a model Christian society.

C. TYPES OF ECONOMIES

1. Virginia developed an agricultural economy based upon the cultivation of tobacco as a cash crop. Planters initially used indentured servants, but then turned to enslaved Africans. Virginia's plantation-based economy created a significant disparity in wealth and power between an elite group of tidewater gentry and a much larger group of small farmers.
2. Massachusetts developed a diversified economy that was based upon small farms, shipbuilding, and fishing. The colony imported very few indentured servants or enslaved Africans. It was initially dominated by Puritan ministers.

D. RELATIONS WITH THE INDIANS

1. The Virginia colony began by establishing peaceful relations with the far more numerous and powerful Powhatan Confederacy. However, land and cultural conflicts led to a series of wars. Defeated in battle and weakened by infectious diseases, the Powhatans became a marginal presence in the Virginia colony.
2. The Massachusetts colony began by establishing peaceful relations with the indigenous native peoples. However, land and cultural conflicts led to a series of wars. Defeated in battle and weakened by infectious diseases, native peoples became a shrinking minority in a land dominated by a rapidly growing colonial population.

KEY TRENDS IN COLONIAL LIFE AND THOUGHT 1607–1754

Chapter 5

I. THE WEST INDIES

A. CONTEXT

1. Cane sugar was the first product in human history that satisfied the universal desire to sweeten food and drink.
2. Columbus introduced sugar cane to Hispaniola. Within a short time, a "white gold" rush began as sugar plantations spread across the island.
3. Other European nations saw the Caribbean sugar islands as a path to acquiring vast wealth.

B. THE BRITISH SUGAR ISLANDS

1. The pursuit of sugar profits drew English colonists to Barbados and Jamaica.
2. In 1650, more white colonists lived on Barbados (30,000) than either the Chesapeake (12,000) or New England colonies (23,000).
3. Sugar was by far the most valuable crop grown in the British Empire. Led by Barbados, in 1700 the English West Indies produced about 25,000 tons of sugar worth four times the value of Chesapeake tobacco.

C. SUGAR AND SLAVERY

1. Sugar plantations required large fields, costly equipment, and a huge labor force working under strict supervision.
2. After beginning with indentured servants, planters in Barbados turned to importing enslaved Africans. In 1644 only about 800 slaves worked on Barbados. Just 16 years later, the number swelled to 27,000.
3. Between 1701 and 1810, sugar planters imported 252,000 enslaved Africans to Barbados and 662,400 to Jamaica.

D. IMPACT ON TRANSATLANTIC TRADE

1. The combination of sugar and slavery fueled the rapid expansion of a transatlantic trading network. By 1700 a complex network of lucrative trade routes interconnected the economies of the West Indies, the mainland colonies, England, and Africa.

2. It is important to note that West Indian planters devoted almost all their land to cultivating sugar cane. They found it less expensive to import lumber, fish, livestock, and grain from the New England and Middle colonies.

Historian Alan Taylor described the West Indies as "the great economic engine of the British empire." Be prepared to discuss the role of the West Indies in the emergence of the transatlantic trade. Also be prepared to compare and contrast the West Indies with the Chesapeake colonies.

II. MERCANTILISM

A. THE ECONOMIC THEORY

1. Great Britain attempted to integrate its North American colonies into a cohesive imperial structure based upon the prevailing economic principles of mercantilism.

2. Mercantilism was intended to enable Great Britain to achieve a favorable balance of trade by exporting more than it imported. Britain expected to achieve this goal by purchasing raw materials from its North American colonies and then selling them more expensive manufactured goods.

3. Mercantilism thus protected English industry while making the colonies dependent upon their mother country.

B. THE NAVIGATION ACTS

1. Parliament enacted a series of Navigation Acts designed to implement its mercantilist policies.

2. Navigation Acts stipulated that no ship could trade in the colonies unless it had been constructed in either England or America. In addition, certain valuable enumerated goods such as sugar, tobacco, rice, and indigo had to be transported from the colonies only to an English or another colony's port.

C. MAKING CONNECTIONS

1. The Navigation Acts had the unintended consequence of encouraging the growth of maritime commerce and shipbuilding in New England.
2. The Navigation Acts were not rigorously enforced. Prior to 1763, a long period of "salutary neglect" enabled enterprising colonial merchants to successfully evade burdensome mercantile regulations. For example, New England merchants reaped great profits trading fish and lumber to French sugar islands. As a result, the colonists developed a growing spirit of economic independence.

III. THE FIRST GREAT AWAKENING

A. CONTEXT

1. The First Great Awakening was a wave of religious revivals that began in New England in the mid-1730s and swept across the colonies during the 1740s.
2. New Light ministers deemphasized ceremony and ritual. Instead, they advocated a spontaneous and emotional religious experience that threatened the authority of traditional Old Light Puritan and Episcopal ministers.

B. JONATHAN EDWARDS AND GEORGE WHITEFIELD

1. Jonathan Edwards helped spark the Great Awakening by delivering emotional sermons warning sinners to repent. His most famous sermon, "Sinners in the Hands of an Angry God," painted a vivid picture of the torments of hell and the certainty of God's justice.
2. George Whitefield was a particularly charismatic preacher who spread New Light fervor to huge audiences from Georgia to Maine. He castigated the learned but boring Old Light sermons claiming that, "The reason why congregations have been dead, is because they had dead men preaching to them."

C. UNDERSTANDING CONSEQUENCES: THE FIRST GREAT AWAKENING

1. It led to a greater appreciation of the emotional experience of faith.
2. It promoted the growth of New Light institutions of higher learning such as Princeton, Brown, and Dartmouth.

3. It added to the growing popularity of itinerant ministers.
4. It led to divisions within both the Presbyterian and Congregational churches, resulting in growing religious diversity.
5. It increased the number of women in church congregations.
6. It sparked a renewed missionary spirit that led to the conversion of many slaves.
7. It promoted greater independence and diversity of thought that encouraged challenges to political authority during the 1760s and 1770s.

IV. DEMOGRAPHIC TRENDS

A. DECLINE OF THE NATIVE AMERICAN POPULATION

1. In 1492, as many as 10 million Native Americans may have lived in the territory that became the United States.
2. By 1700, contagious diseases and warfare reduced the Native American population to less than 2 million people.

B. GROWTH OF THE ENSLAVED AFRICAN POPULATION

1. The number of imported enslaved Africans to North America jumped from 10,000 in the seventeenth century to almost 400,000 in the eighteenth century.
2. Although slavery was legal in all 13 colonies, about 90 percent of enslaved Africans lived and worked in the South.
3. Slaves were able to maintain cultural practices brought from Africa.

C. GROWTH AND DIVERSITY OF THE WHITE COLONIAL POPULATION

1. In 1700, fewer than 300,000 whites inhabited the British North American colonies. By 1775, this figure swelled to 2 million. A soaring birth rate accounted for most of the population increase as the colonists doubled their number every twenty-five years.
2. Emigration from England actually declined between 1700 and 1775 as only 80,000 left their homeland to settle in the 13 colonies.
3. While emigration from England declined, arrivals from Scotland and Germany soared. As a result, the colonial population became increasingly diverse.

College Board test writers often use charts and graphs to generate questions testing your knowledge of key demographic trends. Be sure that you understand the impact the soaring colonial birth rate and the rising dependence upon enslaved African labor had upon Native Americans.

V. THE ENLIGHTENMENT

A. CONTEXT

1. The Enlightenment was an eighteenth century intellectual movement led by a group of English and French thinkers and writers.
2. At first, the Atlantic Ocean posed a formidable barrier that hindered communication between England and her North American colonies. However, as the frequency of transatlantic crossings increased, ships carried more than just goods and people. They also carried a flow of information that included pamphlets and letters written by leading Enlightenment figures.
3. Enlightened leaders formed a cosmopolitan "republic of letters" that included colonial leaders such as Ben Franklin and Thomas Jefferson.

B. CORE BELIEFS

1. Enlightened thinkers rejected superstition, bigotry, and intolerance. They stressed instead humans' ability to become educated and to use reason to understand nature and improve society.
2. Enlightened thinkers believed that reason could be used to discover laws of economics and government that would improve society and make progress inevitable.
3. Enlightened thinkers accepted John Locke's argument that every person was entitled to enjoy natural rights that included life, liberty, and property. The doctrine of natural rights implied a right to change governments that failed to protect a person's life, liberty, and property.
4. Under feudalism, social relationships were considered hierarchical and static. Likewise, under the Navigation Acts, the relationship between the colonies and Great Britain was a static one. In contrast, Enlightenment thinkers such as John Locke viewed static relationships as inherently *un*natural and therefore they advocated individual political rights, which in turn would lead (at least theoretically) to economic and social mobility.

UNIT 3

PERIOD 3
1754–1800

KEY CONCEPTS

KEY CONCEPT 3.1
British attempts to assert tighter control over its North American colonies and the colonial resolve to pursue self-government led to a colonial independence movement and the Revolutionary War.

KEY CONCEPT 3.2
The American Revolution's democratic and republican ideals inspired new experiments with different forms of government.

KEY CONCEPT 3.3
Migration within North America and competition over resources, boundaries, and trade intensified conflicts among peoples and nations.

SEVERING TIES WITH GREAT BRITAIN 1754–1783

I. THE FRENCH AND INDIAN WAR

A. CONTEXT

1. New France included Canada, the entire Mississippi River Valley and Louisiana. The French thus confined the British colonies to territory east of the Appalachians.
2. The French and Indian War began as a struggle for control of the upper Ohio River Valley. The war was part of a wider contest between Great Britain and France in Europe known as the Seven Years' War.

B. ALBANY PLAN OF UNION

1. Promoted by Ben Franklin, the Albany Plan of Union called for the formation of a Grand Council of elected delegates that would oversee a common defense against French and Native American threats to frontier settlements.
2. Franklin's famous "Join, or Die" cartoon dramatically illustrated the need for greater colonial unity.
3. The plan failed because colonial assemblies did not want to give up their autonomy. At the same time, the British feared that colonial unity would undermine their authority.

C. WAR AND PEACE

1. Great Britain won because the 1.2 million people in its thirteen colonies outnumbered the 75,000 inhabitants in New France.
2. The Treaty of Paris of 1763 ended French power in North America as Britain took title to Canada, Spanish Florida, and all the French lands east of the Mississippi River.

D. IMPACT ON NATIVE AMERICANS

1. The French defeat left Native Americans in a vulnerable position by ending long-standing trade and military alliances. Native

Americans could no longer negotiate favorable agreements by playing the French and English against each other.

2. Confident in their superior military position, the British withheld traditional gifts of guns, powder, and lead. Unwilling to submit to the British, Chief Pontiac turned anti-British animosity into an uprising designed to expel the unwanted Redcoats from Indian lands. The British finally suppressed Pontiac's warriors at a cost of over 2,000 lives.

3. Hoping to avoid further conflict with the Native Americans, the British issued the Proclamation of 1763 prohibiting the colonists from settling west of the Appalachians. Land-hungry settlers ignored the Proclamation Line and soon poured into Kentucky.

E. TURNING POINTS IN AMERICAN HISTORY: THE FRENCH AND INDIAN WAR

1. The victorious end to the war sparked strong feelings of colonial pride. Having supplied 20,000 soldiers and spent over 2 million pounds, the colonists viewed themselves as important and loyal partners of the British empire.

2. While the British leaders also celebrated their glorious victory, the long war left Britain with a great empire and an enormous national debt that had doubled to 130 million pounds.

3. The looming financial crisis forced Britain's young and untested King George III and his first minister George Grenville to reassess their colonial policies. Grenville reached a fateful decision when he insisted that the colonies had to begin paying a fair share of the "costs of the empire."

Do not overlook the French and Indian War. It has generated both short and long essay questions. For example, be sure you can explain why it was a turning point and how it affected relations with Native Americans.

II. THE STAMP ACT CRISIS, 1765–1766

A. BRITISH ACTION

1. Parliament passed the Stamp Act to raise revenue to help pay for British troops stationed in America.

2. The Stamp Act required a 1-shilling (about 25 cents) stamp on newspapers and playing cards, a 3-shilling stamp on legal documents, a 2-pound (about 10 dollars) stamp on college diplomas, and a 10-pound (about 50 dollars) stamp on a lawyer's license.

B. COLONIAL REACTION

1. Grenville did not expect opposition to the Stamp Act. He was wrong. Outraged colonial leaders insisted that only their provincial assemblies had the power to raise taxes.
2. British leaders responded by arguing that Parliament was based upon a system of virtual representation in which each member of Parliament represented the interests of all Englishmen, including the colonists.
3. The colonists rejected virtual representation, arguing that as Englishmen they could only be taxed by their own elected representatives. Their defiant slogan, "No taxation without representation" succinctly summarized the colonial position.
4. The colonists did more than shout slogans. In October 1765, nine colonies sent representatives to a Stamp Act Congress in New York City. This marked the first inter-colonial meeting since the Albany Congress. Unlike the earlier meeting, the Stamp Act Congress drafted a petition to Parliament and called for a boycott of imported British goods.

C. PARLIAMENT RESPONDS

1. Parliament used the doctrine of virtual representation to rebut the colonial petition. But they could not ignore the boycott of British goods as exports fell by 15 percent.
2. Pressured by angry merchants and their unemployed workers, Parliament rescinded the Stamp Act while also issuing a little-noticed Declaratory Act reasserting their authority over the colonies.

D. MAKING CONNECTIONS: BOYCOTTS

1. The Stamp Act boycott proved to be a masterful tactic that future American protesters would not forget. Almost 200 years later, Dr. Martin Luther King, Jr., led a successful boycott to protest racial segregation on buses in Montgomery, Alabama. The colonists and the Montgomery protesters both successfully used their economic power to sustain a political protest.

2. The Stamp Act crisis did not galvanize a consensus to declare independence as Americans still remained loyal to King George. However, it did mark the beginning of an increasingly divisive dispute over the relationship between Parliament and the colonies.

III. THE ROAD TO REVOLUTION

A. CONTEXT

1. No single event caused the American Revolution. Instead, it was precipitated by the cumulative effect of a series of British actions and colonial reactions.
2. Before the French and Indian War, John Adams compared the thirteen colonies to "thirteen clocks" each of which kept its own time. However, the once divided colonies began to act in unison as a budget crisis escalated into a fateful dispute that sparked an independence movement.

B. THE TOWNSHEND CRISIS, 1767–1770

1. In 1767, Charles Townshend, the head of the British treasury, persuaded Parliament to enact a new revenue act. The Townshend Act imposed import duties on such everyday items as paint, glass, paper, and tea. Townshend proposed to use the revenue for military expenses to pay the salaries of royal governors and other colonial officials.
2. The Townshend Act reignited the dispute over taxation. The Massachusetts legislature promptly condemned the new taxes and urged other colonial assemblies to join their protest. At the same time, merchants in Boston began a nonimportation movement to boycott British goods.
3. American resistance stiffened Townshend's determination to impose his will on the recalcitrant Bostonians. In late 1768, the first of 4,000 royal troops began to arrive in Boston. Bostonians resented the presence of these troops in their city. On the night of March 5, 1770, a rowdy group of hecklers taunted a squad of British soldiers stationed outside the Boston Customs house. An alarmed soldier fired into the crowd. When the smoke cleared, five townspeople lay on the ground, dead or dying.
4. Led by Sam Adams, enraged patriots branded the incident the "Boston Massacre." Paul Revere's partisan engraving further inflamed colonial opinion by depicting the British soldiers as merciless brutes who killed innocent civilians.

5. On the same day the Boston Massacre occurred, Parliament repealed all the Townshend duties except the one on tea. Although harmony seemed to have been restored, the Townshend Act crisis exacerbated feelings of distrust between British officials and a new, increasingly radical generation of American leaders.

C. THE INTOLERABLE ACTS CRISIS, 1773–1776

1. On December 16, 1773, a group of Boston patriots disguised as Mohawk Indians boarded three British ships and threw 342 chests of tea into the harbor.
2. The so-called Boston Tea Party infuriated British authorities. Parliament promptly passed the Coercive Acts to punish Boston for the wanton destruction of private property.
3. Known in America as the Intolerable Acts, the legislation closed the port of Boston, sharply curtailed town meetings, and authorized the army to quarter troops wherever they were needed.
4. Parliament's punitive actions seemed to confirm the colonists' fear that Britain intended to restrict each colony's right to self-government.
5. The British strategy failed to isolate Boston. In September 1774, fifty-five elected representatives met in Philadelphia to reach a unified colonial response to the Intolerable Acts. The First Continental Congress called for a complete boycott of British goods and urged the colonies to organize militia for defensive purposes.

D. THE SECOND CONTINENTAL CONGRESS

1. The Second Continental Congress convened in Philadelphia in May 1775. The delegates faced an ever-deepening crisis. Bloody battles between colonial militia and British soldiers had just been fought in Lexington and Concord. The Congress responded by creating a Continental Army and naming George Washington its commander.
2. Despite these aggressive actions, the delegates refused to declare war. Like most colonists, they wavered between acts of resistance and attempts at reconciliation.

IV. THE REVOLUTIONARY MINDSET

A. THE IMPACT OF BRITISH TAXES AND REGULATIONS

1. Parliament passed the Stamp Act, the Townshend Act, and the Tea Act to raise revenue to help pay for imperial expenses. Instead,

these tax laws raised questions about Parliament's right to tax the colonies.

2. Parliament passed the Proclamation of 1763, the Quartering Act of 1765, and the Intolerable Acts to tighten its control over the increasingly rebellious colonists. Instead, these regulatory acts intensified the colonists' resistance to British rule and their commitment to republican values.

B. THE IMPORTANCE OF REPUBLICAN VALUES

1. A belief in republican values inspired the American revolutionaries. Republicanism is the belief that government should be based upon the consent of the governed.
2. As resistance to British taxes and regulations intensified, colonial leaders became more and more convinced that a republic is preferable to a monarchy because it would establish a small, limited government responsible to the people.

C. THE INFLUENCE OF *COMMON SENSE*

1. In January 1776, Thomas Paine published a pamphlet entitled *Common Sense* to persuade the colonists to declare their independence from Great Britain.
2. Paine vigorously defended republican principles while denouncing monarchy as a form of government that produced a constant threat to people's liberty. Paine assailed George III as an oppressive "royal brute" who should be scorned and not venerated.
3. Paine rejected calls for a compromise and instead called upon the colonists to declare independence and "begin the world over again."

D. MAKING CONNECTIONS: THE IMPACT OF BEST-SELLING BOOKS

1. *Common Sense* became an instant bestseller as people throughout the colonies agreed with Paine's compelling argument for independence.
2. In the 1850s, Harriet Beecher Stowe's novel *Uncle Tom's Cabin* became an instant bestseller convincing many Americans to oppose the Fugitive Slave Law and support abolitionist efforts to end slavery.

E. TURNING POINTS IN AMERICAN HISTORY: THE DECLARATION OF INDEPENDENCE

1. The Declaration of Independence marked a momentous turning point in American history. Prior to the declaration, the colonists were still subjects of the British Crown. The Declaration of Independence created a new American identity by transforming a dispute over taxes into a fight for independence.

2. Jefferson opened the declaration with a concise and compelling statement of principles and self-evident truths. Inspired by John Locke's philosophy of natural rights, Jefferson asserted that governments derive "their just powers from the consent of the governed." The governed are entitled to "alter or abolish" their ties to a government that denies them their "unalienable rights" to "life, liberty, and the pursuit of happiness."

3. The Declaration of Independence also marked a turning point in American history because it has had enduring consequences that transcended its initial purpose. Jefferson did not base his argument on the narrow "rights of Englishmen." Instead, he left a lasting impression on the conscience of the world by appealing to universal principles derived from "the laws of Nature and Nature's God." Although not originally fulfilled, Jefferson's ringing statement that "all men are created equal" became an integral part of the American dream.

4. The Declaration of Independence did not call for the abolition of the slave trade. The reality of slavery thus contradicted Jefferson's eloquent statement of republican ideals.

V. THE REVOLUTIONARY WAR

A. WHY AMERICA WON

1. British commanders underestimated the fighting ability of American soldiers. Led by George Washington, America's military commanders proved to be resourceful and resilient.

2. The British government was confused, inept, and divided.

3. The French alliance provided indispensible military, financial, and diplomatic support.

4. American soldiers fought for republican ideals. They won because of the power of their ideas, not the idea of their power.

APUSH test writers rarely ask questions about specific battles. However, the Battle of Saratoga may be an exception. Be sure that you know that this pivotal battle led to America's crucial alliance with France.

B. THE TREATY OF PARIS OF 1783

1. The treaty recognized American independence and sovereignty over territories extending from the Mississippi River in the west, to the Great Lakes in the north, and to Spanish Florida in the south.
2. America pledged to compensate Loyalists whose lands had been confiscated by state governments.

CREATING A NEW NATIONAL GOVERNMENT 1781–1789

Chapter 7

I. THE ARTICLES OF CONFEDERATION

A. CONTEXT

1. The victory over Great Britain created a new nation. Unlike the Old World nations of Europe, America had no monarchy or aristocracy. But it did have a sense of mission to lead the world toward liberty and equality.
2. American leaders faced the still unresolved issue of creating a new form of government. The American Revolution thus remained unfinished.

B. A FLAWED "LEAGUE OF FRIENDSHIP"

1. The thirteen original states ratified the Articles of Confederation in 1781. The new government created a confederation or loose union among sovereign states. The Continental Congress created a confederation because it wanted to avoid giving the new government powers it had just denied to Parliament. Instead it formed a "firm league of friendship" that could not exercise powers independent of the states.
2. The Articles of Confederation constructed a government consisting of only a unicameral legislature. It gave the Congress responsibilities that included authority over coinage, the postal service, Indian affairs, and western territories.
3. The new government had little authority to fulfill its responsibilities. The central government included no judicial or executive branches. It had no power to levy taxes or regulate interstate commerce; likewise, it could not enforce its resolutions upon either the states or individual citizens.

C. ACHIEVEMENTS

1. Despite its weaknesses, the Confederate government successfully won the Revolutionary War and negotiated the Treaty of Paris ending the war on terms favorable to the United States.

2. The Northwest Ordinance of 1787 established an orderly procedure for territories to become states. The new states would not be subordinate colonies. They would instead be admitted as equals into the American republic.

3. The ordinance also banned slavery from the Northwest Territory. This fateful decision created a line between freedom and slavery that extended north of the Ohio River and all the way to the Mississippi River.

D. UNDERSTANDING CAUSATION: SHAYS' REBELLION

1. Causes

   a. Impoverished farmers in Massachusetts were losing their land because they did not have enough hard currency to repay their debts to eastern merchants and bankers.

   b. The desperate farmers demanded that the state legislature halt farm foreclosures, lower property taxes, print paper money, and end imprisonment for debt.

   c. Led by Daniel Shays, a former captain in the Continental Army, armed farmers closed a courthouse where creditors were suing to foreclose farm mortgages.

   d. The Massachusetts state legislature and the national Congress were unable to raise a militia to stop Shays. In January 1787, alarmed Bostonians financed a hastily formed army of 4,000 men who quickly crushed the insurrection.

2. Consequences

   a. Just before Shays' Rebellion, five states sent delegates to Annapolis, Maryland, to discuss trade problems. Although the delegates failed to resolve the commercial problems, they did call upon Congress to summon a convention to revise the Articles of Confederation.

   b. Shays' Rebellion frightened conservative leaders who feared that an unchecked democratic mob would destroy orderly government and threaten private property.

   c. The "great commotion" in Massachusetts fueled dissatisfaction with the Articles of Confederation. It convinced George Washington, James Madison, Alexander Hamilton, and other key leaders that the United States needed a stronger national government.

II. THE CONSTITUTIONAL CONVENTION, 1787

A. CONTEXT

1. On May 25, 1787, 55 delegates from every state except Rhode Island met in Philadelphia. The delegates quickly resolved to abandon the Articles of Confederation and create a new government.
2. During about four months of intense negotiations the delegates seized control of America's destiny. They skillfully resolved a series of contentious issues by reaching compromises that distinguished the possible from the impossible.

B. KEY PRINCIPLES

1. The Framers believed that government derives its just powers from the consent of the people. Widespread ownership of property provides a necessary foundation for representative government.
2. Government should be limited and power should be divided into separate legislative, executive, and judicial branches tied together by a complex system of checks and balances.
3. Political parties or factions are undesirable but inevitable. Left unchecked they will threaten the existence of representative government.
4. A large republic will curb factions. Madison reasoned in *Federalist No. 10* that "in an expanding Republic, so many different groups and viewpoints would be included in the Congress that tyranny by the majority would be impossible."
5. American republican principles would be best implemented by a federal system of government in which a written constitution divides power between a central government and state governments.

C. THE GREAT COMPROMISE

1. The Great Compromise resolved a fractious dispute between the large states led by Virginia and the small states led by New Jersey.
2. The Great Compromise created a bicameral, or two-house, Congress. Representation in the House of Representatives would be apportioned on the basis of population, while each state would be allotted two seats in the Senate.

D. KEY PROVISIONS

1. A Congress with the authority to levy taxes, declare war, and regulate interstate commerce.
2. A Necessary and Proper Clause, also known as the elastic clause, that gives Congress the power to make laws necessary for carrying out its enumerated powers.
3. An Electoral College designed to insulate the presidency from the threat of "excessive democracy."
4. An independent Supreme Court with justices appointed by the President and confirmed by the Senate.
5. Senators chosen by the state legislatures. This would help protect Congress from what Hamilton called "the imprudence of democracy."
6. A constitutional process for impeaching the President.
7. An amendment process that made the Constitution a living and flexible document.

E. KEY OMISSIONS

1. A Bill of Rights (added in 1791 as the first ten amendments)
2. Direct election of Senators (added by the Seventeenth Amendment in 1913)
3. Two-term limit for Presidents (added by the Twenty-second Amendment in 1951)

F. TURNING POINTS IN AMERICAN HISTORY: THE CONSTITUTION

1. The Constitution marked a momentous turning point in American political history. In a bold and unprecedented decision, the Framers transferred sovereignty from the states to the people.
2. The Constitution did not mark the beginning of momentous social changes. The revolutionary rhetoric about equality and natural rights did not change the status of enslaved Africans and women.

APUSH test writers often qualify questions on the Constitution with the phrase "as ratified in 1788." Remember, the Bill of Rights was not part of the Constitution ratified in 1788. Be sure you carefully read each question, paying special attention to qualifying phrases.

III. THE CONSTITUTION AND SLAVERY

A. THE FIRST EMANCIPATION

1. As the Framers met in Philadelphia, a "First Emancipation" was already taking place in the North. At that time, Northern states had eliminated or were gradually eliminating slavery.

2. In addition, the Confederation Congress had already excluded slavery from the Northwest Territory. As a result, slavery was becoming a distinctive Southern institution.

B. THE THREE-FIFTHS COMPROMISE

1. The Constitution did not actually use the words "slave" or "slavery." Afraid of alienating the Southern states, the Framers agreed to the Three-Fifths Compromise whereby slaves (euphemistically called "other persons") were treated as three-fifths of a person for purposes of taxation and representation. This gave the Southern states an enlarged vote in the House of Representatives.

2. The Three-Fifths Compromise was later repealed by Section 2 of the Fourteenth Amendment. The amendment process thus enabled the Constitution to be a living document that could advance the democratic principles stated in its Preamble and in the Declaration of Independence.

C. THE SLAVE TRADE

1. Many delegates abhorred the slave trade and wanted to immediately abolish it. Gouverneur Morris underscored slavery's moral outrage by declaring that, "The inhabitant of Georgia and South Carolina who goes to the Coast of Africa, and in defiance of the most sacred laws of humanity tears away his fellow creatures from their dearest connections and damns them to the most cruel bondage, shall have more votes in a Government instituted for the protection of the rights of mankind than the citizens of Pennsylvania and New Jersey."

2. Delegates from South Carolina and Georgia ignored Morris' moral argument pointing out that they needed to continue the slave trade in order to replenish slaves evacuated by the British during the Revolutionary War.

3. Led by Madison, pragmatic delegates wanted to avoid a dispute with the South that would fracture the convention. "Great as the evil is," Madison wrote, "a dismemberment of the union would be worse."

4. The convention resolved the issue by agreeing to a compromise in which Congress would not interfere with the slave trade until 1808.

IV. THE ROLE OF WOMEN

A. WOMEN IN COLONIAL AMERICA

1. A woman usually lost control of her property when she married.
2. A married woman had no separate legal identity apart from her husband.
3. An adult woman could not vote, hold a political office, or serve on a jury.
4. An adult woman had no legal rights over her children. A divorce was very difficult to obtain.

B. "REMEMBER THE LADIES"

1. Abigail Adams and her husband John exchanged over 1,200 letters. This correspondence contains a treasure trove of revealing insights into the thoughts of one of the most prominent and articulate couples in colonial America.
2. On March 31, 1776, Abigail wrote a celebrated letter to John, who was then serving as the Massachusetts representative to the Constitutional Convention in Philadelphia. Keenly aware that the delegates were on the brink of composing a Declaration of Independence, Abigail urged her husband to "remember the Ladies, and be more generous and favorable to them than your ancestors. Do not put such unlimited power into the hands of the Husbands."
3. Like most of his male contemporaries, John Adams refused to apply the logic of liberty to the status of women. He sarcastically replied, "I cannot but laugh."
4. Abigail's famous request underscored the fact that colonial women were treated as second-class citizens. Her letter demonstrated that some colonial women were aware of the discrepancy between the republican ideal of equality and the reality of how women were treated.

C. REPUBLICAN MOTHERHOOD

1. Neither the revolutionary ferment nor the new Constitution changed the legal status of women. But the spirit of republicanism

did lead to the conclusion that every citizen had a stake in maintaining the nation's hard-won liberty.

2. The American Revolution led to expanded support for women's education. In his influential essay, "Thoughts on Female Education," Benjamin Rush argued that women should be educated so they could instruct "their sons in the principles of liberty and government."

3. The idea of republican motherhood began to emerge after the Revolutionary War. Its advocates stressed that the new American republic offered women the important role of raising their children to be virtuous and responsible citizens. By instructing their children, especially their sons, in the principles of liberty, women played a key role in shaping America's moral and political character.

D. MAKING CONNECTIONS: WOMEN'S RIGHTS

1. Like Abigail Adams, other American women petitioned for expanded legal rights. However, their letters and protests led to limited reforms.

2. The Seneca Falls Convention (1848) marked the beginning of the women's rights movement in the United States. The Declaration of Sentiments opened by boldly declaring, "We hold these truths to be self-evident that all men and women are created equal." The document did more than urge the male politicians to remember the ladies; it demanded greater legal rights and the extension of the suffrage to women.

APUSH exams always include a number of questions designed to test your knowledge of both African American and women's history. Be sure that you carefully review the sections on these topics.

V. MAKING COMPARISONS: ANTIFEDERALISTS AND FEDERALISTS

A. CONTEXT

1. The Framers did not submit the proposed Constitution to the state legislatures. Instead they arbitrarily declared it would go into effect when ratified by conventions held in at least nine of the thirteen states.

2. A fiercely contested debate erupted between Antifederalists who opposed the Constitution and Federalists who supported it.

3. Antifederalists drew their primary support from rural areas and small farmers. In contrast, Federalists drew their primary support from urban areas, large landowners, and wealthy merchants.

B. KEY ANTIFEDERALIST ARGUMENTS

1. Warned that the proposed Constitution would create a powerful central government dominated by a "great and mighty President" and a Senate composed of wealthy men who would "swallow up all of us little folks."

2. Argued that the proposed Constitution would not work in a large nation with diverse interests. They maintained that a republican form of government works best in a small nation "close to the people."

3. Insisted that the United States should remain a group of small sovereign states tied together only for trade and defense.

4. Pointed out that the proposed Constitution did not contain a Bill of Rights to safeguard individual liberties.

C. KEY FEDERALIST ARGUMENTS

1. Warned that Shays' Rebellion demonstrated that the Articles of Confederation lacked the power to protect property and preserve domestic tranquility.

2. Argued that the proposed Constitution would work in a large republic by fragmenting political power and thus curbing the threat posed by both the wealthy minority and the turbulent majority.

3. Insisted that the separation of powers and the system of checks and balances would make it difficult for a special interest to dominate the government.

4. Stressed that the proposed Constitution would create a federal system in which power would be shared between state and federal governments.

D. THE *FEDERALIST PAPERS*

1. James Madison, Alexander Hamilton, and John Jay wrote a series of 85 essays now known as the *Federalist Papers* to defend and explain the Constitution.

2. The *Federalist Papers* are considered a definitive explanation of the theoretical underpinnings of the Constitution. For example, in *Federalist No. 10*, Madison argued that political factions are undesirable but inevitable. He believed that a large republic with three branches of government would disperse power and thus curb factionalism.

3. The Federalists prevailed as conventions in all thirteen states ratified the Constitution. But many skeptics questioned if the bold and risky decision to transfer sovereignty from the states to the people would work.

THE FEDERALIST ERA 1789–1800

Chapter 8

I. HAMILTON'S FINANCIAL PROGRAM

A. CONTEXT

1. George Washington commanded unmatched prestige and respect. The Electoral College unanimously elected Washington president in 1789 and again in 1792.
2. Washington named Alexander Hamilton to head the Department of Treasury and Thomas Jefferson to head the Department of State. Widely recognized for their brilliance, both men had served America with distinction during the Revolutionary War and the struggle to create a new national government.
3. Hamilton submitted a series of far-reaching economic reports to Congress. These reports exposed deep divisions within American society, raised significant constitutional issues, and turned political allies into partisan adversaries.

B. HAMILTON'S PROPOSALS

1. To restore confidence in America's credit by funding the federal debt at face value and by assuming state debts incurred during the Revolution.
2. To adopt an excise tax on liquor to aid in raising revenue to fund the national debt.
3. To impose tariffs on imported goods to raise revenue and to protect America's new industries.
4. To charter a national bank that would provide a stable currency and a source of capital for loans to fund the development of business and commerce.

II. THE NATIONAL BANK DEBATE

A. THE ISSUE: IS A NATIONAL BANK CONSTITUTIONAL?

1. Congress passed the bank bill over Madison's objections. Before signing the bill into law, Washington asked Jefferson and Hamilton

to compose written opinions on the constitutionality of creating a national bank.

2. Washington's request sparked America's first debate on whether the Constitution should be interpreted strictly or loosely.

B. JEFFERSON'S ARGUMENTS

1. Jefferson admitted that a bank would be a convenient aid to Congress in regulating the currency and collecting taxes.
2. However, Jefferson forcefully argued that a national bank was not absolutely necessary. The Constitution does not specifically authorize Congress to create a national bank. Jefferson favored a "strict" interpretation of the Constitution, arguing that what the Constitution does not permit, it forbids.

C. HAMILTON'S ARGUMENTS

1. Hamilton countered by pointing out that the Constitution specifically empowers Congress to collect taxes and regulate trade. A national bank would be more than a convenience; it would be a necessary institution for carrying out these powers.
2. Hamilton argued that the Necessary and Proper Clause gave Congress the implied power to charter a national bank. He favored a "loose" interpretation of the Constitution, arguing that what the Constitution does not forbid, it permits.

D. WASHINGTON'S FATEFUL DECISION

1. Hamilton's arguments prevailed and Washington signed the bank bill into law, thus chartering the First National Bank of the United States.
2. Hamilton's "loose construction" theory of the Constitution set an important precedent for the expansion of federal power. Jefferson and his supporters warned that the bank would create a "boundless field of power" for financial interests. The dispute between Jefferson and Hamilton created loose coalitions of leaders with opposing views and interests. The controversy over foreign policy hardened these coalitions into America's first political parties.

Alexander Hamilton is both the star of a Broadway musical and an APUSH exam superstar. Many multiple-choice questions feature a quote illustrating Hamilton's economic and political ideas.

III. UNDERSTANDING CAUSATION: JAY'S TREATY

A. CAUSES

1. A number of issues strained relations between the United States and Great Britain. The British impeded western settlement by refusing to evacuate forts in the Northwest Territory. Angry Americans accused the British of deliberately supporting Indian attacks on frontier settlements. In addition, British naval commanders seized some 250 American merchant ships trading with the French West Indies.
2. Determined to avoid war, Washington sent Chief Justice John Jay to London with orders to negotiate a treaty resolving the issues dividing the two countries.
3. Jay brought back a treaty in which Britain promised to evacuate the Northwest forts and pay damages for seized American ships. In return Jay agreed that the United States would pay the debts owed to British merchants on pre-Revolutionary accounts. Despite these agreements, the British stubbornly refused to renounce their right to make future seizures of ships and to repay Southern planters for slaves taken during the Revolution.

B. CONSEQUENCES

1. Jay's Treaty kept the peace with Great Britain, but strained relations with France.
2. The Treaty had particularly important domestic consequences. Opponents unleashed what Jefferson called "a burst of dissatisfaction." They bitterly complained that the treaty turned its back on America's friendship with France. Southern planters vehemently protested that the treaty forced them to pay the lion's share of pre-Revolutionary debts while New England merchants collected damages for seized ships.
3. After some hesitation, Washington endorsed the treaty and it received the necessary Senate two-thirds approval with no votes to spare. The ratification fight played a key role in exacerbating the increasingly bitter disputes between Hamilton's Federalist supporters and Jefferson's Democratic-Republican supporters.

Don't overlook Jay's Treaty. APUSH test writers expect you to know that it played a significant role in the development of political parties.

IV. THE FIRST PARTY ERA

A. CONTEXT

1. Political parties are not mentioned in the Constitution. Led by James Madison, the Framers opposed political parties as sources of corruption and vehicles for self-interest and personal ambition.
2. During the Washington administration, political parties began to coalesce around the economic policies and political philosophies of Alexander Hamilton and Thomas Jefferson. The Federalist Party supported Hamilton's programs while opponents led by Jefferson founded the Democratic-Republican Party.
3. The emergence of the Federalists and the Democratic-Republicans inaugurated America's two-party system. Historians divide American political history into party eras. The first party era began with the election of John Adams in 1796.

B. THE FEDERALISTS

1. Led by Alexander Hamilton and John Adams, the Federalists drew support from the New England and eastern port cities.
2. The Federalists favored a strong central government and a loose interpretation of the Constitution. They supported the national bank, protective tariffs, commercial interests, and the British over the French.

C. THE DEMOCRATIC-REPUBLICANS

1. Led by Thomas Jefferson and James Madison, the Democratic-Republicans drew support from the South and frontier farmers.
2. The Democratic-Republicans favored a weak central government and a strict interpretation of the Constitution. They opposed the National Bank and protective tariffs while favoring agrarian interests and the French over the British.

V. WASHINGTON'S FAREWELL ADDRESS, 1796

A. THE WARNING

1. In his Farewell Address to the nation in 1796, Washington responded to calls to support the revolutionary government of France by urging future American leaders to avoid forming permanent alliances with foreign nations.

2. "The great rule of conduct for us in regard to foreign nations," Washington advised, "is in extending our commercial relations, to have with them as little political connection as possible. So far as we have already formed engagements, let them be fulfilled with perfect good faith. Here let us stop."

B. MAKING CONNECTIONS: ISOLATIONISM

1. Washington's Farewell Address had a significant impact upon America's foreign policy. For example, following World War I, Republican congressmen used Washington's views to justify their refusal to support the League of Nations. During the 1930s, many congressional leaders used the Farewell Address to justify their support for Neutrality Acts intended to prevent America from becoming entangled in European conflicts.
2. The Second World War ended the influence of Washington's Farewell Address upon American foreign policy. Following the war, the United States adopted a foreign policy designed to contain Soviet expansion. As the leader of the Free World, the United States joined the United Nations and became a founding member of the NATO alliance.

VI THE ADMINISTRATION OF JOHN ADAMS, 1797–1801

A. THE QUASI-WAR WITH FRANCE

1. Foreign policy dominated the Adams presidency. He inherited an undeclared Quasi-War with France.
2. The French resented Jay's Treaty arguing that it favored British interests. They retaliated by announcing that they would no longer honor the neutrality of American ships. In 1797, French corsairs operating in the West Indies seized over 300 American ships.
3. President Adams resisted enormous pressure to declare war on France. He defied Hamilton and other war hawks by sending envoys to France. Now led by Napoleon Bonaparte, the French preferred to avoid war with the United States and concentrate on their conflict with Great Britain.

B. THE ALIEN AND SEDITION ACTS

1. The Federalists took advantage of the anti-French furor to pass a series of laws known as the Alien and Sedition Acts. The acts were intended to punish the Democratic-Republicans.

2. The Naturalization Act raised the residency requirement for U.S. citizenship from 5 to 14 years. Outraged Democratic-Republicans insisted that the act's real purpose was to prevent immigrants from voting for their party.

3. The Alien Acts authorized the President to deport dangerous aliens.

4. The Sedition Act made it illegal to speak, write, or print any statements about the President that would bring him "into contempt or disrepute."

C. THE KENTUCKY AND VIRGINIA RESOLUTIONS

1. The Federalists controlled all three branches of the federal government. Both Jefferson and Madison believed that the Alien and Sedition Acts embodied a threat to individual liberties caused by unchecked Federalist power.

2. Jefferson and Madison anonymously authored a series of resolutions that were approved by the Kentucky and Virginia legislatures. They denounced the Alien and Sedition Acts as "alarming infractions" of the First Amendment.

3. The Virginia and Kentucky Resolutions advanced a states' rights doctrine asserting that the Constitution arose as a compact among sovereign states. The states therefore retained the power to challenge and, if necessary, nullify federal laws.

D. MAKING CONNECTIONS: NULLIFICATION

1. The other states did not support the Virginia and Kentucky Resolutions. Nonetheless, Jefferson and Madison successfully turned public opinion against the Federalists by accusing them of taking steps on the road to tyranny. Jefferson defeated Adams in the 1800 presidential election in part because of his position as a defender of Revolutionary principles.

2. The immediate dispute over the Alien and Sedition Acts faded when the laws expired in 1801. However, their states' rights argument had a deep and lasting impact. During the 1830s, John C. Calhoun promoted the theory of nullification, the idea that a state had the right to veto a federal law it considered unconstitutional. Criticized as "a recipe for disunion," the doctrine of states' rights played an important role in causing the Civil War.

UNIT 4 PERIOD 4
1800–1848

KEY CONCEPTS

KEY CONCEPT 4.1
The United States began to develop a modern democracy and celebrated a new national culture, while Americans sought to define the nation's democratic ideals and change their society and institutions to match them.

KEY CONCEPT 4.2
Innovations in technology, agriculture, and commerce powerfully accelerated the American economy, precipitating profound changes to U.S. society and to national and regional identities.

KEY CONCEPT 4.3
The U.S. interest in increasing foreign trade and expanding its national borders shaped the nation's foreign policy and spurred government and private initiatives.

Chapter 9

THE EARLY REPUBLIC 1800–1828

I. THE JEFFERSON PRESIDENCY, 1801–1809

A. THE REVOLUTION OF 1800

1. Thomas Jefferson and James Madison organized and led the Democratic-Republican Party. Jefferson narrowly defeated John Adams in the election of 1800, thus ending the Federalist decade.
2. The election of 1800 is often called "the Revolution of 1800" because there was a peaceful transfer of political power from the defeated Federalists to the victorious Democratic-Republicans.
3. In his inaugural address, Jefferson stressed that the "essential principles" of American government were above party politics. Striking a conciliatory tone, he reminded his fellow countrymen, "We are all Republicans; we are all Federalists."
4. The Democratic-Republicans dominated the First Party Era as Jefferson and his fellow Virginians, James Madison and James Monroe, won six consecutive presidential elections. The Federalists disappeared on the national level in 1816.

B. JEFFERSONIAN DEMOCRACY

1. Jefferson promised to replace formal ceremonies that characterized the Federalist administration with what he called "republican simplicity." For example, White House guests were encouraged to shake hands with the president rather than bowing as had been the Federalist practice.
2. Republican simplicity meant more than just a new code of presidential etiquette. In his inaugural address, Jefferson promised "a wise and frugal government." Believing that the government governs best that governs least, Jefferson cut the budget, fired federal tax collectors, eliminated the tax on whiskey, and reduced both the army and the navy.
3. Jefferson wanted America to become an agrarian republic. He strongly believed that yeoman farmers exemplified virtue and independence from the corrupting influences of cities, bankers, financiers, and industrialists.

C. THE LOUISIANA PURCHASE, 1803

1. Westerners depended upon the Mississippi River to ship their goods to New Orleans where they were reloaded aboard ocean-going vessels for shipment to the East Coast or to foreign ports.

2. In 1803, the French leader, Napoleon Bonaparte, offered to sell the entire Louisiana Territory, including New Orleans, to the U.S. for just $15 million.

3. Jefferson now faced a dilemma. He recognized that Napoleon's offer was too good to refuse. However, as a strict constructionist Jefferson worried that the Constitution did not give Congress the power to purchase new territory.

4. Jefferson's advisors argued that the President's power to make treaties gave him the implied power to purchase territory. Fearing that the capricious Napoleon might change his mind, Jefferson relented and the Senate overwhelmingly approved the Louisiana Purchase.

5. The Louisiana Purchase doubled the size of the U.S. Jefferson optimistically believed that the purchase would help fulfill his vision of America as an agrarian republic that would become an Empire of Liberty. Ironically, the lands acquired in the Louisiana Purchase later sparked a divisive sectional dispute over the spread of slavery into the western territories.

6. Jefferson sponsored the Lewis and Clark expedition to explore the Louisiana Territory. The expedition mapped the upper reaches of the Missouri River, explored the Columbia River, strengthened America's claim to the Oregon Territory, and increased general scientific knowledge about Northwest America.

D. *MARBURY v. MADISON*

1. As Chief Justice of the Supreme Court from 1801 to 1835, John Marshall issued a number of landmark decisions that strengthened the power of the federal government, upheld the supremacy of federal law over state legislatures, and promoted business enterprise.

2. Marshall established the principle of judicial review in the famous case of *Marbury v. Madison*. Judicial review gave the Supreme Court the power to declare unconstitutional a governmental action found to violate some provision of the Constitution.

APUSH test writers will not expect you to recall the details of Marbury v. Madison, *but they will expect you to know that the case established the principle of judicial review. This power gave the Supreme Court the authority to make definitive rulings on the meaning of the Constitution.*

E. THE EMBARGO OF 1807

1. Although he was an ardent supporter of the French Revolution, Jefferson continued Washington's policy of neutrality.
2. In 1807, Jefferson persuaded Congress to pass an Embargo Act stopping all exports of American goods to Europe. Jefferson hoped the embargo would enable the United States to avoid being drawn into the ongoing conflict between Great Britain and France.
3. As in the Louisiana Purchase, Jefferson once again drew upon the loose constructionist doctrine of implied powers. He argued that the government's power to regulate commerce could be used to justify imposing an embargo.
4. The embargo proved to be very unpopular with New England shippers. Ironically, it had the unforeseen effect of promoting manufacturing in the region.

II. UNDERSTANDING CAUSATION: THE WAR OF 1812

A. CAUSES

1. Both Jefferson and his successor James Madison followed a policy of neutrality hoping to avoid war with either Great Britain or France. However, the British policy of impressing American seamen and forcing them into the Royal Navy outraged Americans. Led by Henry Clay and John C. Calhoun, a group of "War Hawks" in Congress demanded war with Britain as the only recourse to defend American honor.
2. The War Hawks also hoped to drive Britain from Canada and remove Indians from the frontier.

B. CONSEQUENCES

1. The War of 1812 restored American pride and reaffirmed the young republic's independence. It also ensured Canada's independence from the United States.

2. The British defeat dealt a severe blow to Indians living in the Midwest by depriving them of their strongest ally.
3. On January 8, 1815, American forces led by General Andrew Jackson won a decisive battle defending New Orleans from British attack. The victory transformed Jackson into a national hero.
4. While Jackson was preparing to defend New Orleans, a group of disgruntled Federalists were meeting in Hartford, Connecticut, to oppose the war and discuss ways of limiting the power of the federal government. The Hartford Convention released its report as news of Jackson's victory spread across the country. The Hartford Convention contributed to the demise of the Federalist Party by making its leaders appear to be unpatriotic.
5. The War of 1812 interrupted trade, thus contributing to the process of industrialization begun by the Embargo Act of 1807.
6. The War of 1812 intensified a new spirit of nationalism. A newly "federalized" President Madison now supported re-chartering the National Bank and increasing tariffs to protect America's "infant" industries from foreign competition.

III. JAMES MONROE AND THE ERA OF GOOD FEELINGS

A. A SURGE OF NATIONALISM

1. James Monroe overwhelmed his Federalist opponent in the 1816 presidential election. He was then reelected in 1820 without opposition.
2. Monroe's presidency began with a surge of nationalism. One Boston newspaper captured the optimistic spirit of the time when it proclaimed that Monroe's election marked the beginning of an "Era of Good Feelings."

B. THE AMERICAN SYSTEM

1. Sponsored by Henry Clay, the American System supported the national bank to promote economic stability, called for a tariff to raise revenue and protect American industries, and endorsed a program of federal support for internal improvements or transportation projects to unite the country.
2. Clay's American System was similar to Alexander Hamilton's economic vision. Both programs favored a strong federal government to strengthen the Union by promoting commerce and stimulating economic growth.

C. JUDICIAL NATIONALISM

1. The Marshall Court continued to render landmark decisions that opposed states' rights and strengthened the power of the federal government.
2. In *McCulloch v. Maryland,* the Court struck down a Maryland law taxing a branch of the Second Bank of the United States. The decision established the supremacy of federal laws over state laws. Marshall declared the National Bank constitutional by confirming the right of Congress to utilize its implied powers.
3. In *Gibbons v. Ogden,* the Court declared that only Congress has the constitutional power to regulate interstate commerce. The decision established the commerce clause as a key mechanism for the expansion of federal power.

D. THE MONROE DOCTRINE

1. In his final message to Congress on December 2, 1823, Monroe announced a new American foreign policy toward Latin America.
2. Monroe's unilateral declaration of principles stated that republican governments in the Americas were different and separate from the monarchical systems in Europe. As the protector of republican institutions, the United States would not tolerate the creation of new European colonies in the Western Hemisphere. Monroe further demanded that the European powers stay out of the internal affairs of the newly independent American nation.
3. In return, Monroe promised that the United States would not interfere with any established European colonies in the Western Hemisphere or in the internal affairs of any European nation.
4. The Monroe Doctrine had little effect at the time. The European powers refrained from interfering in the New World because of the power of British warships, not the eloquence of Monroe's words.

E. MAKING CONNECTIONS: U.S. POLICY TOWARD LATIN AMERICA

1. Monroe's declaration was a sign of America's growing self-confidence in the Era of Good Feelings. First called the Monroe Doctrine in 1852, the principles Monroe proclaimed became the cornerstone of American foreign policy in the Western Hemisphere.
2. Theodore Roosevelt also worried about European intervention in Latin America. In December 1904, Roosevelt updated the Monroe Doctrine declaring that "flagrant cases of wrongdoing" in Central America and the Caribbean "may force the United States to

exercise an international police power." Known as the Roosevelt Corollary to the Monroe Doctrine, this unilateral declaration changed the Monroe Doctrine from a statement against the intervention of European powers in the affairs of the Western Hemisphere to a justification of the unrestricted American right to regulate affairs in the Caribbean and Central America.

IV. TURNING POINTS IN HISTORY: THE MISSOURI COMPROMISE

A. CONTEXT

1. The spirit of nationalism brought Americans together. But a debate over the extension of slavery into the Louisiana Territory sparked a divisive spirit of sectionalism.
2. When George Washington took office in 1789, the North and South were roughly equal in wealth and population. However, with each passing decade the North steadily outgained the South in population growth. By 1819, the free states in the North had 105 representatives in the House compared with just 81 representatives for the South.
3. While the North controlled a solid majority of votes in the House, the Senate was evenly but precariously balanced between 11 free and 11 slave states.

B. "A SACRED PACT"

1. In 1819, the territory of Missouri applied for statehood as a slave state. The Northern controlled House of Representatives responded by passing the Tallmadge Amendment prohibiting the further introduction of slaves into Missouri and providing for the gradual emancipation of the 10,000 slaves already in the territory.
2. Outraged Southerners believed that the Tallmadge Amendment threatened the future of the plantation system while also implying an attack on the Southern way of life. Although the Senate rejected the Tallmadge Amendment, the issue of extending slavery into the western territories ignited a passionate sectional debate that shattered the harmony of the Era of Good Feelings.
3. House Speaker Henry Clay promoted a compromise that settled the dispute by admitting Missouri as a slave state and Maine as a free state. In addition, the Missouri Compromise prohibited slavery in the remaining portion of the Louisiana Purchase north of latitude 36° 30′.

Many in the North viewed the 36° 30′ line as "a sacred pact" that should never be broken.

C. "A FIRE BELL IN THE NIGHT"

1. Before the Missouri controversy, many thoughtful Southern leaders acknowledged that slavery was a necessary evil inherited from their colonial ancestors. But a new generation of Southern leaders increasingly began to defend slavery as a positive good.
2. While Southerners defended slavery, many in the North began to fear that the institution posed a threat to free labor and industrial expansion. A small but vocal group of critics also began to question the morality of slavery.
3. The Missouri Compromise temporarily defused the political crisis over slavery. However, the debate foreshadowed the sectional controversies that dominated American political life in the 1840s and 1850s. The Congressional power struggle that produced the Missouri Compromise created "the North" and "the South" as rival political sections.
4. An alarmed Thomas Jefferson sensed the future peril when he wrote, "This momentous question, like a fire bell in the night, awakened and filled me with terror."

V. THE END OF THE ERA OF GOOD FEELINGS

A. THE ELECTION OF 1824

1. The Era of Good Feelings proved to be brief. The contentious debate over slavery and the return of partisan political factions within the Democratic-Republican Party eroded the consensus on national goals that had been the hallmark of the Monroe presidency.
2. In 1824, four regional candidates vied for the presidency. Andrew Jackson received more popular and electoral votes than his rivals John Quincy Adams, William Crawford, and Henry Clay. Since Jackson did not receive a majority of the electoral votes, the election went to the House of Representatives, which voted by states.
3. As Speaker of the House, Clay occupied a unique position of power. Clay despised Jackson as a "military chieftain" who was unfit for office. Although Clay was not personally close to Adams, the two men were both nationalists who supported the American System. Clay's influence prevailed and Adams won the presidency.

4. Shortly after winning the House vote, Adams named Clay his new Secretary of State. Jackson's outraged supporters promptly accused Adams and Clay of a "corrupt bargain" that thwarted the will of the people by cheating Jackson out of the presidency.

Be prepared for a short-answer question asking you to define the Era of Good Feelings and provide evidence supporting why this is and is not an appropriate historic label for the period between 1816 and 1824.

B. THE DISAPPOINTING PRESIDENCY OF JOHN Q. ADAMS

1. A confirmed nationalist, Adams hoped to accomplish great projects. He championed an ambitious program of internal improvements and called upon Congress to establish a national university and build an astronomical observatory in Washington.
2. Adams' presidency proved to be disappointing. Although he possessed a brilliant intellect, Adams lacked personal charm and a common touch. His alleged political deal with Clay tarnished his presidency. Jackson's fervent supporters in Congress undermined the Adams presidency by voting down most of his proposals. They eagerly looked forward to the presidential election of 1828 when they fully expected the popular will to prevail.

Chapter 10

THE AGE OF JACKSON 1828–1844

I. THE RISE OF JACKSON

A. CONTEXT

1. To his legion of admirers, Andrew Jackson provided an example of what an able and ambitious man born without privileges might become.
2. Jackson was born in 1767 to a family of poor Scotch-Irish immigrants living in the back country of North Carolina. Forced to make his own way in life, Jackson moved to Tennessee where he became a lawyer and a successful land speculator.
3. Although he was a man of uncommon ability, Jackson nonetheless projected a common touch. He became Tennessee's first representative in Congress and also served the state in the Senate.
4. Jackson won his greatest acclaim as a military hero. He defeated the Creek Indians and triumphed over the British at the Battle of New Orleans. He earned the nickname "Old Hickory" because he seemed as tough as the hardest of American hardwood trees.

B. THE ELECTION OF 1828

1. The First Party System provided political stability by allowing peaceful transfers of power from one set of elite leaders to another. Because of property qualifications, very few white males—and no women, enslaved Africans, or Native Americans—actually voted.
2. During the 1820s, state legislatures eliminated most property qualifications enabling a growing number of white males to vote. Led by Martin Van Buren, Jackson's supporters shrewdly launched a new style of campaigning that included parades, mass rallies, leaflets, barbecues, and, of course, kissing babies.
3. The 1828 presidential election featured a rematch between Jackson and John Quincy Adams. One passionate pro-Jackson newspaper editor captured the spirit of partisan politics by urging voters, "To the polls, to the polls! Let no one stay home. Let not a vote be lost." The appeal worked. Jackson swept the South and West and

easily crushed Adams in both the popular and the electoral vote. His victory began a new era in American history.

II. THE KEY TENETS OF JACKSONIAN DEMOCRACY

A. BELIEF IN THE COMMON MAN

1. The Jacksonians had great respect for the common sense and abilities of the common man.
2. Admirers saw Jackson as a common man who represented the interests of the people.

B. EXPANDED SUFFRAGE

1. The Jacksonians enthusiastically supported the expansion of white male suffrage.
2. During the Federalist Era, caucuses of party leaders selected candidates. During the Jackson administration, nominating conventions replaced legislative caucuses.

C. PATRONAGE

1. The Jacksonians supported patronage—the policy of rewarding political supporters with government positions.
2. Many Jacksonians believed that victorious candidates had a duty to reward their supporters and punish their opponents.

D. OPPOSITION TO PRIVILEGED ELITES

1. As champions of the common man, the Jacksonians despised the special privileges of the Eastern elites.
2. Special privileges were anathema to a government dedicated to promoting and protecting the common man.

III. THE TARIFF OF ABOMINATIONS AND THE NULLIFICATION CRISIS

A. THE TARIFF OF ABOMINATIONS

1. Tariffs traditionally served the dual purposes of raising revenue and protecting American industry from European competitors. For example, the 1816 tariff averaged 25 percent of the value

of imported goods. In 1828, Congress unexpectedly passed a protective tariff that pushed rates to over 50 percent of the value of imports.

2. Led by South Carolina, the Southern states branded the hated law the "Tariff of Abominations." Planters argued that while the industrial Northeast flourished, the South was forced to sell its cotton in an unprotected world market and buy imported goods at exorbitant rates.

B. JOHN C. CALHOUN AND THE DOCTRINE OF NULLIFICATION

1. Vice President John C. Calhoun anonymously responded to the Tariff of Abominations by writing the "South Carolina Exposition and Protest."
2. Calhoun drew upon states' rights arguments first formulated by Jefferson and Madison in the Kentucky and Virginia Resolutions. Insisting that the Union was a compact of sovereign states, Calhoun argued that when a federal law exceeded the delegated powers of Congress, a state or states could declare the law "null and void" within their own borders.

C. JACKSON AND THE FORCE BILL

1. Inspired by Calhoun, the South Carolina legislature adopted an ordinance of nullification repudiating the Tariff of Abominations.
2. Jackson angrily denounced nullification as an "impractical absurdity" and warned South Carolina that "disunion by armed force is treason." He then demanded that Congress pass a "Force Bill" authorizing him to use the army to enforce federal laws in South Carolina.
3. As tensions mounted, Henry Clay proposed a new compromise tariff that would gradually reduce duties over the next ten years. The compromise worked and South Carolina rescinded its nullification ordinance.

D. MAKING CONNECTIONS: NULLIFICATION AND SECESSION

1. Calhoun did not advocate secession. Instead, he saw nullification as a viable option that would prevent disunion.
2. Jackson may have sensed that he had not gone far enough in suppressing nullification. On his deathbed in 1845 he bitterly regretted that he had not executed Calhoun for treason. "My country," he said, "would have sustained me in the act, and his fate would have been a warning to traitors in all time to come."

3. Jackson's intuition proved to be prescient. During the 1850s, South Carolina "fire eaters" abandoned nullification and increasingly embraced the doctrine of secession as the best way to remedy their grievances.

IV. JACKSON AND NATIVE AMERICANS

A. THE INDIAN REMOVAL ACT, 1830

1. In the late 1820s, approximately 125,000 Native Americans lived east of the Mississippi River. Although many Americans felt respect and admiration for the Indians, covetous white settlers surrounded their ancestral lands.
2. In 1830, Congress passed the Indian Removal Act providing for the exchange of Indian lands in the East for government lands in the newly-established Indian Territory in what is today Oklahoma.

B. *WORCESTER v. GEORGIA*, 1832

1. The Cherokee legally challenged President Jackson's removal order. In *Worcester v. Georgia*, Chief Justice John Marshall upheld the Cherokee Nation's legal right to their land.
2. The Supreme Court is dependent upon the President to enforce its decisions. As a famous Indian fighter, Jackson harbored a well-known animosity toward Native Americans. He responded to the *Worcester* decision by defiantly declaring, "John Marshall has made his decision, now let him enforce it."

C. THE TRAIL OF TEARS

1. Jackson defied the Court's decision and pushed forward with his policy of moving the remaining eastern tribes west of the Mississippi.
2. In 1838, about 7,000 troops led by General Winfield Scott began the forcible evacuation of some 17,000 Cherokee from their homes. About one-fourth of the Cherokees died from disease and exhaustion on an 800-mile route that came to be known as the Trail of Tears.

The Trail of Tears has generated a number of APUSH exam questions. Be prepared to locate the trail on a map and analyze the famous painting "The Trail of Tears" by Robert Lindneux. The work depicts the suffering of the Cherokee people as stern blue-coated soldiers refuse to slow the forced march.

V. THE BANK WAR

A. JACKSON'S VETO

1. The Second Bank of the United States included a main office in Philadelphia and 25 branches in cities across the nation. Jackson and his supporters assailed the bank as a "monster" that concentrated special financial advantages in the hands of a few privileged people.

2. The bank's 20-year charter was scheduled to expire in 1836. In July 1832, Jackson vetoed a bill that would have rechartered the bank. He denounced the bank as a vehicle used by "the rich and powerful to bend the acts of government to their selfish purposes."

B. CONSEQUENCES

1. Jackson's war against the bank played a key role in the creation of the new two-party system. Now known as the Democrats, Jackson's party opposed the bank. In contrast, a new party known as the Whigs (which included many former Federalists) supported the bank.
2. Without the bank's restraining policies, state-chartered banks flourished. Often poorly managed by inexperienced officials, these so-called "pet banks" flooded the country with paper currency, thus promoting a speculative bubble in western lands and transportation projects.

VI. THE RISE OF THE WHIGS

A. "KING ANDREW THE FIRST"

1. The South Carolina nullification crisis, the Indian Removal Act, and the battle over the national bank all provoked contentious national disputes.

2. Political opponents led by Henry Clay hated Jackson. They derisively called him "King Andrew the First" pointing to his dubious distinction of using the veto power more than all the previous presidents combined.

3. Jackson's rival left the Democratic Party and drew together in the newly-formed Whig Party.

APUSH exams typically include 2 to 3 political cartoons. Be sure to examine the famous cartoon entitled "King Andrew The First." The cartoonist's point of view is that Jackson is an arbitrary ruler whose political actions are unconstitutional. The Indian Removal Act and the bank veto provide evidence supporting this point of view. Jackson's policies led to the formation of the Whig party and the beginning of the Second Party System.

B. THE ELECTION OF 1836

1. In 1836, the Democratic convention nominated Jackson's loyal Vice President, Martin Van Buren, for the presidency.
2. Still not fully organized, the Whigs did not hold a convention. Instead, they ran three candidates, hoping to throw the election into the House of Representatives. The strategy failed as Van Buren won a solid electoral victory.

C. MAKING CONNECTIONS: THE IMPACT OF HARD TIMES

1. Van Buren's campaign benefitted from an economic boom that had created great prosperity during Jackson's second term. But just two months after he took office, a sudden drop in cotton prices combined with a failure of the wheat crop created a financial panic. As hard times quickly spread, states cancelled transportation projects and many of the new pet banks failed. The financial panic settled into a deep depression as wages fell and unemployment rose. The economic depression doomed Van Buren's presidency.
2. Like Van Buren, Herbert Hoover's 1928 presidential campaign benefitted from a prolonged but vulnerable economic boom. Just six months after he took office, a sudden collapse of stock prices created a financial panic that swept through the American economy. Hard times spread quickly as banks closed, businesses failed, and unemployment soared. The impact of hard times doomed Hoover's presidency as it had that of Van Buren a century before.

D. THE LOG CABIN CAMPAIGN OF 1840

1. Feeling that they had no other choice, the Democrats once again turned to Van Buren as their presidential standard bearer.

2. Sensing victory, the Whigs nominated William Henry Harrison of Ohio. They emphasized his victory over the Indians in the 1811 Battle of Tippecanoe and blamed "Van Ruin" for the continuing economic slump. The strategy worked as Harrison and his running mate, John Tyler, won 234 electoral votes against just 40 for Van Buren.

3. Harrison's election marked a triumph for a new democratic style of running political campaigns. Although Harrison's father was a prominent Virginia planter who signed the Declaration of Independence, the Whigs adopted the log cabin and hard cider as campaign symbols to connect with the common man. Many historians consider the "log cabin and hard cider" campaign of 1840 the first "modern" election because both parties actively campaigned among the voting masses.

VII. MAKING COMPARISONS: THE WHIGS AND THE DEMOCRATS

A. THE WHIGS

1. The Whigs supported a strong federal government, a loose construction of the Constitution, the Second National Bank, and Clay's American System.

2. The Whigs opposed Andrew Jackson, the spoils system, Indian removal, and western expansion.

3. Key leaders included Henry Clay and Daniel Webster. The Whigs drew their greatest support from small businessmen, professionals, manufacturers, and some Southern planters.

B. THE DEMOCRATS

1. The Democrats supported states' rights, a strict construction of the Constitution, Indian removal, and western expansion.

2. The Democrats opposed the Second National Bank and federal support for Clay's American System.

3. Key leaders included Andrew Jackson and Martin Van Buren. The Democrats drew their greatest support from Irish immigrants, poor farmers in the North and Midwest, small planters in the South, skilled and unskilled workers in cities and towns, and the "common man."

THE OLD SOUTH 1800–1848

I. THE COTTON KINGDOM

A. THE COTTON GIN

1. During the late 1700s, a series of technological developments revolutionized the textile industry in Great Britain. The new inventions enabled British factories to turn cotton fibers into a cloth that was cooler and more comfortable than wool. These advances created a seemingly insatiable demand for raw cotton.
2. Southern farms could not meet the demand for raw cotton because of the difficulty of separating the fluffy cotton fiber from its sticky seeds. It required a full day for one laborer to remove the seeds from a pound of cotton.
3. In 1793, Eli Whitney invented a machine that could perform this tedious chore. His cotton engine or "gin" enabled slaves to clean fifty times as much cotton as could be done by hand.
4. The cotton gin revolutionized the Southern economy. Cotton production soared from just 9,000 bales in 1791 to 987,000 in 1831 and 4 million in 1860. This represented a prodigious number since each bale contained 500 pounds of cotton!

B. KING COTTON

1. Cotton quickly became America's most valuable cash crop. By the 1840s, cotton production accounted for over half the value of all American exports.
2. The excessive cultivation of tobacco had depleted the soil in the Chesapeake states. Ambitious planters looked south and west for fertile new land. They found them in a vast region of fertile land stretching from Georgia to Louisiana. Known as the black belt because of its rich black soil, this region soon produced two-thirds of the world's supply of cotton. Proud Southern planters confidently boasted, "Cotton is King."

C. UNDERSTANDING CAUSATION: THE IMPACT OF THE COTTON ECONOMY

1. Cotton irrevocably altered the South's attitude toward slavery. As the South became committed to a one-crop cotton economy, it also became committed to slavery. Of the 2.5 million slaves engaged in agriculture in 1850, 75 percent worked at cotton production.

2. The presence of slavery discouraged immigrants from moving to the South. In 1860 just 4.4 percent of the Southern population was foreign-born. Meanwhile, between 1844 and 1854 over 3 million European immigrants flooded into eastern seaports.

3. As the South devoted more and more resources to growing cotton, the region lagged behind the North in trade and manufacturing. Southern cotton was primarily exported in Northern vessels. While Northern factories produced manufactured goods at an ever-increasing rate, Southern farmers purchased finished goods under a credit system that kept them in debt.

4. The South's commitment to growing cotton slowed urban growth. With the exception of New Orleans and Charleston, the South had few urban centers. Instead, most Southerners lived on widely dispersed farms and plantations.

5. Taken together, the South's reliance upon cotton and slaves and its slow rate of industrialization and urbanization removed it from the dynamic innovations taking place in the North and West. As these forces of change accelerated, the South became committed to preserving and defending its distinctive regional identity.

II. WHITE SOCIETY IN THE OLD SOUTH

A. PLANTERS

1. Planters comprised just 4 percent of the South's adult white male population. This small but powerful group owned more than half of all the slaves and harvested most of the region's cotton and tobacco.

2. A wealthy elite, planters dominated Southern economic and social life. The image of a paternalistic planter who lived in a white-columned mansion came to embody a distinctive way of life that valued tradition, honor, and genteel manners.

B. YEOMAN FARMERS

1. The majority of white families in the antebellum South were independent yeoman farmers who owned few, if any, slaves.

2. Although the South's numerical majority, yeoman farmers did not set the region's political and social tone. Instead, they deferred to the large planters since many aspired to become large planters themselves.

C. POOR WHITES

1. As many as 25 to 40 percent of white Southerners were unskilled laborers who owned no land and no slaves. These "poor whites" often lived in the backwoods where they scratched out a meager living doing odd jobs.

2. Although they did not own slaves and frequently resented the aristocratic planters, poor whites nonetheless supported the South's biracial social structure. The existence of slavery enabled even the most impoverished white to feel superior to black people. Poor whites, yeoman farmers, and planters all shared a sense of white supremacy that bridged class distinctions.

Many students mistakenly believe that most white Southerners owned slaves. This is incorrect. It is important to remember that three-quarters of white Southern families owned no slaves.

III. ASPECTS OF LIFE AMONG SLAVES IN THE OLD SOUTH

A. THE DOMESTIC SLAVE TRADE

1. Congress outlawed the African slave trade in 1808. The spread of cotton plantations into the black belt caused a major change in the movement and distribution of slavery. In 1790, planters in Virginia and Maryland owned 56 percent of all enslaved Africans. Between 1800 and 1860, tobacco-depleted Chesapeake planters sold about one million slaves to planters in a region stretching from western Georgia to eastern Texas known as the Deep South.

2. The domestic slave trade uprooted countless families. Despite forced separation and harsh living conditions, slaves maintained strong kinship networks while creating a distinct African American culture. Religion played a particularly important role. For example,

spiritual songs enabled slaves to express their sorrows, joys, and hopes for a better life.

B. RESISTANCE

1. Slaves tried to escape when they could. For example, in 1841, slaves being shipped from Norfolk, Virginia, to New Orleans forced the captain to sail to the Bahamas where Britain had abolished slavery in 1833.
2. Slave revolts were infrequent. With the exception of Nat Turner's insurrection in 1831, vigilant planters successfully suppressed slave rebellions. Many slaves retaliated against their masters by slowing the pace of work, damaging equipment, and feigning illness.

C. FREE BLACKS

1. Not all blacks were slaves. By 1860, as many as 250,000 free blacks lived in the South. Many of these "free persons of color" were the descendants of men and women who had been freed by idealistic owners following the Revolutionary War. Others successfully purchased their freedom.
2. Free blacks occupied a precarious position in Southern society. For example, they were often subject to discriminatory laws that denied them property rights and forbade them from working in certain professions and testifying against whites in court.

IV. MAKING COMPARISONS: ATTITUDES TOWARD SLAVERY IN THE OLD SOUTH

A. SLAVERY AS A "NECESSARY EVIL"

1. During the late 1700s, many Southern leaders referred to slavery as a "necessary evil" inherited from their colonial past.
2. Leading Southern statesmen such as Thomas Jefferson and James Monroe advocated a policy of gradually emancipating slaves while at the same time compensating their owners.

B. SLAVERY AS A "POSITIVE GOOD"

1. During the early 1830s slaveholders advanced a systematic argument to justify what they called "our peculiar institution." The word "peculiar" did not mean odd or strange. Instead, it referred to something distinctive or characteristic of the Southern way of life.

2. First expressed by John C. Calhoun, the "positive good" argument insisted that slaves benefitted from a benign and paternalistic institution. They argued that well-cared-for slaves actually had lives that were as good or better than the lives of so-called wage slaves working in textile mills in New England.
3. Proslavery advocates pointed to citations in the Bible condoning slavery. They also used "scientific" theories of their day to create a false image of blacks as inferior people who required paternal white guardianship.
4. Planters warned that slavery was vital to the South's and to the nation's economy. They vowed to resist any attempt to interfere with their "peculiar institution."

APUSH exam writers often use quotes by John C. Calhoun and other Southern leaders to illustrate the "positive good" argument. This view contributed to increased sectional tensions between the North and the South during the 1850s.

A BURST OF CHANGE 1815–1848

I. REVOLUTIONARY CHANGES IN AGRICULTURE

A. CONTEXT

1. As ambitious planters and their slaves poured into the Deep South (Chapter 11), a second wave of settlers pushed into the Ohio Valley and the Great Lakes region.
2. In 1800, just 387,000 settlers lived in the trans-Allegheny region. Twenty years later the number swelled to 2.4 million.

B. TECHNOLOGICAL ADVANCES

1. Fertile but thickly matted soil awaited farmers arriving in Ohio, Indiana, and Illinois. They quickly discovered that iron plows that had worked well on East Coast farms proved unable to reliably clear the tough sticky Midwestern soil. John Deere's new polished steel-tipped plow solved the problem. Sharp and durable enough to slice through the soil, Deere's new plow enabled farmers to efficiently till their fields. Deere proved to be a talented publicist as his new company soon sold over 10,000 steel plows a year.
2. Midwestern farmers found that their land supported abundant wheat crops. However, they initially used hand-operated sickles that limited even the most industrious farmer to harvesting just a half-acre of wheat a day. In 1831, Cyrus McCormick invented a mechanical horse-drawn reaper that could harvest twelve acres of wheat a day.
3. Like the cotton gin, the mechanical reaper revolutionized American agriculture. As golden fields of wheat spread across the Northwest, farmers could harvest and sell their crop to East Coast consumers. But first they had to get their produce to these distant markets.

II. REVOLUTIONARY CHANGES IN TRANSPORTATION

A. ROADS

1. The federal government began to finance construction of the National Road in 1811. When finally completed in 1837, the 620-mile road stretched from western Maryland to Vandalia in Illinois.

2. Although the National Road represented a vast improvement over wilderness trails, land travel was still difficult, slow, and expensive. Covered wagons proved to be an inefficient and expensive way to transport wheat, corn, and other bulky Midwestern products across the mountains separating them from lucrative East Coast markets.

B. UNDERSTANDING CAUSATION: THE IMPACT OF THE ERIE CANAL

1. Because of the difficulties of land transportation, Midwestern farmers used a circuitous route that took their produce down the Ohio and Mississippi rivers to New Orleans where it was then loaded onto ships headed for East Coast port cities.

2. DeWitt Clinton, the governor of New York, had an audacious plan that reshaped American commerce. In 1817, crews began the construction of a canal connecting Albany on the Hudson River with Buffalo on Lake Erie. When it opened in 1825, the 363-mile-long Erie Canal created an all-water route that cut travel time from New York City to Buffalo from 20 days to just 6. Mule-drawn barges cut the cost of moving a ton of freight between these two cities from $100.00 to $5.00.

3. The Erie Canal enabled farmers in upstate New York and in Ohio to send their wheat to New York harbor. At the same time, these once isolated farmers could now import clocks, mattresses, curtains, and even Long Island oysters at a fraction of their former cost. During the 1830s, the Erie Canal carried more freight than the Mississippi River.

4. The Erie Canal transformed New York City into America's foremost commercial center. At the same time it tightened economic bonds between the North and the Old Northwest. The success of the Erie Canal inspired a decade-long mania for building canals that witnessed the construction of about 3,000 miles of new waterways.

C. STEAMBOATS

1. The westward flowing Ohio River provided a convenient all-water route to the Mississippi and New Orleans. While reaching New Orleans was relatively straightforward, returning home was not. A farmer could travel north on horseback over the dangerous

Natchez Trail. Most prudent people chose instead to ride back up the Mississippi on safe but slow-moving keelboats.

2. In 1807, Robert Fulton revolutionized water travel by proving that steam could propel a ship. His steamship *Clermont* successfully puffed its way up the Hudson River from New York City to Albany. Steamboats quickly became a common sight in East Coast harbors.

3. Steamboats also revolutionized trade on the Mississippi River. In 1811, the steamboat *New Orleans* powered its way up the Mississippi to Natchez. Soon steamboats capable of traveling ten miles an hour brought two-way traffic to the Mississippi. By the 1840s, more than 1,000 steamboats were carrying freight and people on the Mississippi and its tributaries. New Orleans and St. Louis became great Mississippi ports while Pittsburgh, Cincinnati, and Louisville became major cities along the Ohio River.

D. RAILROADS

1. The use of steam power also revolutionized land travel. During the 1820s, British engineers successfully built a railroad line connecting the port of Liverpool with the industrial city of Manchester.

2. The Liverpool-Manchester Railway inspired business leaders in Baltimore to finance a pioneering railroad line. By 1832, the Baltimore and Ohio (B&O) Railroad extended 72 miles west of Baltimore.

3. The B&O demonstrated that railroads were a cheaper and faster means of moving passengers and freight than canals. As "railroad fever" swept across the country, new lines connected major cities especially across the North.

4. The transformative impact of the railroad can be seen in the presidency of Andrew Jackson. Like other presidents before him, Jackson traveled to his inauguration in 1829 in a horse-drawn carriage. Eight years later he left Washington on a train.

III. REVOLUTIONARY CHANGES IN COMMUNICATIONS

A. CONTEXT

1. Throughout history messages had been limited by how fast messengers could travel. For example, it took riders on horseback a week to deliver the news of Washington's death in Arlington, Virginia, to New York City.

2. Canals, steamboats, and railroads all shortened travel times enabling news to travel more quickly. For example, the Erie Canal

reduced travel times from New York City to Ohio from 2 to 3 weeks to just one week.

B. THE TELEGRAPH

1. Led by Benjamin Franklin's pioneering work, electricity had long fascinated scientists and inventors. During the 1840s, several inventors made telegraph systems using wires that carried low-voltage currents. In 1844, Samuel F. B. Morse tapped out the first telegraph message in history over a line connecting Washington, D.C., to Baltimore.
2. The telegraph allowed instant communications over vast distances. Soon telegraph poles ran alongside the new railroad tracks. The railroads carried passengers and freight; the telegraph carried news. Both worked at previously unprecedented speeds, linking the nation as never before.

C. MAKING CONNECTIONS: COMMUNICATIONS TECHNOLOGY

1. The telegraph initially had little direct impact on most people's daily lives. Owned by companies such as Western Union and operated by trained specialists, the telegraph enabled railroads to create efficient schedules for their trains. The telegraph also enabled businesses to obtain news about the price of goods in distant markets.
2. Each new communications technology has had a greater impact on society than the one before it. The telephone, radio, and television all created an instantaneous flow of voices and images around the world. Today, the digital revolution is creating a fast-paced global market that is reshaping the pace and quality of daily life around the world.

IV. REVOLUTIONARY CHANGES IN COMMERCE

A. THE MARKET REVOLUTION

1. During the Era of Good Feelings, most Americans bought or bartered goods from friends and neighbors in a local economy.
2. The new network of roads, canals, steamship lines, and rail lines enabled merchants, farmers, and planters to reach consumers in other markets of the country. The term "market revolution" in antebellum America refers to the creation of a national economy that linked regions and people who were previously unable to access such a large market.

B. UNDERSTANDING CAUSATION: THE IMPACT OF THE MARKET REVOLUTION

1. Impact on the Northeast
   a. Accelerated the rate of industrial growth beginning with textile mills in New England.
   b. Created a close trading relationship between the Northeast and the Midwest.
   c. Created a wealthy class of urban capitalists.
2. Impact on the Midwest
   a. Accelerated the migration of settlers into the Midwest.
   b. Transformed Chicago into an important rail-center and distributor of agricultural products and machines to the West.
   c. Increased the production of cash crops such as wheat and corn.
3. Impact on the South
   a. Extended a plantation system based upon cotton and slavery southwestward into Alabama, Mississippi, and Louisiana.
   b. Slowed the pace of urbanization and industrialization.
   c. Created an economy dominated by wealthy planters.

The market revolution is a key development in the growth of the American economy. Be prepared to explain why the market revolution marks the beginning of industrialization in the United States.

V. REVOLUTIONARY CHANGES IN INDUSTRY

A. THE BEGINNING OF THE FACTORY SYSTEM

1. The cotton gin, reaper, and growing use of steamships and railroads created an agricultural revolution in the South and Midwest. At the same time, new technologies spurred the rise of the factory system in New England.
2. In 1790, Moses Brown built America's first textile mill in Pawtucket, Rhode Island. The pace of textile production, however, remained slow until the Embargo Act of 1807 and the War of 1812 stimulated domestic production.

3. In 1813, Francis Cabot Lowell and a group of investors known as the Boston Associates constructed a textile factory in Waltham, Massachusetts. The new mill used modern spinning machines and power looms to produce cheap cloth. Investors earned a 20 percent profit as sales soared from $3,000 in 1814 to $300,000 in 1823.

B. THE LOWELL EXPERIMENT

1. Inspired by the success of the Waltham mill, Francis Lowell built a model factory in a village renamed Lowell. Designed to avoid the drab conditions in English mill towns, Lowell featured clean red-brick factories and dormitories.
2. Lowell hired young New England farm women to work and live in his model town. The women worked 12 hours a day, 6 days a week. They lived together in boarding houses under the watchful eyes of older women who enforced mandatory church attendance and strict evening curfews.
3. The Lowell experiment worked well at first. By the early 1830s, young unmarried women from New England comprised the majority of the workers in Massachusetts' textile mills.

C. LOWELL CHANGES

1. Conditions at Lowell soon changed as a new generation of owners stressed efficiency and profit margins. In 1834 and 1836, the owners cut wages without reducing working hours.
2. The women responded by going out on strike. They unsuccessfully petitioned the Massachusetts legislature to pass a law enacting a 10-hour workday.
3. The strike convinced owners that the female workers were too troublesome. Factory owners increasingly hired impoverished Irish immigrants who were pouring into Massachusetts.

D. INDUSTRIALIZATION AND URBANIZATION

1. The factory system quickly spread from the textile industry to the production of shoes and guns.
2. The rise of commerce and industry spurred the growth of cities as the population of places with 8,000 or more inhabitants jumped from 3 percent in 1790 to 16 percent in 1860. During this period, New York City became the first city in America to boast a population of more than a million people.

VI. REVOLUTIONARY CHANGES IN IMMIGRATION PATTERNS

A. CONTEXT

1. Immigration to America slowed dramatically during the four decades between the Revolutionary War and the War of 1812. The French Revolution and the prolonged war between Great Britain and France reduced immigration to a trickle.
2. The first great wave of nineteenth-century immigration took place between 1820 and 1860. During this period, 5 million people immigrated to America. While many immigrants came from England and Scandinavia, over two-thirds of the total came from Ireland and Germany.

B. MAKING COMPARISONS: IRISH AND GERMAN IMMIGRATION

1. The Irish
   a. Desperate living conditions in Ireland made mass immigration inevitable. Beginning in 1845, a blight destroyed three successive potato crops. One million Irish died from starvation and disease, while another 1.7 million immigrated to the United States.
   b. Most Irish immigrants settled in Northeastern port cities. By 1860, the Irish comprised over one-third of the population of New York City and Boston.
   c. Most Irish immigrants were forced to work in the lowest-paying, most demanding unskilled jobs. The percentage of Irish workers employed in the Lowell mills jumped from 8 percent in 1845 to 50 percent in 1860.
   d. Irish voters supported the Democrats as the party of the "common man." Irish bosses soon played a key role in the formation of big city political machines.
   e. The Irish played a major role in the growth of the Catholic Church in the United States. The number of Catholic churches in America increased from 700 in 1840 to over 2,500 in 1860.
2. The Germans
   a. Political instability and economic unrest prompted over 1.5 million Germans to immigrate to America between 1830 and 1860.
   b. German immigrants typically settled in rural areas in the Midwest rather than in East Coast port cities.

c. German immigrants were a very diverse group that included exiled political refugees and displaced farmers. Although the majority of Germans were Protestants, about one-third were Catholics and a significant number were Jewish.

C. MAKING CONNECTIONS: NATIVISM

1. The great wave of Irish immigration sparked a nativist or anti-foreign reaction. Prejudiced employers posted "No Irish Need Apply" signs, while Protestant leaders complained that Irish-sponsored parochial schools would undermine support for public education.
2. Convinced that the Irish would never assimilate into American life, nativists formed groups with the political goal of restricting immigration and making naturalization a much longer process. During the 1850s, a political party known as the Know-Nothings demanded laws that would allow only native-born Americans to hold political office.
3. The Know-Nothings marked the beginning of a recurring pattern of nativist opposition to immigration. During the late 1890s and early 1900s, a wave of so-called "New Immigrants" from southern and eastern Europe sparked a new outburst of nativism. Members of the Immigrant Restriction League believed that the New Immigrants posed a threat to the American way of life because they were racially inferior to Anglo-Saxons. Nativist opposition became so strong that in 1924 Congress passed a law severely cutting the flow of immigration into the United States.

APUSH exams often include a chart depicting immigration patterns from 1820 to 1860. Questions typically ask students to discuss the causes and consequences of Irish and German immigration to the United States.

RELIGION, REFORM, AND ROMANTICISM 1815–1848

I. TURNING POINTS IN AMERICAN HISTORY: THE SECOND GREAT AWAKENING

A. CONTEXT

1. The religious fervor ignited by the First Great Awakening declined as colonial rebellion led to revolution and the eventual ratification and inauguration of the new Constitution dominated American public life.
2. During the early 1800s, a new wave of intense religious feeling called the Second Great Awakening swept across much of the country. Thousands of people attended emotionally charged camp meetings featuring appeals to faith and conversion by charismatic preachers.

B. "MORAL FREE AGENTS"

1. Devout Puritans accepted the Calvinist belief that original sin doomed humanity to a predestined membership in either a small group of "the elect" or a much larger mass of "the damned." In contrast, Second Great Awakening preachers such as Charles Grandison Finney emphasized that each individual was a "moral free agent" who could chart his or her own spiritual course in life.
2. The Second Great Awakening freed Protestants from the Calvinist doctrine of humanity's innate depravity. Instead, a merciful and loving God granted people free will and therefore the freedom to do good. The Second Great Awakening inspired a belief in perfectionism—faith in the human ability to consciously build a just society.

C. THE BURNED-OVER DISTRICT

1. Central and western New York became known as the "Burned-Over District" because of the particularly fervent revivals that crisscrossed the region.

2. The Burned-Over District was the birthplace of the Church of Jesus Christ of Latter-Day Saints, or the Mormons. Joseph Smith provided the initial leadership that galvanized this new faith.

D. IMPORTANCE OF THE SECOND GREAT AWAKENING

1. The Second Great Awakening was a predominantly Christian movement that altered the religious landscape of America. The Congregationalists in New England and the Anglicans in Virginia dominated religious life in colonial America. During the Second Great Awakening these faiths receded. Energized by passionate itinerant ministers, membership in the Baptist and Methodist churches surged.
2. The Second Great Awakening witnessed the birth of a distinctive black church in America. Most enslaved Africans gravitated to the Baptist and Methodist faiths. By the middle of the nineteenth century, white and black Baptist and Methodist denominations constituted two-thirds of the Protestant ministers and churches in America.
3. The Second Great Awakening inspired converts to believe in the possibility of improving their own lives and addressing social problems. It was a short step from the Second Great Awakening's emphasis upon spiritual progress to a belief in social progress. For example, a convert who pledged to give up alcohol could then be persuaded to work for temperance in his or her community.
4. The optimistic belief that Christians have an obligation to improve their society generated a number of reform movements. Denied roles in politics and the new market economy, many women found that they could make a difference by championing social change. Reformers worked to improve public education, promote better care for the mentally ill, limit the sale of alcoholic beverages, abolish slavery, and expand women's rights.
5. The Second Great Awakening played an important role in the ongoing democratization of public life in the early republic. The involvement of Protestants in their churches paralleled the increasing involvement of citizens in their government. Jacksonian democracy and the Second Great Awakening both expressed and reinforced the spirit of egalitarianism shaping American culture.

II. REFORM MOVEMENTS

A. EDUCATIONAL REFORM

1. Horace Mann sponsored many reforms in Massachusetts including a longer school year, higher pay for teachers, and a larger public

school system. As a result of his tireless work, Mann is often called the "Father of the Common School Movement."

2. Emma Willard was an early advocate of women's education. She founded Troy Female Seminary, America's first woman's school of higher education.
3. America's public school children learned about literature from a series of textbooks called *McGuffey Readers*. Also known as *Eclectic Readers*, the books featured stories illustrating the virtues of patriotism, hard work, and honesty.

B. THE MENTALLY ILL

1. Dorothea Dix launched a crusade to create special hospitals for the mentally ill. An indefatigable champion of reform, Dix travelled more than 10,000 miles and visited almost every state.
2. Dix and other reformers created the first generation of American mental asylums. By the 1850s there were special hospitals in 28 states.

C. THE TEMPERANCE MOVEMENT

1. In the early 1800s, America had over 14,000 distilleries producing 25 million gallons of alcoholic beverages each year. By 1830, Americans drank 5 gallons of alcohol per capita.
2. The temperance movement was a widespread campaign to convince Americans to consume less alcohol. Founded in 1826, the American Society for the Promotion of Temperance soon boasted 5,000 state and local temperance groups. Their campaign against "Demon Rum" worked. By the mid-1840s, Americans drank just 2 gallons of alcohol per capita.

D. MAKING CONNECTIONS: REFORM MOVEMENTS

1. Antebellum reform featured a number of voluntary organizations. Inspired by the Second Great Awakening, many reformers strove to eradicate sin from American society.
2. The reform impulse did not vanish from American life. Populists, Progressives, New Dealers, and advocates of the Great Society all sponsored programs designed to address social problems. For example, the Progressives focused on a broad range of problems including the consequences of industrialization, urbanization, and immigration. While the antebellum reformers emphasized voluntary reform organizations, the Progressives wanted government to play an active role in solving social problems and improving the quality of American life.

III. THE CRUSADE AGAINST SLAVERY

A. THE AMERICAN COLONIZATION SOCIETY

1. Founded in 1817, the American Colonization Society (ACS) advocated the gradual abolition of slavery combined with the goal of returning freed slaves to Africa. Although ACS members opposed slavery, many were openly racist and believed that blacks could not be integrated into American society.

2. The ACS was instrumental in founding the colony of Liberia on the west coast of Africa. However, the Society's gradual approach could never resolve the problem of slavery. By 1860, the ACS helped approximately 12,000 freed blacks migrate to Liberia. At that time there were about 4 million slaves in the South.

B. WILLIAM LLOYD GARRISON: "I WILL BE HEARD"

1. William Lloyd Garrison was a mild-looking reformer who at first supported the ACS's gradual approach to ending slavery. But Garrison's youthful appearance belied his strong moral convictions. His contact with slavery in Baltimore transformed him into a radical abolitionist who believed that slavery was a cruel, brutal, and sinful institution that should be immediately abolished.

2. As Garrison's views became more militant, he resolved to move to Boston and begin his own antislavery newspaper, *The Liberator*. On New Year's Day 1831, the 26-year-old Garrison published an open letter rejecting moderation and compromise. He boldly denounced slave owners as oppressors who defended an immoral institution that contradicted the Declaration of Independence's self-evident truth that all men are created equal.

3. Garrison defiantly promised, "I will not retreat a single inch–AND I WILL BE HEARD!" Although *The Liberator* had a modest circulation, Garrison's uncompromising call for immediate and uncompensated emancipation helped galvanize anti-slavery sentiment in the Northeast. In 1833, Garrison co-founded the American Anti-Slavery Society. Within just five years, it claimed to have 250,000 members and 1,350 local affiliates.

C. FREDERICK DOUGLASS: "I STOLE THIS HEAD"

1. Born a slave in Maryland, Frederick Douglass escaped from bondage in 1838 when he was just twenty-one. Recruited by William Lloyd Garrison, Douglass became a gifted orator who captivated anti-slavery audiences with his authentic stories about the horrors of slavery. For example, he told a spellbound audience

in Massachusetts, "I appear before this immense assembly this evening as a thief and a robber. I stole this head, these limbs, this body from my master and ran off with them."

2. Douglass was also a compelling writer. In 1845 he published his *Narrative of the Life of Frederick Douglass* describing his brutal fight with a slave driver and dramatic escape to the North. In 1847, he founded the *North Star*, an influential anti-slavery newspaper.

3. Douglass's eloquent speeches and writings played an important role in persuading a growing number of Northerners that slavery was evil and that its further spread into the western lands should be halted.

Frederick Douglass is part of an important group of African American leaders that includes Booker T. Washington, W.E.B. Du Bois, Marcus Garvey, Malcolm X, and Dr. Martin Luther King, Jr. APUSH exam writers typically devote a multiple choice or short-answer question to one or more of these key historic figures.

IV. WOMEN AND THE FIRST STIRRINGS OF REFORM

A. CONTEXT

1. The new American republic promoted equality and political democracy. However, women could not vote, hold office, or serve on juries. In addition, married women were denied rights to own and manage property, to form contracts, and to exercise legal control over children.

2. Prior to the Industrial Revolution many men and women worked together as an economic unit on small family farms. As the Industrial Revolution gained momentum, it encouraged a division of labor between home and work. While men held jobs in a competitive market economy, the home became the appropriate place or "sphere" for a woman.

B. THE CULT OF DOMESTICITY

1. The cult of domesticity idealized women in their roles as wives and mothers. As a nurturing mother and faithful spouse, the wife created a home that was a "haven in a heartless world." The home thus became a refuge from the world rather than a productive economic unit.

2. The cult of domesticity created a cultural ideal that best applied to upper- and middle-class white families that could afford to maintain separate spheres for their work life and for their home life. There was a wide gap between the ideals of the cult of domesticity and the harsh realities faced by women working in factories and on the frontier. Enslaved black women were completely excluded from any hope of participating in the cult of domesticity.

APUSH test writers often use pictures to see if students can identify and explain the concept of the cult of domesticity. The pictures typically feature a middle-class mother surrounded by her children. Her husband stands to the side watching as his wife instructs their children in music and literature.

C. THE SENECA FALLS CONVENTION

1. During the 1830s and 1840s many women dedicated themselves to working for the abolition of slavery. Led by Elizabeth Cady Stanton and Lucretia Mott, a small but determined group of feminists realized that they were also the victims of injustice. The anti-slavery movement thus helped spark a demand for equal rights for women.

2. Stanton and Mott issued a call for a convention to meet in Seneca Falls, New York, "to discuss the social, civil, and religious condition and rights of women." On July 19, 1848, approximately 300 delegates, including Frederick Douglass, met inside the Wesleyan Chapel to conduct America's first convention devoted to women's rights.

3. After meeting for two days, the convention issued a "Declaration of Sentiments and Resolutions." Written primarily by Stanton, the Declaration opened by declaring, "We hold these truths to be self-evident that all men and women are created equal."

4. The convention unanimously passed resolutions calling for greater divorce and child custody rights, equal opportunities in education, and the right to retain property after marriage. However, a contentious debate erupted over a controversial resolution calling for the extension of the suffrage to women. Douglass made a key speech emphasizing that the right to participate in government is a fundamental principle of equality, from which all other rights would follow. His speech swayed the delegates and the Stanton-Douglass position narrowly prevailed.

D. MAKING CONNECTIONS: FEMINISM

1. The Seneca Falls Convention marked the beginning of the women's rights movement in the United States. The resolutions passed at Seneca Falls formed the agenda for what historians call first-wave feminism. The first-wave agenda was fulfilled in 1920 when Congress passed the Nineteenth Amendment granting women the right to vote.
2. A second wave of feminism began in the United States in the early 1960s. Sparked by Betty Friedan's book *The Feminist Mystique,* the revived feminist movement focused on a new range of issues including workplace discrimination, domestic violence, and reproductive rights.

V. ROMANTICISM AND AMERICAN CULTURE

A. FROM DEISM TO ROMANTICISM

1. Thomas Jefferson, Benjamin Franklin, and many other leading late eighteenth century American intellectuals were Deists. "Deism" is the belief that God created the world but then allowed it to operate through the laws of nature. These natural laws could be discovered by human reason and expressed in mathematical formulas.
2. During the 1820s and '30s, artists and writers in Europe and America began to rebel against Deism's logical and well-ordered world. "Feeling is all!" became the guiding spirit of a new generation of Romantic painters and poets. The Romantic Movement's emphasis upon emotion reinforced the Second Great Awakening's emphasis upon the intense expression of spiritual feelings.

B. TRANSCENDENTALISM

1. The Transcendentalists were a small but influential group of writers and thinkers who lived in and around Boston. The leading Transcendentalists included Ralph Waldo Emerson, Henry David Thoreau, and Margaret Fuller (a brilliant woman who died at an early age in a shipwreck).
2. The Transcendentalists believed that God lived within each individual. Each person possessed an inner soul or spirit and thus a capacity to find spiritual truth.

3. The Transcendentalists believed that truth could be found in nature. They viewed communion with nature as a religious experience that enlightened their souls. For example, Thoreau turned away from the artificiality of "civilized" life and lived for two years in a cabin at the edge of Walden Pond near Concord.

C. THE HUDSON RIVER SCHOOL

1. The Hudson River School was America's first native school of art. Its members concentrated on painting landscapes that portrayed America's natural beauty.

2. For two famous examples of Hudson River School art, see *The Oxbow* by Thomas Cole and *The Rocky Mountains, Lander's Peak* by Albert Bierstadt.

UNIT 5 PERIOD 5
1844–1877

KEY CONCEPTS

KEY CONCEPT 5.1
The United States became more connected with the world, pursued an expansionist foreign policy in the Western Hemisphere, and emerged as the destination for many migrants from other countries.

KEY CONCEPT 5.2
Intensified by expansion and deepening regional divisions, debates over slavery and other economic, cultural, and political issues led the nation into civil war.

KEY CONCEPT 5.3
The Union victory in the Civil War and the contested reconstruction of the South settled the issues of slavery and secession, but left unresolved many questions about the power of the federal government and citizenship rights.

TERRITORIAL EXPANSION 1836–1850

I. THE "LONE STAR REPUBLIC"

A. THE TEXAS REVOLUTION

1. Texas belonged first to Spain and then, after 1821, to Mexico. The Mexican government opened Texas to settlers from the United States. The Anglo-Americans received generous land grants at low prices. In exchange they agreed to become Roman Catholics and citizens of Mexico. By 1830, there were about 30,000 people in Texas, ninety percent of whom were Anglo-Americans. However, few converted to Catholicism and many owned slaves.
2. The rapid growth of the Anglo-American population in Texas alarmed Mexican officials. In 1830, the Mexican government announced that slaves could no longer be brought into any part of Mexico and that Americans could no longer settle in Texas. Faced with these restrictions, the Texans rebelled and declared their independence on March 2, 1836.
3. The Texas revolution lasted less than two months. After suffering defeats at the Alamo and Goliad, Texan forces, led by Sam Houston, crushed the Mexican army at the Battle of San Jacinto on April 21, 1836.

B. THE ANNEXATION ISSUE

1. Most Texans wanted to join the United States. However, antislavery Whigs opposed admitting another slave state into the Union. Other opponents warned that annexing Texas would provoke a war with Mexico.
2. President Jackson feared that a prolonged debate over the admission of a slave state would ignite a divisive campaign issue that could cost his chosen successor Martin Van Buren the presidency. As a result, Jackson postponed annexation and Texas remained an independent "Lone Star Republic."

II. POLK AND TERRITORIAL EXPANSION

A. THE DOCTRINE OF MANIFEST DESTINY

1. During the 1820s many Americans thought the boundaries of the United States would not extend beyond the Rocky Mountains. However, the quest for land, opportunity, and adventure excited a new generation eager to explore and settle the western frontier. By 1860, over 4 million people lived west of the Mississippi River.

2. John L. O'Sullivan, the editor of the *Democratic Review*, gave the nation's expansionist spirit a name when he coined the term "Manifest Destiny." O'Sullivan declared that America's right to territorial expansion lay in "our manifest destiny to occupy and possess the whole of the Continent which Providence has given us." Illinois Representative John Wentworth expressed this optimistic sense of America's special destiny when he told Congress that the original States had a divinely sanctioned mission to become the "great center from which civilization, religion, and liberty should radiate and radiate until the whole continent shall bask in their blessings."

B. POLK AND MANIFEST DESTINY

1. The issue of territorial expansion dominated the 1844 presidential election. As the campaign began, Texas still remained independent, California still belonged to Mexico, and America and Great Britain still shared the Oregon Territory.

2. The Democratic presidential nominee James K. Polk shared Jackson's belief that America was chosen by Providence to be "the guardians of freedom." Polk narrowly defeated the Whig candidate Henry Clay on a platform promising to turn the idea of Manifest Destiny into a geographical reality.

C. TEXAS AND OREGON

1. Shortly after Polk's election, Congress approved a resolution annexing Texas as the nation's 28th state. President Tyler signed the resolution on March 1, 1845, three days before Polk took office.

2. Acquiring Oregon proved to be more difficult than annexing Texas. Both the United States and Great Britain claimed the territory. The Democratic campaign slogan "Fifty-four forty or fight" meant that the United States would go to war with Britain in order to obtain the entire Oregon territory. Despite his belligerent campaign slogan, Polk avoided a conflict by accepting a proposal dividing Oregon at the 49th parallel.

The concept of Manifest Destiny generates a number of APUSH exam questions. Be prepared for a passage followed by multiple-choice questions asking you to identify the causes and consequences of Manifest Destiny. You may even be asked to know that the rationale for Manifest Destiny before the Civil War was similar to the rationale for America's involvement in the Spanish-American War.

III. TURNING POINTS IN AMERICAN HISTORY: THE MEXICAN WAR

A. THE OUTBREAK OF WAR

1. The annexation of Texas outraged Mexico. Polk exacerbated tensions by supporting Texas's claim to the Rio Grande River as its southwestern boundary. The Mexican government denied this claim, insisting that the Texas territory extended no further south than the Nueces River.
2. On April 25, 1846, Mexican cavalry ambushed a U.S. unit in the disputed region between the Rio Grande and the Nueces River, killing 11 soldiers. Polk promptly demanded that Congress declare war on Mexico, stating that Mexico had "invaded our territory and shed American blood on American soil." Congress agreed and approved a declaration of war on May 13, 1846.

B. OPPOSITION TO THE WAR

1. The Mexican War provoked opposition from a small but highly visible group of influential critics. Whigs such as John Quincy Adams and New England abolitionists such as William Lloyd Garrison both denounced the war as an act of aggression designed to help the South expand slavery into new territories.
2. In Congress an obscure Illinois representative named Abraham Lincoln challenged Polk to identify the exact spot on American soil where American blood had been shed. Like other Whigs, Lincoln believed that the skirmish was a pretext for a war to claim new lands.

C. MAKING COMPARISONS: CIVIL DISOBEDIENCE

1. Henry David Thoreau staged the best-known act of protest against the Mexican War. As a gesture of opposition, the Transcendentalist essayist spent a night in jail for refusing to pay a state poll tax.

Thoreau later wrote the classic essay "Civil Disobedience" urging passive resistance to laws that required a citizen "to be an agent of injustice."

2. Thoreau's essay became a source of inspiration for Dr. Martin Luther King Jr.'s philosophy of nonviolent protest. In 1963, authorities in Birmingham, Alabama, arrested the civil rights leader for participating in demonstrations protesting the city's segregation laws. While in jail, Dr. King wrote his classic essay "Letter from Birmingham Jail" defending civil disobedience as a morally justified response to unjust laws.

D. THE CONQUEST OF MEXICO

1. American forces led by Generals Zachary Taylor and Winfield Scott successfully conquered Mexico. Taylor became a national hero when he defeated a much larger Mexican army at the Battle of Buena Vista. Scott won public acclaim when his forces captured Mexico City.
2. While American forces invaded Mexico, Colonel Stephen W. Kearny captured Santa Fe, New Mexico, and then helped secure California.

E. THE TREATY OF GUADALUPE HIDALGO

1. Mexico ceded New Mexico and California to the United States while also accepting the Rio Grande as the Texas border. New Mexico included what is now Arizona, Nevada, Utah, and parts of Colorado and Wyoming.
2. The United States acquired more than 500,000 square miles of new territory while Mexico lost about one-third of its territory.
3. The later Gadsden Purchase was not part of the Treaty of Guadalupe Hidalgo. The purchase included land in the southern portion of the New Mexico Territory intended to facilitate the construction of a transcontinental railroad from Houston, Texas, to Los Angeles, California.

F. MAKING CONNECTIONS: NATIONALISM AND SECTIONALISM

1. The War of 1812 sparked a wave of postwar nationalism that supported a new national bank, protective tariff, and a spirit of political harmony during the Era of Good Feelings. The optimism of this Era soon vanished, however, after the Panic of 1819 and the Missouri Compromise of 1820, both of which led to increased feelings of sectionalism.
2. The Mexican War sparked a brief moment of triumph. The war fulfilled the goal of Manifest Destiny by transforming America into a transcontinental republic. Instead of giving rise to a new era of

harmony, however, the postwar spirit of nationalism quickly faded. The Mexican War marked a turning point in American history because it ignited an increasingly bitter dispute over the extension of slavery into the new western territories. Sectionalism soon threatened to disrupt the fragile balance of power between the North and the South.

IV. THE WILMOT PROVISO

A. CONTEXT

1. Since the passage of the Missouri Compromise of 1820, both the Whigs and the Democrats attempted to suppress divisive questions about the status of slavery in the western territories.
2. On August 8, 1846, David Wilmot, a freshman Democrat from Pennsylvania, attached an amendment, or proviso, to a military appropriations bill. In language deliberately borrowed from the Northwest Ordinance, the proviso stated "neither slavery nor involuntary servitude shall ever exist" in any territory gained from Mexico.

B. "THE RIGHT TO RISE"

1. Wilmot defended his proviso as a necessary means of insuring the "rights of white freemen" to live and work in the new territories without facing the unfair burden of competing with slave labor. He argued that slavery degraded free labor. Wilmot and his supporters believed that "free soil" would guarantee liberty, free competition, social mobility and thus a worker's "right to rise."
2. Supported in the North and opposed in the South, the Wilmot Proviso passed the House twice, but was defeated in the Senate.

C. UNDERSTANDING CAUSATION: CONSEQUENCES OF THE WILMOT PROVISO

1. The votes on the Wilmot Proviso did not divide along party lines between Whigs and Democrats. Instead, they occurred between representatives from the North and the South. This rift exposed an ominous development that would soon destroy the Second Party System.
2. Apprehensive Southern leaders warned that the Wilmot Proviso marked the beginning of a long postponed attack on slavery. Determined to defend their "peculiar institution," they suppressed dissent in the South and denounced all attempts to resist the expansion of slavery.

3. The South's response to the Wilmot Proviso deepened Northern fears of the so-called Slave Power. Abolitionists had long warned that a slaveholding oligarchy intended to dominate the federal government. The defeat of the Wilmot Proviso gave these warnings greater credibility.
4. The debate over the Wilmot Proviso raised issues about slavery, free labor, political power, and the nature of the Constitution that could not be evaded. Despite attempts to resolve them, these issues widened and eventually eroded the bonds holding the Union together.

The debate over the Wilmot Proviso marks an important turning point in the sequence of events leading to the Civil War. Be prepared for a short-answer question asking you to briefly explain three consequences of the Wilmot Proviso.

THE ROAD TO DISUNION 1850–1860

Chapter 15

I. THE COMPROMISE OF 1850

A. THE CALIFORNIA GOLD RUSH

1. On January 24, 1848, a carpenter named James Marshall spotted shiny yellow objects glittering at the bottom of the American River not far from Sacramento, California. The sight "made my heart thump," Marshall later recalled. "I was certain it was gold."
2. Marshall's discovery triggered a frenzied rush of fortune seekers hoping to strike it rich. By the end of 1849, over 80,000 prospectors swarmed into California. The new Californians promptly drew up a constitution asking Congress to admit them into the Union as a free state.

The gold rush transformed San Francisco from a tiny village into a booming port city. APUSH test writers often use a picture of San Francisco harbor as a prompt to test your knowledge of the demographic and economic changes caused by the gold rush. Pictures from this time show San Francisco harbor filled with tall masted clipper ships bringing people and goods from the East Coast cities and Asia.

B. RENEWED DEBATES OVER SLAVERY

1. California's petition for statehood renewed the still unresolved debate over the spread of slavery into the territories won in the Mexican War.
2. Southern leaders feared the North's growing political dominance. Augmented by a surging tide of immigrants from Ireland and Germany, Northern states held a commanding majority in the House of Representatives. However, the equal division of 15 slave states and 15 free states enabled the South to maintain a veto power in the Senate.
3. Reaching an agreement with the South proved to be difficult. Southern senators repeatedly warned that any law threatening

slavery would lead to secession. Sensing that "our country is in danger," Henry Clay lived up to his reputation as the "Great Compromiser" by proposing a series of measures that passed the Senate after months of intense bargaining.

C. CLAY'S COMPROMISE PROPOSALS

1. Clay grouped six proposals into three pairs. Each pair offered one concession to the North and one to the South.
2. The first pair admitted California as a free state while also calling for the establishment of territorial governments in the rest of the Mexican Cession "without the adoption of any restriction or condition on the subject of slavery." This statement conciliated the South by reaffirming the permanence of slavery and rejecting the validity of the Wilmot Proviso.
3. The second pair settled a heated boundary dispute between Texas and New Mexico. Congress assigned the disputed territory to New Mexico but compensated Texas by paying off a $10 million debt it had incurred while an independent republic.
4. The third pair abolished the slave trade but not slavery in the District of Columbia. At the same time, Congress recognized Southern complaints by enacting a strict new Fugitive Slave Law.

D. "A FINAL SETTLEMENT"

1. In a message to Congress in December 1850, President Fillmore described the Compromise of 1850 as "a final settlement." Most Americans agreed, believing the compromise would restore sectional harmony.
2. With the benefit of hindsight, we know that sectional forces would soon gather strength and ultimately lead to disunion. But the Compromise of 1850 should not be dismissed as unimportant. It bought a decade of delay that enabled the North to gain the industrial strength, population growth, and presidential leadership it would need to successfully face the challenge of secession.

II. THE FUGITIVE SLAVE ACT

A. CONTEXT

1. The Compromise of 1850 initially produced unexpected benefits for the South. Although California entered the Union as a free state, it selected conservative Senators who voted with the South

on most issues. Meanwhile, the territorial legislatures in Utah and New Mexico legalized slavery.

2. Despite this promising beginning, the agitation over slavery did not end. About 1,000 slaves escaped to freedom each year. Southern leaders viewed enforcement of the Fugitive Slave Act as a litmus test of the North's good faith in enforcing the Compromise of 1850.

B. PUBLIC OPPOSITION

1. The Fugitive Slave Act intensified antislavery sentiment because it required Northerners to enforce slavery. In Boston, thousands of outraged abolitionists vainly attempted to prevent federal marshals from returning a fugitive slave to his master in Virginia.
2. Demonstrations like the one in Boston dramatized public resistance to enforcing the Fugitive Slave Act. At the same time, a clandestine network of conductors and safe houses known as the Underground Railroad helped escaped slaves flee to the North. Renowned as "The Moses of Her People," Harriet Tubman led more than 300 slaves to freedom.

C. *UNCLE TOM'S CABIN*

1. The Fugitive Slave Act appalled Harriet Beecher Stowe. A dedicated abolitionist, Stowe wrote *Uncle Tom's Cabin* to help her readers understand the morally intolerable impact of slavery upon family life.
2. First published in book form in March 1852, *Uncle Tom's Cabin* sold 300,000 copies within a year. It soon became an international sensation translated into 20 languages while selling 2.5 million copies worldwide.
3. *Uncle Tom's Cabin* intensified antislavery sentiment in the North, and by contrast, aroused deep resentment in the South.

III. TURNING POINTS IN AMERICAN HISTORY: THE KANSAS-NEBRASKA ACT

A. CONTEXT

1. As 1854 began, most Americans believed that the Missouri Compromise line provided a permanent agreement for separating free and slave territory in the Louisiana Purchase. At that time, the Republican Party did not exist and Democrats sympathetic to the

South controlled the White House and Congress. But all this was about to dramatically and irrevocably change.

2. As the slavery issue receded, political leaders and the public focused on the need for a transcontinental railroad to facilitate the movement of people and goods across the nation. While everyone agreed on the need for a transcontinental railroad, cities such as New Orleans, St. Louis, and Chicago vigorously competed for the lucrative position of becoming the eastern terminus for the project.

B. THE KANSAS-NEBRASKA ACT

1. As the senator from Illinois, Stephen A. Douglas wanted Chicago to be the eastern terminus of the transcontinental railroad. In order to achieve his objective, Douglas had to first persuade Congress to organize the Nebraska Territory and then persuade Southern senators to support giving this prize to a Northern city.
2. On January 23, 1854, Douglas introduced a bill that would organize two territories, Kansas and Nebraska. Both territories were north of the line banning slavery. In order to win Southern support, Douglas added an enticing amendment repealing the Missouri Compromise.
3. Douglas's bill included a proposal calling for popular sovereignty granting the people of Kansas and Nebraska the sole right to allow or forbid slavery.
4. Douglas predicted that his bill would "raise a hell of a storm." However, he believed that passions would subside when the public recognized that climate and soil conditions in the Great Plains would serve as permanent barriers to the expansion of plantation crops and slavery into Kansas and Nebraska. Given these geographic conditions, settlers would inevitably use popular sovereignty to remain free.
5. After a prolonged and bitter debate, Congress passed the Kansas-Nebraska Act on May 22, 1854. President Pierce signed it into law eight days later. "Few events," wrote historian David M. Potter, "have swung American history away from its charted course so suddenly and so sharply as the Kansas-Nebraska Act."

C. MOMENTOUS CONSEQUENCES

1. The Kansas-Nebraska Act broke the uneasy truce between the North and the South. Indignant Northern Democrats denounced the act as a violation of the Missouri Compromise's "sacred pledge" to ban slavery north of the 36° 30′ line.

2. Kansas marked the first important test of popular sovereignty. Within a short time, "Bleeding Kansas" became a battleground between rival proslavery and antislavery settlers.
3. The Democrats and Whigs had formed a Second Party System that dominated American politics from the 1830s to the early 1850s. The furor over the Kansas-Nebraska Act and the violence in Kansas led to the demise of the Whig Party.
4. The Kansas-Nebraska Act galvanized a spontaneous outpouring of popular opposition in the North that led to the formation of the Republican Party in 1854. Within a short time, Whigs, antislavery Democrats, Free Soilers, and former Know-Nothings joined the rapidly growing Republican coalition. The rise of the Republican Party began a new Third Party System that dominated American politics until the 1896 presidential election.
5. The Kansas-Nebraska Act dealt a severe blow to Douglas's presidential aspirations. At the same time, it revitalized Abraham Lincoln's political career. Realizing that his opposition to the Kansas-Nebraska Act had gone beyond the confines of Whig policy, Lincoln declared himself a Republican.

Make sure that you understand the consequences of the Kansas-Nebraska Act. APUSH test writers can use this watershed act to generate either a long-essay turning point question or a short-essay three-part listing question.

IV. THE *DRED SCOTT* CASE, 1857

A. THE CASE

1. Dred Scott was a slave who belonged to John Emerson, an army surgeon assigned to a post in Missouri. When the Army transferred Emerson from the slave state of Missouri to the free state of Illinois, he took Scott with him as a servant. The pair then moved to the Wisconsin Territory, an area where the Missouri Compromise expressly forbade slavery.
2. When Emerson died, Scott returned to Missouri where he was placed under the authority of his former master's wife. Helped by abolitionists, Scott sued for his freedom. He contended that living in a free state and a free territory made him a free man.

B. THE DECISION

1. Led by Chief Justice Roger B. Taney, the Supreme Court ruled that neither slaves nor free blacks were citizens in the political community created by the Constitution. Taney declared that slaves were "chattel property ... so far inferior that they have no rights which the white man is bound to respect."

2. The Court ruled that as a constitutionally protected form of property, slaves could be taken into any state or territory. The decision therefore declared the Missouri Compromise to be unconstitutional. This marked the first time the Supreme Court struck down an act of Congress since the *Marbury v. Madison* decision in 1803.

C. UNDERSTANDING CAUSATION: CONSEQUENCES OF THE *DRED SCOTT* DECISION

1. The *Dred Scott* decision invalidated the Missouri Compromise. It also cast doubt on the validity of popular sovereignty.

2. The decision worsened sectional tensions. It strengthened the Southern view that the Constitution safeguarded slavery. It strengthened the Northern view that a relentless Slave Power intended to impose slavery upon the entire nation.

3. The decision invalidated the Republican Party's platform pledge opposing the extension of slavery into the territories. Although this initially appeared to be a serious setback, Republicans redoubled their efforts to win the presidency. They promised that a victory would enable them to change the composition of the Southern dominated Supreme Court and reverse the *Dred Scott* decision.

D. MAKING CONNECTIONS: AFRICAN AMERICAN CITIZENSHIP

1. The Thirteenth Amendment overturned the *Dred Scott* decision.

2. In modern times, the Court has ruled that the Thirteenth Amendment prohibits any action that recognizes a "badge" or "condition" of slavery, such as housing discrimination and certain forms of employment discrimination.

V. THE UNION IN PERIL

A. JOHN BROWN'S RAID ON HARPERS FERRY, 1859

1. John Brown's doomed raid on Harpers Ferry set off a wave of fear throughout the slaveholding South. As rumors of slave

insurrections swept across the region, frightened Southerners suppressed all criticism of slavery. Southern "fire eaters" incorrectly linked John Brown to the now-hated Republican Party.

2. Although his raid was a military failure, John Brown's capture, trial, and execution mesmerized the nation. His death aroused great sympathy in the North where he became an antislavery martyr celebrated in the song "John Brown's Body." Perplexed and angered Southerners accused the North of lionizing a fiend who intended to instigate a bloody slave rebellion.

B. THE ELECTION OF 1860

1. Unable to bridge the division over slavery, the Democratic Party split into two factions. Northern Democrats nominated Stephen A. Douglas on a platform promising congressional noninterference with slavery. Deep South Democrats nominated John C. Breckinridge on a platform calling for a national slave code that would protect slavery in the territories.
2. Republicans sensed that they had an excellent opportunity to defeat the divided Democrats. The Lincoln-Douglas debates transformed Abraham Lincoln into a nationally known figure. The party nominated Lincoln on the third ballot.
3. The Republican platform stated that slavery would continue to be protected in the states where it already existed. However, the Republican Party firmly opposed the expansion of slavery into the western territories.
4. Lincoln won the election by carrying all 18 free states. He did not win a single state in the South.

C. THE CRITTENDEN COMPROMISE

1. Lincoln's election prompted South Carolina and six other Deep South states to secede from the Union.
2. In a final desperate effort to save the Union, Senator John Crittenden of Kentucky proposed a binding constitutional amendment to extend the Missouri Compromise line to the West coast.
3. Lincoln rejected the Crittenden Compromise because it violated the Republican Party's steadfast position against the further extension of slavery into the Western territories. The nation thus continued on an inexorable path to disunion and a bloody Civil War.

THE CIVIL WAR 1861–1865

I. THE SECESSION CRISIS

A. THE CONFEDERATE STATES OF AMERICA

1. Led by South Carolina, seven Deep South states seceded before Lincoln took office on March 4, 1861. These seven cotton belt states left the Union because they believed Lincoln was an enemy of the South and its slave system.
2. The seven seceded states sent delegates to Montgomery, Alabama, where they founded the Confederate States of America. The delegates adopted a constitution based upon states' rights and elected Jefferson Davis of Mississippi as president.

B. LINCOLN TAKES CHARGE

1. Lincoln faced a grave crisis. In his inaugural address he struck a conciliatory tone by repeating his pledge not "to interfere with the institution of slavery in the states where it exists." Lincoln reminded the seceded states, "We are not enemies, but friends."
2. Lincoln nonetheless denied that states had any lawful right to leave the Union, insisting "the Union of these states is perpetual." The issue of civil war therefore lay, he said, with the people of the South: "The Government will not assail you. You can have no conflict, without being yourselves the aggressors."

C. FORT SUMTER

1. The nation's attention swiftly became riveted to the sixty-nine Union soldiers stationed at Fort Sumter in Charleston Harbor. On April 6th, Lincoln notified the governor of South Carolina that he intended to resupply the Union garrison with food. Six days later, before the supply ships arrived, Confederate guns opened fire on Fort Sumter. The shelling continued for 34 hours before the Union forces lowered their flag. One day later, Lincoln called upon the loyal states to supply 75,000 militiamen to subdue the rebellion.
2. The firing on Fort Sumter and Lincoln's call for troops persuaded Virginia, Arkansas, Tennessee, and North Carolina to join the

Confederacy. The Confederate Congress meeting in Montgomery welcomed these states and moved its capital to Richmond, Virginia. The noted Civil War historian Bruce Catton underscored the significance of this move when he wrote, "American history has known few events more momentous than the secession of Virginia, which turned what started out to be a simple suppression of a rebellion into a four-year cataclysm."

D. THE BORDER STATES

1. Delaware, Maryland, Kentucky, and Missouri were all slaveholding Border States that remained in the Union.
2. Kentucky provided industrial and agricultural resources that proved vital to the Union. Lincoln recognized Kentucky's strategic importance when he declared, "I hope to have God on my side, but I must have Kentucky."

E. MAKING CONNECTIONS: MILITARISM

1. Militarism, the glorification of armed strength, quickly won support in both the North and the South. To many people, splendid uniforms, waving flags, and rousing songs all seemed the purest forms of patriotism. People on both sides believed their armies would win a quick and decisive victory. This proved to be an illusion as the Civil War lasted four years and claimed over 620,000 lives.
2. Like Americans in 1861, Europeans in 1914 also forgot the horrors of war. In August 1914, armies in Europe marched off to battle convinced that the war would be short and glorious. Few foresaw the horrors ahead as the First World War toppled empires and claimed the lives of a whole generation of young men including over 100,000 Americans.

II. MAKING COMPARISONS: THE BALANCE OF FORCES

A. THE NORTH

1. Advantages
   a. The North enjoyed a significant population advantage. In 1861, the 23 states in the Union had a population of about 22 million people. In contrast, the 11 Confederate states had just 9 million people, 4 million of whom were slaves.

   b. The North enjoyed an enormous advantage in industrial capacity. The Union produced over 90 percent of the nation's manufactured goods. In addition, the Union had far more wagons, horses, ships, and miles of railroad track.

c. The North enjoyed a significant advantage in presidential leadership. Lincoln proved to be an inspiring leader and a forceful commander-in-chief. He successfully held the Republican Party together despite its internal conflicts.

d. Northern farms produced 140 million bushels of wheat, seven times the harvest in the South. Because of crop failures and drought in Europe, wheat supplanted cotton as the nation's most important export.

2. Disadvantages

a. When the war began, the North lacked an able group of military commanders. Lincoln had to frequently replace generals as he searched for commanders who could rival those of the South.

b. At first, the North did not enjoy a consensus on its war aims. While Lincoln's announced goal was to save the Union, abolitionists argued that the Union should also abolish slavery. At the same time, a vocal group of "Copperheads" called for a negotiated peace.

B. THE SOUTH

1. Advantages

a. The South enjoyed the advantage of fighting a defensive war to protect its homeland. It only needed to hold back the invading Union armies and wait for Northern public opinion to tire of fighting a prolonged and costly war.

b. The South boasted a strong military tradition that produced an exceptional group of experienced commanders, including Robert E. Lee and Stonewall Jackson.

c. Great Britain and France imported three-quarters of their cotton from the South. Southern leaders confidently, but inaccurately, predicted that a cotton famine would cause massive unemployment that would force these two European powers to recognize the Confederacy and break the Union blockade.

2. Disadvantages

a. The disparities in population, industrial capacity, and railroad mileage meant that the South could not sustain a prolonged war.

b. Jefferson Davis proved to be an ineffective political and military leader. He frequently quarreled with his Cabinet and failed to implement a consistent military strategy.

c. The Confederacy was founded on the principle of states' rights. But the South needed a strong central government to conduct an efficient war effort. Independent-minded Confederate governors often frustrated the Davis government's attempts to raise the money and troops it needed to fight the war.

Antietam is the Civil War battle most likely to generate test questions. The Union's narrow victory convinced England and France to remain neutral while enabling Lincoln to issue the Emancipation Proclamation.

III. THE EMANCIPATION PROCLAMATION

A. "CONTRABAND OF WAR"

1. The Civil War disrupted plantation life throughout the South. As Federal forces pushed into the Confederacy, fugitive slaves sought refuge behind Union lines.
2. Union generals labeled the escaped slaves "contraband of war"—enemy property that could be legitimately seized according to international law. The 1861 Confiscation Act authorized Union troops to seize all Confederate property including slaves.
3. Radical Republicans persuaded Congress to abolish slavery in the District of Columbia and to exclude it from all federal territories.

B. EMANCIPATION

1. President Lincoln signed the Emancipation Proclamation on New Year's Day, 1863. The Proclamation was not a law passed by Congress. Instead, it was based on the President's constitutional authority as commander-in-chief of the armed forces.
2. The Emancipation Proclamation only freed slaves living in states that rebelled against the Union. It did not free slaves in the Union-controlled Border States.
3. Slavery was not completely abolished until the ratification of the Thirteenth Amendment on December 6, 1865.

C. IMPORTANCE

1. The Emancipation Proclamation strengthened the Union's moral cause. The Civil War was now widened into a crusade against slavery. Advancing Union troops thus became liberators who freed human beings from slavery.

2. With slavery doomed, public opinion in Britain and France swung decisively behind the Union cause. The Emancipation Proclamation thus ended any chance that these two European powers would support the Confederacy.

D. "BLACKS IN BLUE"

1. The Emancipation Proclamation permitted blacks to join the Federal army. Frederick Douglass urged blacks to rally to the Union cause. "The iron gate of our prison," he told them, "stands half open."

2. Approximately 180,000 African Americans served in the Union army. Although these "blacks in blue" fought with great valor, they were paid less than white soldiers of equal rank. More than 38,000 black soldiers lost their lives during the Civil War.

E. MAKING CONNECTIONS: "A GREAT BEACON LIGHT OF HOPE"

1. Dr. Martin Luther King, Jr. frequently used the Emancipation Proclamation as a point of historic reference. For example, he linked it to the "imperishable" and self-evident truths proclaimed in the Declaration of Independence that "electrified the free world."

2. Dr. King began his famous "I Have a Dream" speech by saying, "Five score years ago, a great American, in whose symbolic shadow we stand, signed the Emancipation Proclamation. This momentous decree came as a great beacon light of hope to millions of Negro slaves." Dr. King reminded his vast audience that one hundred years later Negroes were still "crippled by the manacles of segregation and the chains of discrimination." Less than one year later, Congress passed the Civil Rights Act barring discrimination in public facilities.

IV. THE REPUBLICAN ECONOMIC AGENDA

A. THE REPUBLICAN CONGRESS

1. During the 1840s and 1850s, Southern congressmen repeatedly blocked tariff, railroad, banking, and land policies favored by the North and West.

2. The secession of the Southern states enabled the Republicans to dominate Congress. They promptly passed a series of landmark acts with far-reaching social and economic consequences.

B. THE HOMESTEAD ACT, 1862

1. The Homestead Act enabled settlers to acquire a free tract of 160 acres of surveyed public land. Settlers acquired title to the land after five years of continuous residence.
2. The Homestead Act opened the Great Plains to settlers. By 1935, 1.6 million homesteaders received 270 million acres of federal lands.

C. THE MORRILL LAND-GRANT COLLEGE ACT, 1862

1. The act conveyed 30,000 acres of federal land per member of Congress from each state. The sales of the land provided funds to create colleges of "agriculture and mechanical arts."
2. The land-grant colleges played an important role in promoting agriculture, engineering, and veterinary medicine.

D. THE PACIFIC RAILROAD ACT, 1862

1. Prior to the Civil War, Southern congressmen supported a transcontinental railroad that would link New Orleans with California.
2. Following the outbreak of the Civil War, Congress approved a transcontinental route that would run along a north-central route linking Omaha, Nebraska, with Sacramento, California.

E. THE NATIONAL BANKING ACT OF 1863

1. Banking policies had been a source of contention since the formation of the First National Bank in 1791. The rising cost of financing the Civil War highlighted the urgent need for a national currency and an orderly banking system.
2. The National Banking Act of 1863 established a national banking system to provide a uniform currency. No additional important changes were made in the nation's banking system until Congress passed the Federal Reserve Act in 1913.

V. UNDERSTANDING CAUSATION: CONSEQUENCES OF THE CIVIL WAR

A. FOR THE FEDERAL GOVERNMENT

1. The Civil War ended the long-held Southern principle of state sovereignty. States could no longer threaten to nullify a federal law or claim the right to secede.

2. The Civil War broadened the definition of federal power. The adoption of the Thirteenth Amendment affirmed the supreme power of the federal government to abolish slavery, ensure the liberty of all Americans, and act on matters affecting "the general welfare."

B. FOR THE SOUTH

1. Prior to the Civil War, the Southern planter elite played a disproportionate role in national affairs. For example, a Southern slaveholder occupied the presidency during two-thirds of the years from 1789 to 1861. The Civil War ended this long era of power. No native of a Southern state occupied the White House for fifty years after 1861.
2. The South suffered devastating human losses. More than 258,000 Confederate soldiers died in the war. This constituted over 20 percent of the South's adult white male population.
3. The South suffered devastating economic losses. In 1860, the South contributed 30 percent of the nation's wealth. The Civil War destroyed Southern homes, crops, livestock, and railroad lines. In 1870, the South contributed just 12 percent of the nation's wealth.
4. The Civil War caused a severe reduction in the South's political influence and economic prosperity. However, it left the region's commitment to white supremacy unbroken. This would create a problem that would not be successfully confronted until the Civil Rights Movement in the 1950s and 1960s.

C. FOR THE NORTH

1. The Civil War solidified the alliance of Northern business interests and Western farmers with the Republican Party.
2. The war accelerated the creation of powerful corporate enterprises. This enhanced the economic and political influence of a rising class of Northern "captains of industry."

D. FOR WOMEN

1. Women in both the Union and Confederacy accepted new responsibilities as more and more men left their homes and jobs to fight in the army. In the South, planters' wives and daughters learned how to manage their plantations. Women on smaller farms plowed the fields and harvested their crops. In the North, women took paying jobs in business and government.
2. Women pushed the boundaries of their traditional roles by serving as nurses. The North set up a training program for nurses under

Dr. Elizabeth Blackwell, the first American woman to graduate from medical school. Clara Barton, who later founded the American Red Cross, helped overcome resistance to women working in military hospitals. Over 3,000 women served as nurses in Northern frontline hospitals.

3. The Civil War did not remove barriers to sexual equality that had existed since the nation's founding. However, it did broaden beliefs about what women could accomplish outside the home.

E. FOR THE FREED SLAVES

1. The Civil War emancipated about 4 million slaves. However, existing laws still denied them legal equality and the right to vote.
2. Frederick Douglass succinctly described the plight of freed slaves: "He had neither money, property, nor friends. He was free from the old plantation, but he had nothing but the dusty road under his feet. ... He was turned loose, naked, hungry, and destitute to the open sky."

The Civil War was a pivotal turning point that can generate a long-essay question. Be sure you are familiar with the impact of the war on the federal government, South, North, women, and freed slaves.

Chapter 17

RECONSTRUCTION AND THE NEW SOUTH 1865–1900

I. PRESIDENTIAL RECONSTRUCTION

A. LINCOLN'S TEN PERCENT PLAN

1. Abraham Lincoln led the United States through a long and bloody Civil War. When the conflict finally ended, Lincoln faced the daunting challenge of overcoming Southern resentment, restoring the Union, and determining the meaning of black freedom.
2. Lincoln's Ten Percent Plan proposed a generous settlement. He offered a full pardon (except for high-ranking Confederate leaders) to Southerners who pledged loyalty to the Union and to the Constitution. Southern states in which 10 percent of the 1860 electorate took such an oath and accepted emancipation would be restored to the Union.
3. Lincoln concluded his Second Inaugural Address by promising "malice toward none, with charity for all." We will never know if Lincoln could have fulfilled his inspiring pledge. On April 14, 1865, John Wilkes Booth assassinated Lincoln while the president was watching a play at Ford's Theatre in Washington.

B. THE THIRTEENTH AMENDMENT

1. Ratified on December 6, 1865, the Thirteenth Amendment formally abolished slavery and involuntary servitude.
2. Lincoln believed that the freedmen should receive suffrage because their military contribution during the Civil War "demonstrated in blood their right to the ballot." Lincoln felt confident that the states would fulfill this important responsibility.

C. JOHNSON'S PLAN

1. Lincoln's tragic death placed the burden of reconstructing the South on the untested shoulders of his former Vice President, Andrew Johnson.
2. Johnson favored a swift return to political and racial normalcy. Like Lincoln, he offered amnesty to most Confederates who took an oath of loyalty to the Union. Whites in each Southern state

could then elect delegates to a state convention. A state could reenter the Union when its convention repealed all secession laws, repudiated Confederate debts, and ratified the Thirteenth Amendment.

3. Johnson did not support racial equality. His idea of racial normalcy was grounded in a firm belief in white supremacy. Declaring, "White men alone must manage the South," Johnson stood aside as former rebels regained political power across the South.

II. RADICAL RECONSTRUCTION

A. THE BLACK CODES

1. Slavery left an entrenched legacy of prejudice and discrimination that would be difficult to eliminate. Unwilling to accept blacks as equals, Southern legislatures enacted laws known as Black Codes to limit the freedmen's basic civil and economic rights.
2. Black Codes continued the legal distinction between whites and blacks. For example, laws barred blacks from carrying weapons, marrying whites, assembling in groups, serving on juries, and pursuing any occupation other than agricultural work.

B. THE CIVIL RIGHTS ACT OF 1866

1. President Johnson did not object to the Black Codes. His lenient view of Reconstruction placed the president on a collision course with Congress.
2. Led by Thaddeus Stevens and Charles Sumner, Radical Republicans insisted on protecting the basic rights of the newly-freed blacks. Congress promptly passed the Civil Rights Act of 1866 declaring that blacks were American citizens who had the same rights as whites.
3. Johnson stunned Congress by vetoing the bill, claiming it was an unwarranted extension of federal power that would "foment discord among the races." Johnson's veto infuriated the Republicans who successfully overrode his veto. The struggle over the Black Codes and the Civil Rights Act marked the beginning of a contest of wills between Johnson and Congress.

C. THE FOURTEENTH AMENDMENT

1. The Republican majority in Congress feared that Johnson would not enforce the Civil Rights Act. They also worried that the courts would declare the law unconstitutional. These concerns prompted

Congress to pass the Fourteenth Amendment in June 1866. Many constitutional scholars believe the Fourteenth Amendment is the most important addition to the Constitution since the Bill of Rights was ratified in 1791.

2. The Fourteenth Amendment defines national citizenship for the first time as extending to "all persons born or naturalized in the United States."

3. The amendment gave the federal government responsibility for guaranteeing equal rights under the law to all Americans. The amendment prohibited the states from depriving "any person of life, liberty, or property, without due process of law; nor deny to any person within its jurisdiction equal protection of the laws."

4. Making Connections: The Incorporation Doctrine
   a. The Founders wrote the Bill of Rights to restrict the powers of the new national government. For example, the First Amendment begins by stating, "Congress shall make no laws . . ." Prior to the Fourteenth Amendment, the Supreme Court ruled that the Bill of Rights restrained only the national government, not states and cities.
   b. In the 1925 *Gitlow v. New York* decision, the Supreme Court ruled that freedom of speech and press "were fundamental personal rights and liberties protected by the due process clause of the Fourteenth Amendment from impairment by the states." This landmark decision began the development of the incorporation doctrine, the legal concept under which the Supreme Court has nationalized the Bill of Rights, by making most of its provisions applicable to the states through the Fourteenth Amendment.

D. THE RECONSTRUCTION ACT OF 1867

1. The Fourteenth Amendment intensified the struggle for power between President Johnson and Congress. Saying that blacks were unfit to receive "the coveted prize" of citizenship, Johnson campaigned for Congressional candidates who supported his policies. His strategy backfired. Voters repudiated the president by giving his Republican opponents a solid two-thirds majority in both houses of Congress.

2. The victorious Republicans promptly passed the Reconstruction Act of 1867 eliminating the state governments created by Johnson's plan. It divided the South into five military districts, each under the command of a Union general. In order to be readmitted into the Union, a state had to approve the Fourteenth Amendment.

3. Johnson vetoed the Reconstruction Act thus deepening his growing rift with Congress. Firmly in control of Capitol Hill, the Republicans overrode his veto.

E. THE IMPEACHMENT CRISIS

1. Congress escalated the struggle for power by passing the Tenure of Office Act. It required Senate consent for the removal of any official whose appointment had required Senate confirmation. Convinced the law was unconstitutional, Johnson fired Secretary of War Edwin Stanton, a leading Radical Republican ally.
2. Johnson's provocative action prompted the Radical Republicans to pass a resolution declaring that the president should be impeached. On February 24, 1868, the Republican-dominated House of Representatives impeached Johnson for "high crimes and misdemeanors in office," which included violating the Tenure of Office Act. After a tense trial, the Senate failed to convict Johnson by one vote.
3. Although Johnson escaped conviction, the trial crippled his presidency. Ten months later, voters sent the Union war hero Ulysses S. Grant to the White House. The Republicans completed their overwhelming victory by retaining two-thirds majorities in both houses of Congress.

F. THE FIFTEENTH AMENDMENT

1. The Fifteenth Amendment marked the last of the three Reconstruction Amendments. Ratified on February 3, 1870, it forbade either the federal government or the states from denying citizens the right to vote on the basis of "race, color, or previous condition of servitude."
2. Taken together, the three Reconstruction Amendments constitute what modern historians call a "Second Founding." The Republicans who wrote these amendments believed that the new constitutional provisions would fully protect the newly-freed slaves by granting them the liberties and legal equality promised in the Declaration of Independence.
3. Making Connections: Women's Suffrage
   a. The Fifteenth Amendment left leading women's rights activists feeling outraged and abandoned. They angrily demanded to know why Congress granted the suffrage to ex-slaves and not to women. Julia Ward Howe and other leaders of the women's suffrage movement finally accepted that this was "the Negro's hour." However, both Susan B. Anthony and Elizabeth Cady Stanton actively opposed passage of the Fifteenth Amendment.

b. During the early 1900s, the Progressive movement sharpened the nation's social conscience and motivated a new generation of suffragists. Led by Carrie Chapman Catt and Alice Paul, women organized rallies, signed petitions, and demonstrated in public marches. Their campaign of mounting pressure finally became irresistible. On June 4, 1919, Congress passed the Nineteenth Amendment stating that no citizen could be denied the right to vote "on account of sex."

The three Reconstruction Amendments have generated a significant number of APUSH exam questions. Be sure you can identify the short- and long-term consequences of each amendment.

III. RECONSTRUCTION IN THE SOUTH

A. RADICAL REPUBLICAN GOVERNMENTS

1. The period when Republicans ruled the South is called Radical Reconstruction. The word "radical" underscores the Republicans' attempt to transform the South by extending civil and political equality to African Americans.
2. The Fifteenth Amendment enabled African Americans to exercise political influence for the first time. This produced a significant change in voting patterns and office holding in the South. Freedmen provided about 80 percent of Republican votes in the South. Over 600 blacks served as state legislators in the new state governments. In addition, voters elected 14 blacks to the House of Representatives and 2 to the Senate. Black voters supported the Republican Party by loyally casting votes that helped elect Grant in 1868 and reelect him in 1872.
3. The Republicans launched an ambitious program of reforms. They started a public school system that included about 600,000 black students. They also built new hospitals and orphanages and began to reform the criminal justice system. Republican officials raised taxes to finance the construction of roads, bridges, and railroad lines.

B. MAKING CONNECTIONS: BLACK COLLEGES

1. The growth of educational opportunities also led to the founding of a number of black colleges including Howard University in Washington, D.C., Morehouse College and Spelman College in Atlanta, Georgia, and Fisk University in Nashville, Tennessee.

2. These historically black colleges later played a crucial role in training African American leaders who led the fight against segregation. For example, W.E.B. Du Bois and Ida B. Wells attended Fisk, Thurgood Marshall and Stokely Carmichael attended Howard, and Dr. Martin Luther King, Jr., attended Morehouse.

C. CRITICISM OF RECONSTRUCTION IN THE SOUTH

1. Critics complained that the new Republican state governments misused public funds by accepting absurdly high bids for contracts. In addition, Democrats charged that corrupt Republican politicians accepted kickbacks and bribes from construction and railroad companies.

2. White Southerners reserved their greatest scorn for carpetbaggers and scalawags. Carpetbaggers were Northerners who supposedly packed their belongings in a carpetbag suitcase and then headed south to seek power and profit. The much-maligned scalawags were Southerners who "betrayed" the South by supporting and then benefitting from Radical Republican policies.

D. UNDERSTANDING CAUSATION: THE END OF RECONSTRUCTION

1. "Slavery is not honestly dead."

   a. In 1869, members of the American Antislavery Society gathered to celebrate the abolition of slavery, passage of the Reconstruction Amendments, and the beginning of racial justice in the South. Frederick Douglass, however, did not share their optimism. He warned his listeners that "slavery is not honestly dead." Douglass pointed out that slavery did not die because of moral convictions; it died because of overwhelming military force in a bloody civil war.

   b. Douglass's insight proved to be prescient. Two centuries of slavery created deeply rooted racial prejudices that Constitutional amendments could not eradicate. White Southerners bitterly resented Republican governments that repealed Black Codes and guaranteed voting rights to African Americans.

2. The Ku Klux Klan

   a. The Ku Klux Klan began in Tennessee in 1866 and then quickly spread across the South. The Klan sought to maintain white supremacy by aiding the revival of the Democratic Party and by overthrowing of Radical Republicans.

b. Anonymous Klansmen dressed in white robes and pointed cowls burned black homes, schools, and churches and committed hundreds of murders. The Klan lynched as many as 400 African Americans between 1868 and 1871.

c. The Klan's reign of terror worked. Political intimidation and violence helped weaken Republican governments. By 1876, Democrats replaced Republicans as governors and state legislators in eight of the eleven former Confederate states. Only South Carolina, Louisiana, and Florida remained under Republican control.

3. The Erosion of Northern Support

a. Radical Republicans had long been the driving force behind the program to reconstruct Southern society. Sympathy for the freedmen began to wane as these leaders died or left office. A new generation of "politicos" began to focus their attention on Western expansion, Indian wars, tariffs, and the construction of transcontinental railroads.

b. President Grant showed little enthusiasm for Reconstruction. His administration soon became distracted by scandals. In addition, a business panic in 1873 followed by a crippling economic depression further undermined public support for Reconstruction.

4. The Compromise of 1877

a. The presidential election of 1876 created a potential constitutional crisis when Democratic candidate Samuel Tilden won the popular vote over his Republican rival Rutherford B. Hayes. However, the outcome remained unclear because of disputed electoral votes from three Southern states.

b. Congress created an electoral commission to determine which candidate would receive the disputed electoral votes. As tensions mounted, Democrat and Republican leaders reached an agreement known as the Compromise of 1877. The Democrats agreed to support Hayes. In return, Hayes and the Republicans agreed to withdraw all federal troops from the South, appoint at least one Southerner to the cabinet, and grant federal funds for internal improvements in the South.

c. The Compromise of 1877 ended Reconstruction. Republican governments in Louisiana and South Carolina quickly collapsed as Southern Democrats proclaimed a return to "home rule" and white supremacy.

IV. THE NEW SOUTH

A. HENRY GRADY'S VISION

1. Henry Grady, editor of the *Atlanta Constitution*, called for a "New South" that would be home to thriving cities, bustling factories, and rewarding business opportunities.
2. Grady inspired a new generation of Southern leaders who strove to fulfill his vision of building a more diversified Southern economy.

B. THE INDUSTRIAL SOUTH

1. Investors recognized that the South's ready supply of cheap labor, low taxes, and proximity to vast cotton fields created ideal conditions for building a profitable textile industry. Cotton mills soon flourished in small towns across the Piedmont region of North Carolina, South Carolina, and Georgia. By 1900, the South had about 400 cotton mills employing 100,000 workers.
2. James Buchanan Duke launched one of the South's great industrial successes when he founded the American Tobacco Company. By 1900, Duke's company produced 80 percent of the cigarettes manufactured in the United States.
3. During the 1870s and '80s, Birmingham, Alabama, quickly became a major industrial center and manufacturing hub. The city's thriving iron and steel mills led boosters to proclaim their city "The Pittsburgh of the South."

C. THE LIMITS OF DEVELOPMENT

1. Despite pockets of industrial development, Grady's dream of a diversified Southern economy remained elusive.
2. In 1900, two-thirds of all Southern men still earned their living in farming. At that time, the average income in the South was only 40 percent of that in the North.

V. SOUTHERN AGRICULTURE

A. DEPENDENCE UPON COTTON

1. Cotton continued to be the South's most important cash crop. Between 1870 and 1900, the number of acres devoted to cotton production doubled as production soared to almost 10 million bales.

2. The Southern economy became increasingly vulnerable to fluctuations in the global price of cotton. During the 1890s, a global glut of cotton caused a 50 percent drop in prices that shook the Southern economy as debts and unemployment rose.

B. SHARECROPPING

1. Cotton planters continued to own most of the land, while landless blacks were forced to sell their labor. During the 1860s, cotton planters and blacks formed a new labor system called sharecropping. Under this arrangement, blacks (and some whites) exchanged their labor for the use of land, tools, and seed. The croppers typically gave the landowner half of the crop as payment for using his property.
2. In addition to beginning with a debt to the landowner, sharecroppers had to borrow food, clothing, and other supplies from local storekeepers. These merchants then took a lien or mortgage on the crops.

C. A CYCLE OF DEBT AND POVERTY

1. Sharecropping did not lead to economic independence. Facing interest rates as high as 50 percent, sharecroppers became entrapped in a seemingly endless cycle of debt and poverty.
2. Sharecropping offered little hope for black or white tenants. During the 1890s, the problem of perpetual debt produced a harvest of discontent that led to the formation of farmers' alliances and the beginning of the black migration out of the South.

VI. THE RESTORATION OF WHITE SUPREMACY

A. THE REDEEMERS

1. The end of Reconstruction left political control in the South in the hands of a group of white Democratic Party leaders known collectively as "Redeemers" because they "redeemed" or saved the region from Republican rule.
2. The Redeemers included merchants, financiers, and politicians who promoted economic growth based upon industrialization and railroad expansion. At the same time, they also supported policies intended to restore a social system based upon white supremacy.

B. THE DISENFRANCHISEMENT OF BLACK VOTERS

1. The Fifteenth Amendment prohibited states from denying anyone the right to vote because of race. Redeemer governments used

literacy tests and poll taxes to evade the amendment. For example, poll taxes ranged from $1.00 in Georgia to $3.00 in Florida. Voters who skipped an election found that the tax accumulated from one election to the next.

2. The Redeemers' tactics worked. During the 1890s, the number of black voters plummeted. For example, in 1896, 130,000 blacks were registered to vote in Louisiana. Just four years later the number plunged to 5,320. By the early 1900s, African Americans had effectively lost their political rights in the South.

C. "SEPARATE BUT EQUAL"

1. The Civil Rights Act of 1875 guaranteed blacks "full and equal enjoyment" of public facilities. As more and more white Southerners rejected the idea of racial equality, Southern towns and companies began to enact Jim Crow laws mandating racial segregation in public facilities.
2. In the 1883 *Civil Rights Cases,* the Supreme Court ruled that the equal protection clause of the Fourteenth Amendment only applied to state action and could not be used to regulate the behavior of private individuals or private organizations.
3. In 1896, the Supreme Court carried the logic of legal segregation a significant step further. In *Plessy v. Ferguson*, the Court upheld segregation by approving "separate but equal" railroad facilities for African Americans.
4. *Plessy v. Ferguson* allowed Jim Crow segregation laws to spread across the South. Within a few years, state and local statutes required segregated schools, restaurants, and hotels. Ubiquitous signs mandating "Whites only" or "Colored" appeared on restroom doors, above water fountains, and inside stores.

D. MAKING CONNECTIONS: SEGREGATED PUBLIC SCHOOLS

1. *Plessy v. Ferguson* sanctioned a pattern of court-supported segregation that lasted almost 60 years. Segregated schools in the South were consistently inferior and underfunded compared with schools attended by white students.
2. In 1954, the Supreme Court, led by Chief Justice Earl Warren, overturned *Plessy v. Ferguson*. Basing its decision in *Brown v. Board of Education* on the equal protection clause of the Fourteenth Amendment, the Court concluded that "in the field of public education the doctrine of separate but equal has no place. Separate educational facilities are inherently unequal." The decision

helped galvanize the modern Civil Rights Movement. Led by Dr. King, civil rights activists began to demand "Freedom Now!"

VII. MAKING COMPARISONS: BOOKER T. WASHINGTON AND W.E.B. DU BOIS

A. CONTEXT

1. African Americans living in the South had to adjust to the oppressive reality of white supremacy and Jim Crow laws. Many chose to "walk a quiet life" shielded by a mask of public deference. Excluded from the dominant white society, African Americans increasingly turned to black churches as centers of community life.

2. The resurgence of racism forced African American leaders to speak out. Booker T. Washington and W.E.B. Du Bois offered very different approaches to finding a place in Southern society.

B. BOOKER T. WASHINGTON

1. Believed that white racism was a consequence of slavery.
2. Advocated black economic self-help. Washington called upon African Americans to master trades. He believed that economic progress would earn white respect and gradually overcome racism.
3. Supported accommodation to white society. In his Atlanta Compromise Speech, Washington offered a conciliatory approach welcomed by his white audience: "In all things purely social we can be as separate as the fingers, yet one as the hand in all things essential to mutual progress."
4. Supported vocational education. Washington helped found Tuskegee Institute in Alabama to provide industrial education for African American students.
5. Opposed public political agitation to challenge Jim Crow segregation. Washington recognized that African Americans faced a wall of discrimination that could only be overcome by gradual and patient progress. He believed that political rights would follow economic success.

C. W.E.B. DU BOIS

1. Believed white racism was the cause of slavery and the primary reason why African Americans were forced into a subordinate position in American society.

2. Advocated the intellectual development of a "talented tenth" of the African American population. The talented tenth would become a vanguard of influential leaders who would fight for social change.

3. Supported legal action to oppose Jim Crow segregation. Du Bois helped found the National Association for the Advancement of Colored People. The NAACP adopted a strategy of using lawsuits in federal courts to fight Jim Crow segregation.

4. Opposed Booker T. Washington's policy of gradualism and accommodation. In *The Souls of Black Folk*, Du Bois called upon African Americans to "insist continually, in season and out of season, that voting is necessary to modern manhood, that color discrimination is barbarism, and that black boys need education as well as white boys."

5. Believed that economic success would only be possible if African Americans first won political rights. Du Bois therefore advocated a strategy of "ceaseless agitation" and litigation to achieve equal rights.

AP® test writers expect students to be able to compare and contrast the views of Booker T. Washington and W.E.B. Du Bois. Be sure that you can cite specific events that illustrate Washington's accommodationist program and Du Bois's commitment to "ceaseless agitation."

UNIT 6 PERIOD 6

1865–1898

KEY CONCEPTS

KEY CONCEPT 6.1

Technological advances, large-scale production methods, and the opening of new markets encouraged the rise of industrial capitalism in the United States.

KEY CONCEPT 6.2

The migrations that accompanied industrialization transformed both urban and rural areas of the United States and caused dramatic social and cultural change.

KEY CONCEPT 6.3

The Gilded Age produced new cultural and intellectual movements, public reform efforts, and political debates over economic and social policies.

THE NEW WEST 1865–1900

I. DIVERSITY IN THE AMERICAN WEST

A. CONTEXT

1. Most people moving westward before the Civil War traveled directly from the Midwest to the Far West. Based upon reports from early trailblazers, Americans believed that a sparsely inhabited desert filled the vast prairies between the Mississippi and the Rocky Mountains.
2. The West was neither a desert nor uninhabited. The region was in fact a diverse land inhabited by Indians, Hispanics, Asians, and a growing number of American settlers.

B. THE WESTERN TRIBES

1. The Great Plains were home to about 250,000 of the Indians who remained in the United States.
2. First brought to North America by the Spanish, horses thrived on the western grasslands. Once tamed, the small but powerful horses quickly transformed the Plains Indians into superb hunters who followed vast herds containing millions of buffalos. The Indians ate the creature's meat, fashioned its hides into clothes, and even turned its sinews and tendons into string for their bows.
3. In 1851, representatives of the United States government and a number of Plains tribes signed the Fort Laramie Treaty. The tribes guaranteed safe passage for settlers on the Oregon Trail and allowed the construction of roads and forts. In exchange they received defined lands that would be theirs forever. But "forever" lasted less than four decades.

C. THE HISPANIC WEST

1. Much of the land from Texas to California began as part of the Spanish Empire and then became part of the Mexican Republic. Following the Mexican-American War thousands of Hispanic people living in this region became residents of American territory.

2. The Hispanic elite lost much of their political authority and economic prosperity as American settlers moved into the region. By the late nineteenth century, Hispanics became part of a large working class.

D. THE CHINESE

1. The gold rush and demand for railroad construction workers sparked a mass migration of Chinese workers to California. By the 1870s, Chinese immigrants comprised the largest non-European group in California.
2. At first, Californians welcomed the Chinese, praising their work ethic. But as the Chinese communities became larger and more conspicuous, many Californians began to view them as economic rivals who worked for low wages.
3. As anti-Chinese agitation spread up and down the Pacific coast, calls for immigration restriction grew louder. Congress responded to this nativist pressure by passing the Chinese Exclusion Act of 1882. The law suspended immigration of all Chinese laborers for ten years. Congress renewed the legislation in 1892 and then made it permanent in 1902. The Chinese Exclusion Act marked the first law enacted to exclude a specific ethnic or racial group from immigrating to the United States.

E. MIGRATION FROM THE EAST

1. By 1860, California, Oregon, and Texas were established states with large and growing Anglo-American populations. Traders, farmers, and ranchers from Texas had already begun to establish outposts in New Mexico and Arizona.
2. The three decades between 1870 and 1900 witnessed an unprecedented migration of miners, ranchers, and farmers into the West.

II. TURNING POINTS IN AMERICAN HISTORY: THE TRANSCONTINENTAL RAILROADS

A. "THE LAST RAIL IS LAID"

1. In 1862, President Lincoln signed the Pacific Railroad Act authorizing the construction of a transcontinental railroad. The Central Pacific started at Sacramento, California, and with a labor force made up largely of Chinese workers, pushed east over the rugged Sierra Nevada Mountains. At the same time, the Union

Pacific started in Omaha, Nebraska, and with a labor force made up largely of Irish workers, pushed west across the gently sloping Great Plains.

2. The two lines linked on May 10, 1869, at Promontory Summit, Utah, when an official used a silver hammer to drive in a ceremonial golden spike. At 3:05 PM, officials in New York received a telegram triumphantly announcing, "The last rail is laid; the last spike is driven; the Pacific Railroad is completed." The news sparked nationwide celebrations as jubilant citizens rang church bells, unfurled flags, and fired cannons.
3. The completion of the first transcontinental railroad marked the beginning of a building boom across the West. By 1893, five transcontinental lines linked the east and west coasts with what one railroad financier called "a strong band of iron."

B. UNDERSTANDING CAUSATION: THE IMPACT OF THE TRANSCONTINENTALS

1. Before the transcontinentals, it took almost six months to travel from New York to California. The new railroads cut travel time between the two coasts to just one week. The world as Americans experienced it had now grown smaller and faster.
2. The transcontinental railroads became a visible symbol of national union. After 1869, goods and people could freely move across the entire country without passing through customs or a passport control. This created a vast integrated national market for raw materials and manufactured goods. Within ten years of its completion, the Pacific Railroad annually shipped $50 million worth of freight coast to coast.
3. Before the transcontinental railroads, every town in America had its own "local" time. The national rail lines required a uniform schedule so that passengers and freight could arrive and depart on time. The need for coordination led to the creation of four standardized time zones that still regulate daily life today.
4. The rails carried more than just raw materials and manufactured goods. As the lines grew bigger and safer, companies encouraged eastern settlers by offering to carry whole families to their new homes in the West for free. The railroads did not limit their appeals to Americans. They set up offices in Europe and distributed pamphlets containing glowing descriptions of the wonders waiting for immigrants willing to seek new lives in the great American West. For example, one pamphlet stretched the truth by describing the normally dry Platte Valley as "a flowing meadow of great

fertility clothed in nutritious grasses and watered by numerous streams." Attracted by promises of fertile land, large numbers of Swedes, Norwegians, Danes, and Germans immigrated to the United States.

5. The transcontinental railroads did not benefit everyone. The buffalo had been the center of the Plains Indian way of life for centuries. The railroads enabled hunters to nearly exterminate the vast herds that roamed the Great Plains. This wanton slaughter dealt a catastrophic blow to the culture of the Plains Indians.

C. MAKING CONNECTIONS: NATIONAL TRANSPORTATION NETWORKS

1. The transcontinental railroads created America's first nationwide transportation system. Their success doomed the pony express, wagon trains, stagecoach lines, and even the fast clipper ships that sailed around the tip of South America and up the California coast.
2. Less than a century after the completion of the first transcontinental, the Federal Aid Highway Act of 1956 authorized the construction of a 40,000-mile network of four-lane interstate highways. The new interstates promoted automobile traffic and gave a huge boost to the trucking industry. The loss of passengers and freight dealt a serious setback to the nation's railroad industry.

The numerous consequences of the transcontinental railroads make them an ideal subject for a turning point long essay. Be sure that you can discuss the impact the transcontinentals had upon the American West.

III. THE TRANSFORMATION OF THE WEST

A. THE MINERS' FRONTIER

1. The California Gold Rush demonstrated that the discovery of precious metals would spark a frenetic rush of prospectors into a region. This pattern repeated itself across the Sierra Nevada and Rocky Mountains. For example, the Comstock Lode near Virginia City, Nevada, yielded deposits of gold and silver worth more than $300 million, the richest single strike in American history. At its peak in the 1870s, Virginia City had 30,000 people and 100 saloons. Deserted in the 1880s, the town survives today as a tourist attraction.

2. Mining towns attracted a diverse and combustible mix of white, black, American Indian, Mexican, and Chinese miners. Wild and unregulated mining towns often verged on anarchy. "There are duels, shooting affrays, and hangings by mob law most every week," wrote one astonished traveler from Pennsylvania.

3. Most miners hoped to get rich and then get out. The heyday of gold and silver rushes exploited by individual miners ended by the 1890s. Although virtually all the placer or surface gold and silver has been discovered, the West continues to be a mineral-rich region. Today, large corporations dominate mining operations. Led by Nevada, the United States currently produces almost 7 percent of the world's gold production.

B. THE COWBOYS' FRONTIER

1. The vast stretches of grassland in southwest Texas supported herds containing about five million head of longhorn cattle. By the mid-1860s, fast-growing cities in the East created a growing demand for meat. Getting Texas cattle to these markets posed a challenging problem. The famous long drives from Texas to railheads in Kansas provided a lucrative solution.

2. During the twenty years after the Civil War, cowboys drove herds of 2,000 to 2,500 steers on long drives to "cow towns" in Kansas. For example, the Chisholm Trail provided a well-traveled route from San Antonio to the railhead in Abilene, Kansas.

3. During the peak years of the 1870s, as many as 40,000 cowboys roamed the Great Plains. Mexicans and African Americans comprised about one-third of this total.

4. The era of the long drives ended by the late 1880s. Open-range cattle ranching became less profitable as beef prices fell. In addition, many ranchers lost half or more of their herds because of unusually cold winters that struck the Great Plains in 1886 and 1887.

C. THE FARMERS' FRONTIER

1. The Homestead Act of 1862 and the completion of the transcontinental railroads opened the West to farming. In the 30 years between 1870 and 1900, more land was made into farms than in all the previous 250 years.

2. Great Plains agriculture posed new challenges for farmers. Blizzards, fires, and swarms of locusts swept across the arid and treeless prairies. Farmers accustomed to log cabins had to

learn how to build sod houses. A series of new tools including mechanical reapers, wind-driven water pumps, and barbed-wire fences enabled determined farmers to overcome natural obstacles and build successful homesteads.

3. The population of the Great Plains steadily increased. For example, during the 1870s over 600,000 people settled in Kansas. This population included about 25,000 black pioneers called exodusters. By 1890, over 500,000 African Americans lived west of the Mississippi River.

IV. THE DEFEAT AND TRANSFORMATION OF THE PLAINS INDIANS

A. THE INDIANS' LAST STAND

1. The construction of the transcontinental railroads, the slaughter of the buffalo, the spread of epidemic diseases, and the destructive effects of constant warfare all threatened to end the autonomy of the Plains Indians.
2. The U.S. government no longer honored its Fort Laramie promises. Instead of trying to concentrate the Plains Indians on large blocks of land, the government moved the Indians onto small reservations in out-of-the-way areas. One Indian leader bitterly complained, "Since the Great Father promised that we should never be removed, we have been moved five times . . . I think you had better put the Indians on wheels, and you can run them about wherever you wish."
3. In 1875, thousands of gold prospectors rushed onto Sioux lands in the Black Hills of the Dakota Territory. The unwanted invasion combined with a harsh winter forced starving Sioux and Cheyenne to leave their reservations. When the Indians refused orders to return, the army ordered General George A. Custer to force them to obey. On June 25, 1876, warriors led by Crazy Horse and Sitting Bull annihilated Custer's Seventh Cavalry at the Battle of the Little Bighorn.
4. The Indian victory hastened their ultimate defeat. News of the disaster reached the East on July 4, 1876, as Americans celebrated the nation's centennial. An outraged public now demanded that the full force of the U.S. Army be used to subdue the Plains Indians. America's overwhelming military power prevailed. One proud but forlorn chief sadly observed, "We have reached the end of our rule, and a new one has come . . . Of our once powerful nation there are now but a few left."

B. *A CENTURY OF DISHONOR*

1. Although the government could defeat the Plains Indians, it could not suppress the truth about how it had mistreated them. In 1881, Helen Hunt Jackson published *A Century of Dishonor* documenting the misdeeds of corrupt Indian agents, duplicitous government officials, and land-hungry settlers. Jackson castigated the government for its role in "a tale of wrongs and oppressions . . . that is too monstrous to be believed."
2. Like many other well-meaning reformers, Jackson supported policies designed to bring Native Americans into the mainstream of American life. *A Century of Dishonor* played a key role in mobilizing public support for the Dawes Act.

C. THE DAWES ACT, 1887

1. Well-meaning but ethnocentric reformers believed that the Indians' traditional tribal culture was an obstacle preventing them from assimilating into mainstream white society. The Dawes Act tried to "civilize" Native Americans by turning them into independent self-supporting farmers.
2. The Dawes Act dissolved the tribes as legal entities and divided their tribal lands into individual homesteads of 160 acres. Reservation lands not allocated to the Indians were sold to the railroads and to white settlers.
3. The Dawes Act ignored the importance traditional Indian culture placed on tribally held land. Instead of transforming Native Americans into self-supporting farmers, the Dawes Act undermined their culture and cost them their land.

D. MAKING CONNECTIONS: OFFICIAL INDIAN POLICY

1. By 1900, Native Americans lost 50 percent of the 156 million acres they held before the Dawes Act became law.
2. In 1934, Congress enacted the Indian Reorganization Act as the centerpiece of the "Indian New Deal." The act reversed the assimilationist policies set in motion by the Dawes Act by recognizing, strengthening, and preserving the tribes' historic traditions and culture. The law also restored the Indians' right to manage their land and mineral rights.

It is very unlikely that your APUSH exam will contain questions on Crazy Horse and Custer. But that does not mean the exam will ignore Native American history. It won't. Be sure you can identify Helen Hunt Jackson's book* A Century of Dishonor *and the impact of the Dawes Act.

V. MAKING COMPARISONS: THE FRONTIER IN AMERICAN HISTORY

A. TURNER'S FRONTIER THESIS

1. In 1890, the Superintendent of the U.S. Census issued a statement declaring that the western frontier had closed. The finding surprised and intrigued Frederick Jackson Turner, a young history professor at the University of Wisconsin. He concluded that the closing of the frontier symbolized the end of a great historic movement.
2. In a seminal paper entitled "The Significance of the Frontier in American History," Turner contended that the frontier experience profoundly shaped the American character. According to Turner, the frontier promoted democracy and encouraged individualism. It produced a unique combination of traits including resilience, self-reliance, and an optimistic faith in democratic institutions. The western frontier also promoted opportunity by providing an open society where rigid class lines did not block social mobility.
3. Turner's thesis justified and reinforced the view of Manifest Destiny as a positive force that extended American democratic ideals across the continent.

B. LIMERICK'S CRITIQUE

1. Patricia Nelson Limerick is an American historian who is one of the nation's foremost scholars of the American West.
2. Published in 1986, her influential book *The Legacy of Conquest* offered a critique of Turner's thesis and a new view of the West.
3. Turner viewed the West as an open, untamed space with few inhabitants. In contrast, Limerick described the West as inhabited by a diverse group of people and cultures including Native Americans, Hispanics, Asians, African Americans, and White Americans. These groups collided in a process marked by conquest and uneasy bargains.
4. Limerick views the forcible conquest and annexation of the West as an example of American expansionism that opposed and even undermined the nation's democratic spirit.

Chapter 19

INDUSTRY AND LABOR 1865–1900

I. THE SECOND INDUSTRIAL REVOLUTION

A. CONTEXT

1. Before the Industrial Revolution, Americans planted crops, wove cloth, and made shoes by hand. The Industrial Revolution in America began in Rhode Island and Massachusetts in the late 1790s and early 1800s. Waterpower, once used only to run tiny grain mills, powered textile machines in Lowell and other nearby New England towns.
2. Innovations in transportation such as steamboats, the Erie Canal, and the early railroads sparked a market revolution linking once isolated communities into regional trading areas.
3. A second Industrial Revolution began in the years following the Civil War. By 1913, the United States produced one-third of the world's industrial output, more than Great Britain, France, and Germany combined.

B. UNDERSTANDING CAUSATION: THE CAUSES OF THE SECOND INDUSTRIAL REVOLUTION IN AMERICA

1. Natural Resources
   a. The United States was blessed with abundant supplies of coal, iron ore, petroleum, and timber. For example, America had more recoverable coal reserves than any other nation. In addition, the Mesabi Range in Minnesota contained the world's largest deposits of iron ore.
   b. Coal burns hotter and longer than wood. These qualities made coal a particularly important reason for of America's surge in industrial production. Prior to the Civil War, wood provided almost half of America's energy. However, as the Industrial Revolution gathered momentum, America became a mineral-intensive economy based upon coal. American railroads and steamships took the lead in replacing wood with coal. In addition, steel mills used vast quantities of coal to fire their furnaces.

2. Human Resources

   a. Labor was both plentiful and inexpensive. America's huge pool of unskilled workers included many women and children. In addition, waves of European immigrants provided a seemingly inexhaustible supply of low-wage laborers.

   b. America's growing population became increasingly concentrated in its cities. Rapidly growing urban areas became centers for the mass consumption of food, clothing, and manufactured goods.

3. Government Support

   a. Nineteenth century federal and state governments were committed to the concept of private property and limited regulation of business activity.

   b. While the federal government adopted a laissez-faire policy towards business regulation, it did enact high protective tariffs to protect American industry from foreign competition.

   c. A group of ambitious, shrewd, and sometimes ruthless entrepreneurs took advantage of this stable and supportive business environment to build a number of enormously profitable corporations.

4. The Golden Age of Railroads

   a. America's railroad network increased from 35,000 miles in 1865 to 193,000 miles in 1900. Railroad construction stimulated industrial growth by consuming vast quantities of iron, steel, coal, and lumber. Other industries flourished as railroads brought them raw materials and carried their finished products to distant markets.

   b. The railroads played a key role in creating an interconnected national transportation and communication network. As railroad and telegraph lines spread across the continent, they increased the pace of commerce by ushering in a new era of instantaneous communication.

5. New Inventions

   a. A series of inventions created new industries that transformed American life. The typewriter, cash register, and adding machine aided merchants by accelerating accurate business transactions. Elevators and structural steel enabled architects to design the first skyscrapers. Refrigerators and washing machines helped families by easing the burden of time-consuming chores.

b. No inventor captured the public's imagination more than Thomas Edison. His list of inventions included the first phonograph and the first commercially successful incandescent light bulb. Reflecting upon his record 1,093 patents, Edison said, "I am proud of the fact that I never invented weapons to kill."

6. Making Connections: The Business of Invention

   a. In 1876, Edison opened an "invention factory" at Menlo Park, New Jersey. This facility became the prototype for the modern research laboratory.

   b. Today most major American corporations fund special research and development departments dedicated to creating new products. For example, California's Silicon Valley is home to Google, Facebook, Apple, and many other high-tech corporations. Silicon Valley's list of high-tech innovations includes the silicon-based integrated circuit, the microprocessor, and the iPhone.

II. KEY ENTREPRENEURS

A. CONTEXT

1. The factors producing America's post–Civil War industrial expansion unleashed a new entrepreneurial spirit. A generation of ambitious and often unscrupulous entrepreneurs took advantage of America's natural resources, growing population, and stable government to create powerful and immensely profitable corporations.

2. Steel and petroleum products played a particularly important role in spearheading America's rapidly growing economy. Andrew Carnegie and John D. Rockefeller helped organize and promote these key industries.

B. ANDREW CARNEGIE AND STEEL

1. Steel is stronger, harder, and more durable than iron. But it was also much more expensive to manufacture in the mid-nineteenth century. As a result, America produced only 13,000 tons of steel in 1860.

2. In 1857, Henry Bessemer discovered that shooting a blast of cold air through hot molten iron would remove impurities. Both inexpensive and efficient, the Bessemer process enabled

manufacturers to produce steel 20 times as durable as iron. Steel soon replaced iron to build railroads, machinery, plows, and buildings.

3. Andrew Carnegie became convinced that steel represented the metal of the future. Although Carnegie was not an inventor, he was a gifted organizer. Under his leadership, Carnegie Steel became a model of vertical integration in which a single company owns and controls the entire productive process from the unearthing of raw materials to the manufacture and sale of finished products. Carnegie employed this model by buying mines that produced iron ore and the ships and railroads that carried it to and from his steel plants near Pittsburgh.

4. By 1900, Carnegie Steel became the largest industrial company in the world. It employed 20,000 workers and produced more steel than Great Britain. Company profits totaled $40 million a year with $25 million going to Andrew Carnegie.

C. JOHN D. ROCKEFELLER AND OIL

1. In 1859, Edwin L. Drake drilled the first oil well near Titusville in northwestern Pennsylvania. Chemists soon discovered that oil could be refined into kerosene that could be used in lighting, heating, and cooking, and into petroleum that could be turned into lubricating oil, grease, and paint.

2. John D. Rockefeller neither discovered oil nor invented ways to refine it. Instead, he focused on refining the oil that others produced. Recognizing the potential profits of refining oil, Rockefeller built his first refinery in Cleveland, Ohio. Situated beside Lake Erie's key shipping lanes and near the Pennsylvania oil fields, Cleveland provided a strategic location from which Rockefeller's Standard Oil Company could dominate the refining market.

3. Horizontal integration is the process by which one company gains control over other firms that produce the same product. Rockefeller believed that his rivals reduced profits by flooding the market with too much refined oil. A ruthless competitor, Rockefeller used horizontal integration to take over 22 of his 26 competitors. Within a short time, Standard Oil controlled 95 percent of the oil refining in America. His control over a vital industry helped to make Rockefeller the world's first billionaire.

4. Under Rockefeller's leadership, Standard Oil evolved into a powerful trust or monopoly. Although Edison's light bulb reduced the demand for kerosene, the automobile soon created an insatiable demand for gasoline.

III. MAKING COMPARISONS: RESPONSES TO THE UNEQUAL DISTRIBUTION OF WEALTH

A. CONTEXT

1. Between 1869 and 1899 the value of American manufactures increased by 600 percent. America's booming economy produced unprecedented personal fortunes. The new millionaires filled their mansions with fine furniture and precious works of art.
2. In 1900, the richest 2 percent of American households owned over one-third of the nation's physical wealth.

B. SOCIAL DARWINISM

1. Social Darwinism was a set of beliefs that explained and justified how a small group of business and industrial leaders could accumulate such great wealth. Social Darwinists applied Charles Darwin's theory that plants and animals are engaged in a constant "struggle for existence" to society. According to Social Darwinists, individuals and corporations are also engaged in a ruthless struggle for profit in which only the fit survive and succeed.
2. Industrial titans such as Carnegie and Rockefeller used the "law of competition" to explain their wealth and praise the free market economic system. They believed that wealth is a reward for hard work and talent, while poverty is a punishment for laziness and bad judgment. Governments must therefore resist the temptation to regulate economic activities by supporting wage increases and social welfare programs.

C. THE GOSPEL OF WEALTH

1. Andrew Carnegie believed that disparities in wealth were inevitable in a free market system. However, he also believed that great wealth brought great responsibility.
2. In his 1889 "The Gospel of Wealth" essay, Carnegie warned that men who die wealthy would pass away "unwept, unhonored, and unsung." The public would justly condemn these men because, "The man who dies thus rich dies disgraced." Instead of squandering their money on passing fantasies, men of wealth have a duty to regard their surplus fortunes as a trust to be administered for the benefit of the community. Carnegie encouraged philanthropists to support public libraries, universities, museums, and other "ladders upon which the aspiring can rise."

3. Carnegie practiced what he preached. After selling Carnegie Steel to J.P. Morgan for almost $500 million, Carnegie devoted the rest of his life to promoting the public good.

D. HORATIO ALGER AND THE SELF-MADE MAN

1. Horatio Alger was a prolific writer who published over 100 novels that together sold more than 20 million copies. Each novel responds to America's unequal distribution of wealth by telling a formulaic story of how an impoverished young boy became successful through hard work, honesty, and luck.
2. Alger's name soon became synonymous with finding fame and fortune through "luck and pluck." Indeed, Alger believed his novels owed their success to stories that brought to life "inspiring examples of what energy, ambition, and honest purpose may achieve."
3. Historians believe that Alger's books are more than just instructive adventure stories for young readers. Written as America made the difficult transition from an agrarian society to an industrial society, Alger's stories reassured Americans that the poor but determined "self-made man" could still achieve success in an economy increasingly dominated by huge bureaucratic corporations.

E. THE SOCIALIST CRITIQUE

1. During the period from 1870 to 1900, a small but vocal group of socialists rejected the responses to income inequality offered by the Social Darwinists, Andrew Carnegie, and Horatio Alger. Socialists argued that the captains of industry were actually greedy robber barons who exploited their workers. Socialists believed that the close links between big business and government enabled wealthy industrialists to drive down wages, ignore hazardous working conditions, and enjoy immense financial rewards.
2. Although socialists agreed on the causes of the unequal distribution of wealth, they were deeply divided over tactics to achieve greater income equality. Many socialists favored the creation of trade unions to demand shorter hours, higher wages, and better working conditions. Others favored political activism by founding political parties dedicated to achieving greater government regulation of private industry.

Be prepared to discuss the different responses to the growing disparity of wealth in industrial America. APUSH test writers have used political cartoons and passages by "dueling historians" to generate short-answer questions designed to test your ability to compare and contrast Social Darwinism, Carnegie's **Gospel of Wealth,** ***the Horatio Alger stories, and the Socialist critique.***

IV. LABOR UNIONS

A. WAGE AND WORKING CONDITIONS

1. Owners enjoyed enormous profits while their workers earned meager salaries. For example, Marshall Field, the founder of a Chicago-based chain of department stores, earned $600.00 an hour while his shop girls survived on a salary of just $3.00 to $5.00 a week.
2. Factory laborers typically worked ten-hour days, six days a week. Hours were even longer in steel mills where workers put in 12-hour shifts for $1.25 a day.
3. America's poorly paid workers were also unprotected by safety regulations. American industry had the highest accident rate in the world. For example, in 1890 railroad accidents injured one railroader for every 30 employed workers.

B. THE KNIGHTS OF LABOR

1. Founded in 1869, the Knights of Labor attempted to unify all working men and women into a national union under the motto, "An injury to one is the concern of all."
2. The Knights denounced "wage-slavery" and were dedicated to achieving a "cooperative commonwealth" of independent workers. The union hoped to achieve this idealistic goal by encouraging workers to combine their wages so that they could collectively purchase mines, factories, and stores.
3. The Knights' open-membership and a few successful strikes contributed to a period of rapid growth during the 1880s as membership rolls swelled from 42,000 in 1882 to over 700,000 in 1886.

4. The Knights began to lose strength when newspapers unjustly blamed them for causing the Haymarket Square riot. As a result of this misrepresentation, the public erroneously linked the Knights with violent anarchists who opposed all forms of government. The economic depression following the Panic of 1893 ended the union's importance.

C. THE AMERICAN FEDERATION OF LABOR

1. Founded in 1886, the American Federation of Labor (AFL) was an alliance of skilled workers in craft unions. Unlike the Knights of Labor, the AFL did not welcome unskilled workers, women, or racial minorities.
2. Led for 37 years by Samuel Gompers, the AFL opposed political activity not directly related to the union. Instead, Gompers advocated using collective bargaining and, if necessary, strikes to win concrete "bread and butter" goals such as higher wages, shorter hours, and better working conditions.
3. Membership in the AFL grew steadily as it replaced the Knights as America's most powerful union. By 1904, it had 1.7 million members and Gompers was recognized as a national spokesperson for American laborers.

D. THE INDUSTRIAL WORKERS OF THE WORLD

1. The AFL's commitment to craft unionism excluded many workers. Like the Knights of Labor, the Industrial Workers of the World (IWW or Wobblies) was intended to be "One Big Union" that would unite all skilled and unskilled workers.
2. While the AFL pursued "bread and butter" issues, the IWW was founded on what one of its early leaders called "the irrepressible conflict between the capitalist class and the working class." The IWW advocated a socialist economic system in which the government would own the basic industries and natural resources.
3. The Wobblies never attracted more than 150,000 members. Branded as dangerous radicals and agitators, they faded from the national scene by the end of World War I.

It is important to understand the similarities and differences among the Knights of Labor, AFL, and IWW. Remember, all three were dedicated to organizing laborers. The Knights and the IWW both attempted to organize all skilled and unskilled workers into one union. However, the Knights strove for a cooperative society, while the IWW embraced class conflict. In contrast, the AFL organized skilled workers, repudiated violence, and fought for higher wages and better working conditions.

V. LABOR STRIKES AND UNREST

A. THE GREAT RAILROAD STRIKE OF 1877

1. The Panic of 1873 triggered a severe depression that bankrupted 47,000 firms and drove wholesale prices down by 30 percent. As orders for industrial goods fell, railroad lines in the East began a series of pay cuts. On July 16, 1877, railroad workers spontaneously walked off their jobs to protest a second wage cut by the Baltimore & Ohio Railroad. Walkouts and sympathy demonstrations quickly followed as the strike spread from Maryland to California.
2. The Great Railroad Strike of 1877 was the first major interstate strike in American history. As the strike rippled across the country it paralyzed rail service. Looters and rioters destroyed millions of dollars of property. State militia and federal troops called out by President Hayes finally crushed the strike and restored order.
3. The Great Railroad Strike of 1877 signaled the beginning of a period of strikes and violent confrontations between labor and management. Between 1880 and 1900 over 23,000 strikes, the most in the industrial world, disrupted the American economy.

B. THE HOMESTEAD STRIKE, 1892

1. The Amalgamated Association of Iron and Steel Workers was the largest craft union in the AFL. The union's history of friendly relations with Andrew Carnegie's company abruptly changed in 1892 when Henry Clay Frick became president of the Homestead plant outside of Pittsburgh. Frick was determined to replace expensive skilled workers with new labor-saving machinery. He reduced the number of workers and slashed salaries by nearly 20 percent in a deliberate attempt to break the union.
2. When the Amalgamated called for a strike, Frick closed the Homestead plant and hired 300 union-busting Pinkerton detectives

to protect the nonunion workers. Enraged strikers fired at barges carrying Pinkertons to the plant. Three detectives and ten workers died before the Pinkertons finally surrendered.

3. The workers' victory proved to be short-lived. The governor of Pennsylvania ordered the state's entire contingent of 8,000 National Guard troops to Homestead to protect the plant. The strike finally ended four months later, leaving the union broken and defeated.

C. THE PULLMAN STRIKE, 1894

1. The Pullman Strike began as a dispute between the Pullman Palace Car Company and its 3,000 employees. Following the Panic of 1893, the Pullman company cut the wages of its workers by about 25 percent. However, the company did not reduce the rent or prices it charged workers in company-run stores at the "model" town of Pullman just outside of Chicago.
2. As tensions mounted and negotiations failed, many workers joined the American Railway Union led by Eugene Debs. Fearing that they had no alternative, desperate Pullman workers walked off their jobs. The American Railway Union then staged a nationwide boycott of Pullman cars. Since most railroad companies used Pullman cars, rail traffic ground to a halt in Chicago and across 27 states and territories.
3. President Cleveland called out federal troops to break the strike on the grounds that it obstructed delivery of the U.S. mail. The Pullman Strike once again demonstrated that the federal government would actively intervene to crush strikes and protect management.
4. The outcome of the Pullman Strike left Debs disillusioned and embittered. Within a few years, he became a key leader of the Socialist Party of America.

URBAN AMERICA 1865–1900

I. URBAN GROWTH

A. THE NEW URBAN REALITY

1. Between 1870 and 1900, urban centers assumed a dominant role in American life and culture. Just after the Civil War only one in six Americans lived in communities with a population of 8,000 or more. By 1900, one in three Americans made their homes in cities.

2. A large number of the new urban dwellers came from small towns and rural areas. New mechanical farm equipment pushed many workers off the land. Still others wanted to exchange the drudgery of farm life for the excitement of living in cities. Electricity, indoor plumbing, telephones, and department stores all combined to make cities an irresistible magnet that promised an exciting new life.

B. INDUSTRY AND URBAN GROWTH

1. Before the Civil War, factories were dependent upon water for their power. As a result, they were usually built near swift rivers and waterfalls. However, in the late nineteenth century, factories increasingly used steam and then electrical power. Factory owners could now build their plants near growing centers of population.

2. During the post–Civil War period transportation centers became booming industrial cities. Meat-packing plants in Chicago, flour mills in Minneapolis, and oil refineries in Cleveland all offered jobs for unskilled workers.

C. SKYSCRAPERS AND VERTICAL GROWTH

1. Before the 1860s, few buildings reached heights greater than three or four stories. Soaring urban populations and rising urban property values placed pressure on engineers and architects to find ways to design taller buildings.

2. Steel-frames and electric elevators enabled architects to design buildings so tall they were called skyscrapers. The nine-story

Wainwright Building in St. Louis paved the way for a new generation of multi-story factories, apartment buildings, and department stores. Soon bigger and better skyscrapers were rising over American cities topped in 1892 by Chicago's soaring 22-story Masonic Temple, then the tallest building in the world.

D. ELECTRIC TROLLEYS AND HORIZONTAL EXPANSION

1. Before the 1890s, horses and mule-drawn streetcars provided the chief sources of urban transportation. In 1888, Richmond, Virginia, successfully tested the first electric trolley system. Within two years, 200 other cities opened trolley lines. By 1900, 30,000 cars carried passengers on 15,000 miles of track.
2. The new electric streetcars promoted the horizontal expansion of cities. The growing middle-class could now live in tree-lined "streetcar suburbs" and commute into the central city for business or entertainment. This first ring of suburbs began the process of segregating urban residents by class, race, and ethnicity.

II. THE NEW IMMIGRANTS

A. A NEW WAVE OF IMMIGRATION

1. Before the 1880s, most immigrants to the United States came from countries in Western Europe and Scandinavia. However, the last two decades of the nineteenth century witnessed a massive wave of immigrants from Southern and Eastern Europe. The overwhelming majority of these "new" immigrants came from Italy, Poland, Russia, and Greece.
2. Europe's new industrial economy replaced the older agricultural way of life, uprooting millions of people. Most of the immigrants from Italy were pushed out by unemployment, crushing poverty, and epidemics of cholera and malaria. Immigrants from Poland and Russia fled government-condoned pogroms, acts of violence in which vandals burned and pillaged Jewish homes and shops. Almost all of these uprooted people viewed America as a land of freedom and opportunity.

B. A HARD NEW LIFE

1. The overwhelming majority of the new immigrants settled in large cities in the Northeast and Midwest. Two-thirds of all the new immigrants found homes in New York, New England, Pennsylvania, and New Jersey. Very few went to the South.

2. The new immigrants quickly faced a grim reality that tested their optimistic faith in America as the "land of opportunity." Many immigrants lived in crowded tenements and worked 12-hour days in grimy factories, dangerous coal mines, and crowded sweatshops where they stitched clothing and rolled cigars. One Italian saying expressed the sense of disillusionment felt by many immigrants: "I came to America because I heard the streets were paved with gold. When I got here, I found out three things: First, the streets weren't paved with gold; second, they weren't paved at all; and third, I was expected to pave them."

3. Bewildered immigrants often congregated into urban enclaves. The "Little Italys," "Little Hungarys" and other ethnic neighborhoods provided close-knit communities where the new immigrants could speak their native language and practice their religious faith.

C. IMMIGRANTS AND POLITICAL MACHINES

1. Most immigrants were politically inexperienced. America's federal system with its local, state, and national governments seemed complex and overwhelming. As a result, many immigrants became clients of big city political machines.

2. The boss and his ward leaders provided poor immigrants with services such as free food, clothing, and coal in exchange for their votes. "If a family is burned out," explained one candid machine boss, "I don't ask whether they are Republicans or Democrats. I just get quarters for them, bring clothes for them if their clothes were burned up and fix them up till they get things runnin' again. Who can tell how many votes these fires bring me? . . . The poor are the most grateful people in the world."

3. The political machines provided the new immigrants with a rudimentary form of welfare. At the same time, venal bosses often engaged in illegal schemes that cost their cities millions of dollars. New York City, for example, fell under the control of a group of corrupt politicians known as the "Tweed Ring." Boss Tweed and his cronies stole as much as $200 million from the public treasury.

4. Tweed's reign of unbridled greed and theft finally came to an end from an unexpected source. Thomas Nast exposed Tweed's fraudulent practices in a series of political cartoons that mercilessly portrayed the boss as the leader of a group of thieves and scoundrels. In one particularly devastating cartoon, Nast gave the rotund Tweed a moneybag for a head!

D. MAKING COMPARISONS: NATIVIST REACTIONS

1. The wave of Irish and German immigrants in the 1840s and 1850s sparked a nativist reaction against Catholics. The Know-Nothing Party raised the issue of restricting immigration and excluding Catholics from holding political office. Although the party enjoyed brief support, it quickly disappeared as Americans shifted their focus to the impending crisis over slavery and disunion.
2. The wave of new immigrants also provoked an intense nativist response. The new immigrants spoke different languages, practiced different religions, and worked for low wages. Alarmed nativists formed the American Protective Association (APA) to demand more restrictive immigration laws. Although the APA claimed 2.5 million members, it never formed a political party.
3. Even though the APA faded from the scene, opposition to immigration did not vanish. Led by the newly formed Immigration Restriction League, nativists supported a literacy test as a way to stem the tide of unwanted immigrants. When Congress passed a literacy test in 1896, President Cleveland vetoed the bill, insisting that America should remain an asylum for the oppressed of Europe.

APUSH exams often include a graph to generate questions about immigration trends between 1820 and 1900. It is important to remember that the industrial revolution played a key role in contributing to the rising rate of immigration to the United States. The flood of people into the Midwest and Northeast provoked a strong nativist reaction that ultimately led to restrictions on immigration from Southern and Eastern Europe in the 1920s.

III. URBAN REFORMERS

A. JACOB RIIS AND *HOW THE OTHER HALF LIVES*

1. Immigrant families packed into rows of squalid tenement buildings. A single square mile in New York City's Lower East Side contained 334,000 people, making it the most densely populated place in the world.
2. Jacob Riis was a journalist and photographer who exposed the poverty and despair of the Lower East Side. Published in 1890, his book *How the Other Half Lives* included deeply troubling pictures of destitute families crammed into overcrowded tenements where

60 or more people might share one stopped-up toilet and a single water tap.

3. Riis was not content to simply document the wretched conditions in New York's disease-ridden tenements. He hoped that his photographs would shock a complacent public into calling for reforms. Riis's concern was not in vain. *How the Other Half Lives* prompted a public outcry that led to improvements in sewers, garbage collection, and indoor plumbing. New York City tore down some of the worse slums replacing them with new parks and playgrounds.

B. JANE ADDAMS AND THE SETTLEMENT HOUSE MOVEMENT

1. Jane Addams, like Jacob Riis, chose to devote her life to bettering the condition of the urban poor. In 1889, Addams rented Hull House, an old mansion in one of Chicago's poorest immigrant neighborhoods. Addams began by providing day nurseries for working mothers and offering adult-education classes for immigrants who wanted to learn English. As Hull House became more successful, Addams offered practical courses on cooking, dressmaking, and personal hygiene. At its peak, Hull House expanded to a dozen buildings and served 2,000 people a week.

2. Hull House served as a model for other middle-class women who founded over 400 settlement houses in cities across America. The settlement houses often extended their mission to include lobbying local governments to enact reform legislation. Settlement houses thus gave a new generation of women organizational and leadership skills that transcended their traditional roles as mothers and wives.

C. WALTER RAUSCHENBUSCH AND THE SOCIAL GOSPEL MOVEMENT

1. Walter Rauschenbusch, a Baptist theologian, was deeply stirred by the plight of his parishioners in the Hell's Kitchen section of New York City. Convinced that something had to be done, he advocated applying the Christian principles of love and justice to the nation's pressing urban problems. He inspired his followers by preaching that the Kingdom of God "is not a matter of getting individuals to heaven, but of transforming the life on earth into the harmony of heaven."

2. Rauschenbusch's religious philosophy became known as the Social Gospel. Supporters of the Social Gospel movement believed that America's churches had a moral responsibility to take the lead in actively confronting social problems and in helping the poor.

Carnegie's Gospel of Wealth *and Rauschenbusch's Social Gospel are easily confused. Remember, Carnegie believed that the rich have a duty to serve their communities, while Rauschenbusch believed that Christian ministers and their congregations must play an active role in helping the unfortunate.*

IV. POPULAR CULTURE

A. CONTEXT

1. Prior to the Industrial Revolution, organized leisure was a luxury reserved for the upper class. The Industrial Revolution created a new middle class of corporate managers and urban professionals who earned disposable income beyond their basic needs of food, clothing, and rent. They also had leisure time on weekends and even the possibility of a week-long vacation.
2. In a popular ballad in the 1890s, a country mother warns her daughter to be wary of the temptations "in the city's giddy whirl" of amusements. The young city-bound daughter probably shrugged off her mother's well-meaning admonition. During the Gilded Age, America's fast-changing cities offered residents and visitors an alluring popular culture that included glamorous department stores, professional sports, and mass-circulation newspapers.

B. DEPARTMENT STORES

1. During the late 1870s and early 1880s, R. H. Macy in New York City, John Wanamaker in Philadelphia, and Marshall Field in Chicago opened huge stores offering a wide range of consumer goods in different categories called "departments."
2. The new department stores revolutionized the urban shopping experience. Well-dressed clerks provided "service with a smile" as shoppers examined displays of stylish wardrobes and counters filled with ready-made products from America's booming industries. When customers tired of shopping, they could ride plush elevators to rooftop restaurants and tearooms.

C. SPECTATOR SPORTS

1. Baseball began its reign as America's pastime during the last quarter of the nineteenth century. Formed in 1869, the Cincinnati

Red Stockings became America's first salaried team. Within a few years eight teams formed the National League. By 1889, two million fans cheered for their local teams at major league games.

2. Football quickly emerged as America's second most popular spectator game. Unlike baseball, football originated on college and university campuses. Princeton and Rutgers played the first intercollegiate game in 1869. Within a short time football became an integral part of college life.

D. NEWSPAPERS

1. Traditional American newspapers featured pages called "tombstones" because they were filled with long columns of gray print devoted to dry topics. Joseph Pulitzer believed these staid journals needed a remodeling to fit the needs and interests of citizens living in America's bustling cities. Pulitzer transformed the once dull pages of the *New York World* into a modern newspaper by adding headlines, comic strips, and sensational stories about celebrity scandals, natural disasters, and corrupt politicians. Typewriters, telephones, and high-capacity rotary presses all helped Pulitzer reach a mass urban audience.
2. Paid advertisements enabled the *New York World* to only charge a few pennies for each newspaper. Department stores were especially committed to using newspaper ads to promote their latest special sales. By 1900, American businesses spent $500 million on ads, ten times more than they spent just 30 years before.

V. REALISTIC ART AND LITERATURE

A. A NEW REALISM

1. Romanticism dominated American art and literature during most of the nineteenth century. However, the twin forces of industrialization and urbanization created harsh new social realities that conflicted with Romanticism's emphasis upon nature and intuitive feelings. A talented group of American artists and authors rejected Romanticism turning instead to Realism's hard-edged portraits of urban life.
2. Realism's artists and authors focused on the facets of the modern world they could personally experience. Idealized landscapes and sentimental love stories seemed out of touch with America's raw and raucous cities.

B. THE ASHCAN ARTISTS AND REALISTIC AUTHORS

1. A new generation of young artists relished portraying New York City's vibrant and unruly life. They typically painted working class taverns, prize fights, bleak tenements, and dark alleys. Shocked critics insisted that these "raw" scenes were only fit for an ash can. The artists soon adopted the name "Ashcan" as a badge of honor. For a famous example of Ashcan art, see *Cliff Dwellers* by George Bellows.

2. Talented authors also rejected Romanticism. Stephen Crane and Theodore Dreiser strove to create a more authentic or realistic portrayal of American urban life. For example, in *Maggie: A Girl of the Streets*, Crane tells the story of a beautiful young girl enduring harsh conditions in a New York City slum.

UNIT 7 PERIOD 7
1890–1945

KEY CONCEPTS

KEY CONCEPT 7.1
Growth expanded opportunity, while economic instability led to new efforts to reform U.S. society and its economic system.

KEY CONCEPT 7.2
Innovations in communications and technology contributed to the growth of mass culture, while significant changes occurred in internal and international migration patterns.

KEY CONCEPT 7.3
Participation in a series of global conflicts propelled the United States into a position of international power while renewing domestic debates over the nation's proper role in the world.

POPULISTS AND PROGRESSIVES 1890–1919

Chapter 21

I. THE RISE AND FALL OF THE POPULIST PARTY

A. UNDERSTANDING CAUSATION: CAUSES OF THE POPULIST REVOLT

1. The laws of supply and demand worked against American farmers. The more wheat, corn, and cotton they produced, the lower prices fell. For example, the price of a bushel of wheat plummeted from $1.19 in 1881 to just 49 cents in 1894.

2. Angry farmers blamed the railroads for many of their problems. Most farmers depended upon the railroads to transport their crops to urban markets and then return with heavy machinery. Farmers bitterly complained that the railroads used their monopoly power to charge unfair rates. For example, the Burlington line charged its customers west of the Mississippi four times what they charged customers east of the river.

3. Farmers had to borrow money to build homes, fertilize fields, and buy new equipment. Following the Civil War, America experienced a prolonged period of deflation in which both prices and the money supply fell. As a result, a farmer had to pay back loans with dollars that had doubled in value since he or she borrowed them.

4. Debt-ridden farmers believed that America's strict adherence to the gold standard reduced the supply of money in circulation, thus limiting economic activity. This policy benefitted bankers and creditors while punishing debtors. Farmers argued that the free and unlimited coinage of silver would bring back prosperity by increasing the money supply, thereby spurring inflation and making it easier to repay debts.

B. THE BIRTH OF THE POPULIST PARTY

1. America's increasingly militant farmers believed they had good reasons to organize a third party. Once praised as the backbone of American democracy, farmers now saw themselves as victims of an unjust system that penalized them with low crop prices and predatory railroad rates while rewarding Wall Street financiers with

extravagant profits. Mary Ellen Lease captured the farmers' militant mood when she advised them to "raise less corn and more hell."

2. The wave of agrarian discontent gave birth to the People's or Populist Party. Although spearheaded by farmers, the movement included labor leaders, women's rights activists, and socialists. In July 1892, 1,300 delegates met in Omaha, Nebraska, to formulate a platform and nominate a candidate for the fall election.

3. The Populist Party platform emphatically demanded government control over the railroads and the free and unlimited coinage of silver. The platform also endorsed the eight-hour workday and the direct election of senators by voters instead of state legislators. A graduated income tax also ranked high on the list of Populist objectives. This meant that the more money a person earned, the more taxes he or she would pay. Populists believed that a graduated income tax would narrow the growing gap between the rich and the poor.

4. The Populists nominated former congressman and Union general James B. Weaver of Iowa to run for president. Weaver received about 9 percent of the popular vote, more than any previous third-party candidate. In addition, the Populists elected 10 congressmen, 5 senators, and almost 1,500 members of different state legislatures. Buoyed by their success, the Populists eagerly looked forward to the 1896 presidential election.

C. THE ELECTION OF 1896

1. The Republicans nominated William McKinley, the affable and well-liked governor of Ohio. The Republican platform supported both the gold standard and high protective tariffs.

2. The Democrats nominated William Jennings Bryan, a 36-year-old former congressman from Nebraska. Bryan was committed to a policy of free silver that would devalue money and help debtors. In a famous speech at the Democratic convention, Bryan galvanized cheering delegates by defiantly warning wealthy creditors, "You shall not crucify mankind on a cross of gold!"

3. The Democrats' decision to nominate a pro-silver candidate presented Populists with a difficult choice. Nominating their own candidate would divide the silver vote and ensure McKinley's election. Endorsing Bryan would mean giving up their identity as a separate party. After much debate, the Populists chose to support Bryan.

4. The charismatic Bryan broke with the tradition that a candidate did not go out and seek votes for himself. Instead, Bryan crisscrossed the country taking his campaign directly to the voters. The "Boy Orator" conveyed boundless energy as he delivered over 600 speeches extolling the benefits of free silver.

5. Bryan won the battle of speeches, but McKinley won the fight for votes. The Republicans captured all of the Northeast and the upper Midwest including the key states of Ohio and Illinois. As a result, McKinley won a solid victory in both the electoral college and the popular vote.

D. UNDERSTANDING CAUSATION: CONSEQUENCES OF THE ELECTION OF 1896

1. The election of 1896 led to the swift collapse of the Populist Party. The silver issue melted away as gold strikes in South Africa, the Yukon, and Australia enlarged the money supply and reversed the deflationary spiral. In addition, crop failure in Europe led to an increase in American grain exports. As commodity prices rose, farmers entered a period of renewed prosperity lasting until the end of World War I.

2. Industrialization and urbanization were the driving forces reshaping American life. Bryan did not carry a single industrial state or large city. The election of 1896 began a generation of almost unbroken Republican dominance that lasted until the election of Franklin Roosevelt in 1932.

3. The defeat of the Populists and the return of prosperity did not end the spirit of reform. A new generation of Progressives successfully fought for many reforms.

Recent APUSH exams have used excerpts from the Populist Party platform and a political cartoon as stimulus sources to generate a number of multiple-choice questions. It is important to remember that the Populist Party was a response to the growth of corporate power over that of agriculture and economic instability in farming. Populists had the most in common with the ideas advanced by the Progressives.

II. THE PROGRESSIVE SPIRIT

A. FROM POPULISM TO PROGRESSIVISM

1. After the collapse of the Populist Party, the reform spirit shifted to the cities where a new generation of middle and upper-middle class reformers focused on a broad range of problems caused by industrialization and urbanization.
2. The term *progressivism* embraced a widespread, many faceted effort to build a more democratic and just society. The Progressive Era is usually dated from 1900 to America's entry into World War I in 1917.

B. KEY ELEMENTS OF THE PROGRESSIVE SPIRIT

1. Both the Populists and the Progressives rejected laissez-faire government policies. Instead, they wanted government to play an active role in public life. Progressives believed that complex social problems required a broad range of government responses. "The real heart of the movement," declared one Progressive reformer, was "to use the government as an agency of human welfare."
2. Progressives were idealists who rejected the main tenets of Social Darwinism. They believed that conflict and competition would not inevitably improve society. Instead, they optimistically believed that informed citizens could create a just society that would reduce poverty, regulate corporations, protect the environment, and elect honest leaders.

C. THE MUCKRAKERS

1. During the early 1900s, popular magazines such as *Collier's* and *McClure's* began to hire writers to expose corrupt practices in business and politics. Known as muckrakers, these investigative reporters expressed the new spirit of Progressive reform by uncovering social wrongs.
2. Muckraking magazines published more than 2,000 investigative reports between 1903 and 1912. For example, Ida Tarbell wrote a devastating exposé of the ruthless practices John D. Rockefeller used to eliminate competitors and build the Standard Oil Company into the "Mother of Trusts." Muckraking articles by Tarbell and others enabled the spirit of Progressive reform to mobilize public opinion to demand and support needed reforms.

III. TURNING POINTS IN AMERICAN HISTORY: WOMEN AND PROGRESSIVE REFORM

A. THE "NEW WOMAN"

1. When the Progressive Era began, men ran the nation's businesses and cast all of its votes. The prevailing belief in the cult of domesticity restricted women to their homes. There were very few female lawyers, physicians, engineers, or scientists.
2. During the Progressive Era, a generation of middle class "New Women" extended their roles as guardians of the home to include becoming activists who fought to improve their communities. Women thus became a major force behind many Progressive Era reforms.

B. CLUBS AND SETTLEMENT HOUSES

1. By 1910 about 1 million women belonged to clubs. They embraced a new ideal called maternalism that expressed itself in a desire to improve their communities. Women's clubs pressed local governments to build community playgrounds, enforce strict fire codes, open public libraries, and improve sanitation by purifying public water and instituting regular trash collection.
2. Women's commitment to social reform extended to addressing problems faced by immigrants living in America's crowded cities. Begun by Jane Addams in Chicago, the settlement house movement spread to hundreds of cities across America. Settlement houses gave women an opportunity to develop leadership skills and to build satisfying careers devoted to service and professional accomplishment.

C. THE TEMPERANCE MOVEMENT

1. Women played a leading role in the temperance movement to outlaw the sale of alcoholic beverages. The Women's Christian Temperance Movement (WCTU) boasted 150,000 dues-paying members, making it one of the largest organizations of women in the world. Under the dynamic leadership of Frances Willard, the WCTU convinced many women that they had a moral duty to eliminate alcohol abuse and thus strengthen the stability of American families.
2. As the crusade against alcohol gathered momentum, more and more states outlawed saloons. In 1918, Congress passed the

Eighteenth Amendment outlawing the manufacture, sale, and transportation of intoxicating liquors.

D. WOMEN'S SUFFRAGE

1. When the Progressive Era began, the law denied criminals, lunatics, idiots, and women the right to vote. Beginning with the Seneca Falls Convention in 1848, a determined group of women fought a long and at times frustrating battle for female suffrage.
2. The Progressive movement sharpened the nation's social conscience and motivated a new generation of suffragists. Led by Carrie Chapman Catt and Alice Paul, women organized rallies, signed petitions, and demonstrated in public marches. Their campaign of mounting pressure proved to be irresistible. On June 4, 1919, Congress passed the Nineteenth Amendment stating that no citizen could be denied the right to vote "on account of sex." The amendment constituted the largest single extension of democratic voting rights in American history.

E. CONTINUITY AND CHANGE

1. When the Progressive Era ended, women still lacked significant political influence and remained largely absent from professional fields and management. At the same time, the lives of the vast majority of African American women remained the same.
2. During the 1920s public attention turned from social activism to a new "normalcy" defined by a focus on leisure, mass entertainment, and material consumption. However, the Wall Street Crash and the resulting Great Depression reawakened interest in social reform. The reform efforts by women during the Progressive Era helped establish precedents for government to play an active role in public life. They thus provided a bridge between the Progressive Era and the New Deal. In addition, the pioneering "New Women" of the Progressive Era provided important role models for the feminist movement in the 1960s and '70s.

IV. ROOSEVELT AND THE SQUARE DEAL

A. A DYNAMIC NEW PRESIDENT

1. An assassin's bullet took President McKinley's life just six months after his second inauguration. At age 42, Theodore Roosevelt became the youngest president in American history.

2. Roosevelt quickly became a major voice in the Progressive movement. Like other Progressives, TR believed that government should be used to solve the nation's pressing problems. The dynamic force of his personality revitalized the presidency and established the White House as the focal point in American life.

B. THE ANTHRACITE COAL STRIKE, 1902

1. On May 12, 1902, 147,000 members of the United Mine Workers (UMW) struck coal mines across Pennsylvania and West Virginia. TR invited both management and labor to the White House. When the owners refused to negotiate, TR threatened to order the Army to seize and operate the mines. Stunned by Roosevelt's unprecedented threat, the owners reluctantly accepted federal arbitration.
2. The Anthracite Coal Strike marked the first time that a President had successfully intervened in a labor dispute as an impartial arbiter. The settlement established TR's reputation as a fearless champion of the working class. TR later wrote that his purpose was "to see to it that every man has a square deal."

C. TR AND THE TRUSTS

1. A trust is a large business combination formed by merging several smaller companies under the control of a single governing board. By 1901, giant trusts dominated the American economy. Like the Populists before them, Progressives complained that trusts restrained trade, fixed prices, and posed a threat to free markets.
2. The Sherman Antitrust Act of 1890 forbade unreasonable combinations "in restraint of trade or commerce." The law, however, had been applied more vigorously to curb labor unions than to breakup trusts.
3. In 1902, TR used his executive power to order the attorney general to breakup the Northern Securities Company, a giant trust that monopolized rail traffic in the Northwest. Two years later, the Supreme Court upheld the antitrust suit and dissolved the company. This victory established TR's reputation as a "trust buster."

D. CONSUMER PROTECTION

1. Upton Sinclair's muckraking novel *The Jungle* dealt with conditions in the Chicago meatpacking industry. Sinclair included a particularly graphic account of the filthy conditions in the packing houses: "There would be meat stored in great piles in rooms; and

the water from leaky roofs would drip over it, and thousands of rats would race about on it."

2. *The Jungle* illustrates the relationship between muckraking and reform legislation during the Progressive Era. When federal inspectors confirmed Sinclair's charges, an indignant public demanded action. Congress promptly passed the Meat Inspection Act and the Pure Food and Drug Act. These laws set strict new Federal standards for food and drugs destined for interstate commerce.

V. ROOSEVELT AND THE ENVIRONMENT

A. CONTEXT

1. During the second half of the nineteenth century, America's westward expansion revealed the nation's wealth of natural resources. Settlers, railroads, and lumber companies acted as if the nation's forests and wildlife resources were inexhaustible. Lumber companies clear-cut richly forested regions while hunters annually killed 5 million birds to decorate women's hats with prized feathers. By 1900, 24 species of mammals and 33 species of birds faced possible extinction.

2. The wanton waste of forest and wildlife resources sparked a growing public awareness that strong steps had to be taken to protect the nation's endangered forests, wildlife, and scenic wonders. Congress took the first steps when it created Yellowstone National Park in 1872 and Yosemite National Park in 1890. Presidents Harrison, Cleveland, and McKinley used the Forest Reserve Act of 1891 to preserve 45 million acres of timberland.

B. ROOSEVELT AND THE CONSERVATIONISTS

1. The appalling exploitation of America's wilderness areas outraged Roosevelt. As a dedicated outdoorsman, he became a leader in the conservation movement. Conservationists believed that the environment and its resources should be managed in a responsible and sustainable manner.

2. Gifford Pinchot, TR's first head of the National Forest Service, endorsed the conservationist perspective. With Roosevelt's enthusiastic support, the federal government tripled the number of acres in its forest preserves.

C. ROOSEVELT AND THE PRESERVATIONISTS

1. Roosevelt also sympathized with the viewpoint of a naturalist group known as preservationists. In contrast to the conservationists' managed "hands-on" approach, preservationists advocated a strict "hands-off" approach to nature. They believed that people can have access to the land, but should only utilize it for beauty and inspiration.

2. John Muir, the founder of the Sierra Club, was America's foremost advocate of the preservationist viewpoint. He wrote that national parks should be places for "rest, inspiration, and prayers." He and TR spent four days camping together in Yosemite Valley. Inspired by the experience and by Muir's writings, Roosevelt fulfilled many preservationist goals by adding 5 national parks, 4 national game preserves, 51 federal bird preserves, and 18 national monuments.

D. THE HETCH HETCHY CONTROVERSY

1. The Hetch Hetchy Valley is a spectacular river valley located in the northwest corner of Yosemite National Park. Pinchot and the conservationists viewed the valley as an ideal spot for a dam to supply water for San Francisco. Muir and the preservationists viewed the valley as "one of God's best gifts [that] ought to be faithfully guarded."

2. The battle between the conservationists and the preservationists left TR with divided loyalties. After some indecision, he turned the issue to Pinchot who approved constructing the dam. Finally completed in 1934, the Hetch Hetchy Project includes a dam, reservoir, and a series of aqueducts that supply San Francisco with 80 percent of its water.

E. MAKING CONNECTIONS: LAND USE POLICY

1. Pinchot's conservationist viewpoint has had a significant impact on America's land use policy. The Hoover Dam, Tennessee Valley Authority (TVA), and Civilian Conservation Corps (CCC) are all examples of managed land use projects.

2. Muir's preservationist viewpoint has also had a significant impact on America's land use policy. The creation of national monuments, historic sites, and national parks are all examples of preserving America's natural and historic heritage.

The environment is one of the key themes covered in the APUSH course. Be sure to study Pinchot and Muir's contrasting viewpoints on environmental policy. They have generated a set of multiple-choice questions and a short-answer question.

VI. WILSON AND PROGRESSIVE REFORM

A. CONTEXT

1. TR believed his hand-picked successor William Howard Taft would continue his progressive reforms. However, Taft was an inept politician who soon alienated Roosevelt's Progressive supporters. When the Republican convention renominated Taft, Roosevelt formed the new Progressive or Bull Moose Party.

2. Sensing an opportunity to defeat the divided Republicans, the Democrats nominated New Jersey's popular reform governor Woodrow Wilson. Wilson won the election thus becoming only the second Democrat elected since the Civil War.

B. "THE TRIPLE WALL OF PRIVILEGE"

1. Once in office, Wilson launched a vigorous legislative offensive against what he called "the triple wall of privilege"—the tariff, the banks, and the trusts.

2. Roosevelt failed to address the issue of tariff reform. In contrast, Wilson successfully persuaded Congress to lower tariff rates by 8 percent.

3. Wilson next turned to reform of the nation's banking system. The landmark Federal Reserve Act of 1913 established a system of twelve district banks coordinated by a Federal Reserve Board appointed by the President. The "Fed" had the power to raise and lower interest rates and issue paper currency. These financial tools enabled the Federal Reserve Board to control both credit and the supply of money.

4. Elated by his tariff and banking reforms, Wilson focused on the final wall of privilege—the trusts. The Clayton Antitrust Act of 1914 strengthened the Sherman Antitrust Act by prohibiting price discrimination and forbidding interlocking directorates between large companies. The Clayton Antitrust Act specifically exempted labor unions from antitrust prosecution.

C. RACIAL DISCRIMINATION

1. Wilson did not include racial discrimination and white supremacy in his wall of privileges. As we have seen (Chapter 17), Jim Crow laws, sanctioned by the Supreme Court's "separate but equal" doctrine, created a wall of discrimination in the South. Despite their concern for social justice, Progressives largely ignored racial discrimination in the South.

2. Wilson reflected the entrenched racial attitudes of his time. In 1915, Hollywood director D.W. Griffith released *The Birth of a Nation*, an explicitly racist film glorifying the Ku Klux Klan. Wilson allowed the film to be the first movie screened inside the White House. He enthusiastically endorsed the film's racist message saying, "It is like writing history with lightning, and my only regret is that it is so terribly true."

BECOMING A WORLD POWER

1890–1919

Chapter 22

I. THE ROOTS OF AMERICAN IMPERIALISM

A. CONTEXT

1. In 1890, the United States still played a minor role in the game of global power politics. With the exception of its Revolutionary War alliance with France, America carefully followed Washington's admonition to avoid becoming entangled in foreign alliances. For most of the nineteenth century, America had been a continental republic focused on settling the western frontier and building democratic institutions.
2. In less than a decade America became an imperial republic with interests in the Caribbean, Latin America, and the Pacific. The speed of this change astonished President McKinley. The proud but perhaps slightly perplexed president correctly observed that "in a few short months we have become a world power."

B. THE QUEST FOR NEW MARKETS AND RAW MATERIALS

1. American business leaders worried that they were producing more products than Americans could buy. Many corporate executives looked to Latin America, Asia, and the Pacific for new markets and new sources of raw materials.
2. The deep depression from 1893 to 1897 exerted a powerful influence on American political leaders. Fearing renewed labor unrest, they linked economic growth and social stability to their quest for foreign markets and raw materials.

C. ALFRED MAHAN AND THE NEW STRATEGIC THINKING

1. In his seminal book *The Influence of Sea Power upon History*, Captain Alfred T. Mahan argued that control of the sea shaped the destinies of history's greatest empires. He forcefully argued that the United States must build a powerful oceangoing navy, construct a canal across the isthmus to link the East Coast with the Pacific, and acquire strategically located colonies to provide coaling stations and repair facilities for its military and commercial fleets.

2. Mahan's ideas influenced a generation of American policy makers led by Theodore Roosevelt and Henry Cabot Lodge. As a result, his views on the importance of sea power became the cornerstone of American strategic thinking.

D. THE IDEOLOGY OF EXPANSION: SOCIAL DARWINISM AND THE WHITE MAN'S BURDEN

1. Social Darwinists believed that Darwin's theory of the survival of the fittest could be applied to the rise and fall of nations. During the late nineteenth century, strong European powers led by England, France, and Germany began to dominate weak nations in Africa and Asia. Proponents of expansion warned that the United States had to play a more aggressive role in world affairs. If the U.S. failed to accept this challenge, it risked falling behind its rivals in the global race for markets and natural resources.
2. Americans believed in the inherent superiority of their political and economic systems. During most of the nineteenth century, America fulfilled its Manifest Destiny by spreading its civilization from the Atlantic to the Pacific. Now America had a responsibility articulated by the British poet Rudyard Kipling to "take up the White Man's Burden" and embark on a mission to "civilize non-Europeans."

II. MAKING COMPARISONS: MANIFEST DESTINY AND IMPERIALISM

A. CONTINUITIES

1. Manifest Destiny and American imperialism both led to territorial expansion and the acquisition of natural resources and new markets.
2. Both Manifest Destiny and imperialism led to military conflicts. The war with Mexico resulted in the acquisition of California and the New Mexico Territory. The war with Spain resulted in the acquisition of Puerto Rico, Guam, and the Philippines.

B. CHANGES

1. The United States did not justify its expansion across the continent as a mission to civilize Native Americans. In contrast, American expansionists and missionaries embraced the notion of a white man's burden to justify imperialist actions.

2. During the 1840s and '50s, the United States spread into a sparsely populated territory that was being settled by waves of migrants from other states. In contrast, during the age of imperialism the United States took possession of densely populated lands inhabited by populations with different ethnic backgrounds and cultural traditions.

Be prepared for a short-answer question asking you to compare and contrast Manifest Destiny and Imperialism. It is important to remember that both attempted to justify American territorial expansion.

III. THE SPANISH-AMERICAN WAR

A. THE MARCH TO WAR

1. Cuban rebels waged a guerilla war against Spanish rule. The Spanish commander Valeriano Weyler herded Cubans into detention centers in a brutal attempt to suppress the rebellion.
2. Joseph Pulitzer's *New York World* and William Randolph Hearst's *New York Journal* were locked in a furious circulation war for readers. Both papers published daily stories about the atrocities committed by "Butcher" Weyler. Known as yellow journalism, these sensational stories sparked widespread public indignation against Spain.
3. The 7,000-ton *U.S.S. Maine*, the navy's newest battleship, arrived in Havana harbor on January 25, 1898, on what Washington called a visit of "friendly courtesy." Three weeks later a deafening explosion tore through the vessel, sinking the ship and killing over 260 sailors. Although the cause of the blast was never fully determined, the press and most Americans blamed the Spanish.

B. MAKING CONNECTIONS: WAR AND PEACE

1. In 1799 America and France approached the brink of war. As a wave of war hysteria swept across the nation, President Adams' popularity soared. Militant Federalists led by Alexander Hamilton urged Adams to ask Congress for a declaration of war. But Adams resisted pressure from his party and the public. Instead of asking for war, he ordered American envoys in Paris to make a final effort to reach an agreement with the French government. They did and America avoided war.

2. In 1898 America and Spain approached the brink of war. As a wave of war hysteria swept across the nation, President McKinley's popularity soared. Militant Republicans led by Theodore Roosevelt and Henry Cabot Lodge urged McKinley to ask Congress for a declaration of war. Even though Spain yielded to almost every American demand, McKinley decided that the political risk of ignoring an aroused public was too high. On April 11, 1898, he sent a war message to Congress urging armed intervention in Cuba.

C. "A SPLENDID LITTLE WAR"

1. Hostilities in what Secretary of State John Hay called "a splendid little war" lasted just 114 days. The United States suffered minimal casualties as it quickly defeated Spanish forces in the Philippines and Cuba.

2. In a famous battle, Lieutenant-Colonel Theodore Roosevelt led a volunteer regiment known as the "Rough Riders" in a dramatic charge up San Juan Hill. Now a war hero, TR was soon elected governor of New York.

D. UNDERSTANDING CAUSATION: CONSEQUENCES OF THE SPANISH-AMERICAN WAR

1. The war marked the end of Spain's once vast New World empire.

2. The war marked the emergence of the United States as a world power.

3. The Treaty of Paris ceded Puerto Rico and Guam to the United States. Spain agreed to cede the Philippine Islands to the United States for $20 million. This marked the first time that the United States acquired overseas territory. The war also gave McKinley a pretext to annex Hawaii.

4. The Teller Amendment guaranteed that the United States would respect Cuba's sovereignty as an independent nation. However, in 1901, Congress made the withdrawal of U.S. troops contingent upon Cuba's acceptance of the Platt Amendment. This amendment prohibited Cuba from making any foreign treaties that might "impair" its independence or involve it in a public debt it could not pay. The amendment also gave the United States the right to maintain a naval station at Guantanamo Bay on the southeast corner of Cuba. Incorporated into the Cuban constitution, the Platt Amendment provided legal grounds for repeated American interventions in the island.

IV. AMERICAN INVOLVEMENT IN THE PHILIPPINES

A. THE DEBATE OVER THE PHILIPPINES

1. The provision in the Treaty of Paris ceding the Philippines to the United States aroused a powerful anti-imperialist movement to block ratification of the treaty. The Anti-Imperialist League pointed out the inconsistency between liberating Cuba and annexing the Philippines. They stressed that annexation would violate America's longstanding commitment to human freedom and rule by the "consent of the governed." Critics also pointed out that while America's industrial economy did require markets, this could be accomplished without acquiring colonies.
2. Expansionists countered by arguing that the Philippines would provide a strategic base from which the United States could trade with China. President McKinley also stressed America's duty "to educate the Filipinos, and uplift and civilize and Christianize them." Although McKinley's argument ignored the fact that most Filipinos were already Christians, his views prevailed. After a heated debate, the Senate approved the Treaty of Paris with one vote to spare.

B. THE PHILIPPINE INSURRECTION

1. Despite strong evidence that the Filipinos wanted independence, the McKinley administration decided that they were not ready for self-government. Led by Emilio Aguinaldo, the Filipinos resisted American control of their country.
2. Called the War for Independence by Filipinos, the Philippine Insurrection foreshadowed the guerrilla wars fought in the twentieth century. After three years of fighting, America's overwhelming military power finally crushed the rebels.
3. In 1916, Congress passed the Jones Act formally committing the United States to eventually granting the Philippines independence. The island nation finally gained its full independence on July 4, 1946.

V. AMERICA'S EMERGING INFLUENCE AND POWER

A. THE OPEN DOOR IN CHINA

1. American business leaders looked to China's "illimitable markets" to spur American economic growth. Strategic coaling stations in

Guam and the Philippines enabled American commercial ships to reach the fabled Chinese market.

2. During the 1880s and '90s, Britain, Germany, France, Russia, and Japan all began to carve out spheres of influence in an ever-weakening China. Each power controlled trade, tariffs, harbor duties, and railroad rates within its sphere of influence.

3. Secretary of State John Hay became increasingly worried that the European powers and Japan would restrict American trading opportunities in China. On September 6, 1899, he dispatched a series of diplomatic notes asking the governments of these nations to respect the rights of other nations within their spheres of influence.

4. Hay's Open Door policy was designed to protect American commercial interests in China. The European powers and Japan neither accepted nor rejected Hay's Open Door Notes. Although America's Open Door policy had no legal standing, Hay boldly announced that all of the powers had agreed and that their consent was therefore "final and definitive."

B. THE PANAMA CANAL

1. Led by Theodore Roosevelt, expansionists placed a high priority on the need to construct a canal through Central America. They pointed out that a canal would reduce the 12,000-mile voyage from San Francisco to the East Coast to just 4,000 miles.

2. After much debate Congress approved a canal through the Isthmus of Panama. At that time Panama was a province of Colombia. The Colombian Senate appeared to thwart TR's plan when it rejected America's offer to pay $10 million for the right to dig a canal across the isthmus.

3. The Colombian refusal did not deter Roosevelt. Rather than continue frustrating negotiations with Colombia, TR implemented his policy that in foreign affairs the President should "speak softly and carry a big stick."

4. Encouraged and supported by Roosevelt, Panama revolted against Colombia and declared itself an independent nation. Roosevelt promptly recognized Panama. He then signed a treaty with the new nation guaranteeing its independence and granting the United States a lease on a ten-mile wide canal zone.

5. Construction of the Panama Canal began in 1904. A work force of about 30,000 laborers completed the 51-mile "Big Ditch" in just

ten years. When it opened in 1914, the Panama Canal gave the United States a commanding position in the Western Hemisphere.

C. THE ROOSEVELT COROLLARY

1. The construction of the Panama Canal made the security of the Caribbean a vital American interest.
2. The Dominican Republic confronted TR with a difficult problem. In 1903 the Dominican government stopped payments on its debts of more than $32 million to France and other European powers. Roosevelt feared that the European powers would intervene in the Dominican Republic and other Caribbean nations to collect their debts. Although the nations would come as creditors, Roosevelt worried that they might remain as occupying powers, thus violating the Monroe Doctrine.
3. In his annual message to Congress in December 1904, Roosevelt urged Latin American nations to stabilize their finances. He warned that failure to repay their debts would force the United States to intervene by taking over a nation's customs house and then paying off its debts. Known as the Roosevelt Corollary, this policy extended the Monroe Doctrine by stating that the United States claimed the right to act as an international police power that could unilaterally intervene in Central America and the Caribbean to remedy what TR called "chronic wrongdoing."

D. MAKING CONNECTIONS: RELATIONS WITH LATIN AMERICA

1. The Roosevelt Corollary changed the Monroe Doctrine from a statement against the intervention of European powers in the affairs of the Western Hemisphere to a justification for the unrestricted American right to regulate Caribbean affairs. Between 1904 and 1917, Presidents Roosevelt, Taft, and Wilson ordered American troops into the Dominican Republic, Cuba, Panama, Nicaragua, and Haiti. These repeated interventions protected American interests but antagonized the local populations.
2. In his inaugural address on March 4, 1933, Franklin Roosevelt repudiated the Roosevelt Corollary declaring, "In the field of World policy, I would dedicate this nation to the policy of the good neighbor." The Good Neighbor Policy led to the withdrawal of U.S. troops from Nicaragua and Haiti and the annulment of the Platt Amendment with Cuba. The era of the Good Neighbor Policy ended with the onset of the Cold War and America's need to protect the Western Hemisphere from Soviet influence.

VI. THE ROAD TO WORLD WAR I

A. "NEUTRAL IN FACT AS WELL AS NAME"

1. The nations of Europe enjoyed an extended period of prosperity and progress in the century following the defeat of Napoleon in 1815. But an arms race between Germany and Great Britain, competition for colonies in Africa, and the formation of rival alliances created an atmosphere of tension and suspicion. The assassination of Archduke Francis Ferdinand on June 28, 1914, set in motion an inexorable chain of events leading to the outbreak of World War I less than six weeks later.

2. The explosive events in Europe stunned President Wilson. He was now forced to shift his focus from his domestic Progressive agenda to how the United States would respond to the war in Europe. On August 19, 1917, Wilson announced, "The United States must be neutral in fact as well as name."

B. FREEDOM OF THE SEAS

1. As a neutral nation, the United States could legally trade with all nations involved in World War I. Enforcing America's neutral rights proved to be difficult. On May 7, 1915, a German submarine sank the *Lusitania*, a British passenger liner. Almost 1,200 people died, including 128 Americans. The sinking of the *Lusitania* forcibly raised the issue of freedom of the seas while also raising the issue of American military preparedness.

2. Following the sinking of the *Lusitania*, the Germans pledged not to launch further attacks on merchant vessels without warning. Wilson sternly warned Germany that a violation of this pledge would risk war with the United States.

3. On January 31, 1917, Germany announced that it would resume unrestricted submarine warfare. The Germans understood that this action would bring the United States into the war. However, they gambled they could defeat France and Great Britain before America could mobilize, train, and transport an army large enough to thwart their offensive along the Western Front.

C. "THE WORLD MUST BE MADE SAFE FOR DEMOCRACY"

1. Events now pushed the United States to the brink of war. In early February 1917, Wilson broke diplomatic relations with Germany. Less than a month later, the British intercepted a telegram from the German Foreign Secretary Arthur Zimmermann to the German

minister in Mexico. The note tried to rekindle Mexican resentment over the loss of its territory to the United States in the Mexican-American War by offering to help Mexico regain its "lost territories in New Mexico, Texas, and Arizona."

2. The Zimmermann telegram and the sinking of several unarmed American ships compelled Wilson to ask a special session of Congress for a declaration of war against Germany. Wilson told Congress that the United States "had no selfish ends to serve" by entering the war. "The world," Wilson proclaimed, "must be made safe for democracy."

VII. THE HOMEFRONT

A. THE COMMITTEE ON PUBLIC INFORMATION

1. President Wilson recognized that the American public had to be mobilized to support a war against an enemy that did not represent a direct threat to the nation's homeland.
2. Wilson issued an executive order creating a Committee on Public Information. Led by George Creel, the committee used films, posters, and an army of speakers to convince the public that America was fighting a righteous war for freedom and democracy.

B. CIVIL LIBERTIES

1. The Committee on Public Information's propaganda campaign promoted a national mood of suspicion and distrust. Wilson promised that any disloyalty would be corrected with "a firm hand of stern repression." Upon the president's request, Congress passed the Espionage and Sedition Acts outlawing criticism of government leaders and war policies.
2. Designed to curtail constitutionally guaranteed freedoms of speech and press, the Espionage and Sedition Acts constituted the greatest attack on civil liberties since the Federalist-inspired Sedition Act of 1798. Ironically, while the United States embarked on a crusade to "make the world safe for democracy," these two acts stifled dissent and encouraged intolerance.

C. *SCHENCK v. UNITED STATES*

1. During the war, Charles T. Schenck, a member of the Executive Committee of the Socialist Party in Philadelphia, oversaw the printing and distribution of 15,000 leaflets urging young men to resist the draft. The government promptly charged Schenck with

violating the Espionage Act by obstructing military recruiting. Schenck argued that his actions were protected by the First Amendment guarantee of free speech.

2. The Supreme Court upheld Schenck's conviction in *Schenck v. United States*. Speaking for a unanimous court, Justice Holmes declared that government could limit speech if it provokes a "clear and present danger" of substantive evils.

D. THE GREAT MIGRATION

1. World War I created a labor shortage by moving about 4 million men from the nation's farms and factories to the armed services.
2. The wartime demand for industrial workers encouraged over 400,000 southern blacks to migrate to Northern cities. Known as the Great Migration, this mass movement opened new opportunities for African Americans while also exacerbating racial tensions in many cities. (For additional information on the causes and consequences of the Great Migration, see the annotated DBQ essay in Chapter 35.)

APUSH test writers typically devote much more attention to home developments than to battles and generals. World War I is no exception to this pattern. Be sure you are familiar with both the background and legal principles of the **Schenck** ***case and the causes and consequences of the Great Migration.***

VIII. TRIUMPH AND DISILLUSIONMENT

A. TRIUMPH ON THE BATTLEFIELD

1. The United States successfully raised and trained an army of 4 million men. By the spring of 1918 troopships carried 100,000 American soldiers a month across the Atlantic Ocean. In addition, American food and munitions poured into Europe.
2. The American Expeditionary Forces (AEF) arrived in time to help block the last great German offensive. Faced with the Allies overwhelming strength, the exhausted Germans accepted the Allied peace offer. All fighting ended at 11:00 am on November 11, 1918.

B. DISILLUSIONMENT AT VERSAILLES

1. The peace conference opened at Versailles, outside Paris, on January 18, 1919. Woodrow Wilson personally led the American delegation.
2. Wilson came prepared to implement his vision of a just and lasting peace based upon the principles in his Fourteen Points. His fourteenth and most famous point called for a League of Nations that would mediate disputes, supervise arms reduction, and curb aggressor nations through collective military action.
3. The Fourteen Points articulated the hopes of people for a just settlement that would ensure a lasting peace. But Wilson soon faced the grim realities of European power politics. Both Great Britain and France wanted to make Germany pay for the terrible suffering their people endured during the war. The Treaty of Versailles contained the Covenant of the League of Nations, but it also forced Germany to accept full blame for starting the war and pay reparations later set at $33 billion.

C. DEFEAT IN THE SENATE

1. Wilson faced a difficult fight to win Senate approval for the Treaty of Versailles. Opponents led by Senate Majority Leader Henry Cabot Lodge objected to the League's collective security provision arguing that it would limit American sovereignty and undermine the power of Congress in foreign affairs.
2. Wilson denounced his critics predicting that, "Unless America takes part in this treaty, the World is going to lose heart." Frustrated by his Senate opponents, Wilson left Washington to take his case to the American people. He traveled 8,000 miles and made 37 speeches in 29 cities, pleading that America is "the Nation upon which the whole world depends to hold the scales of justice even."
3. Three weeks into the grueling trip Wilson collapsed from exhaustion. A few days later he suffered a severe stroke that partly paralyzed his left side. For weeks he could not sit up or even sign his name.
4. The Senate never approved the Treaty of Versailles and the United States never joined the League of Nations. Wilson left office a beaten and embittered man.

THE NEW ERA 1919–1929

I. THE RED SCARE

A. CONTEXT

1. In November 1917, Bolsheviks led by Vladimir Lenin seized power in Russia and promptly created a communist dictatorship. The revolutionary upheaval in Russia alarmed many Americans who believed that communist sympathizers and other radicals were secretly planning to undermine the U.S. government.
2. A sudden postwar recession unsettled Americans as prices rose more than 15 percent, 100,000 businesses declared bankruptcy, and 5 million workers lost their jobs.

B. STRIKES AND BOMBS

1. The recession triggered an unprecedented wave of 3,600 strikes as over 4 million workers walked off their jobs.
2. Public apprehension increased after unions in Seattle co-operated in a general strike, a phenomenon new to America. The public became further unnerved when Boston police staged a walkout leaving the city temporarily unprotected.
3. The press demonized the strikes as "crimes against society," "conspiracies against the government," and most ominously "plots to establish communism." Alarmed citizens cheered when Massachusetts Governor Calvin Coolidge called the National Guard into Boston to restore order. Coolidge won national acclaim by declaring, "There is no right to strike against the public safety by anybody, anywhere, anytime."
4. The wave of strikes coincided with a sudden outbreak of anarchist violence. In April 1919, alert postal workers discovered and defused over thirty mail bombs addressed to leading businessmen and politicians. Just two months later, eight bombs exploded in eight cities, suggesting a nationwide conspiracy. One of the bombs damaged the façade of Attorney General A. Mitchell Palmer's home in Washington.

C. THE PALMER RAIDS

1. The Red Scare, or nationwide fear of radicals, forced Palmer to act. Although no more than one-tenth of one percent of adult Americans belonged to the domestic communist movement, Palmer launched a massive roundup of aliens and alleged communists.

2. On January 2, 1920, agents of the Department of Justice arrested some 5,000 suspects in a dozen cities across America. The Palmer Raids violated civil liberties as government agents broke into private homes, clubs, coffee shops, and union offices without arrest warrants. Although the Department of Justice released most of those arrested, they nonetheless deported about 500 aliens without hearings or trials.

D. BACK TO "NORMALCY"

1. The Palmer Raids marked the end of the Red Scare. The excess of the raids aroused opposition from defenders of American civil liberties. For example, lawyers from the newly formed American Civil Liberties Union (ACLU) and prominent members of the Supreme Court voiced strong support for upholding the American tradition of tolerance and freedom of expression.

2. The 1920 presidential campaign offered very different views of America's future direction. The Democratic candidates, Ohio Governor James M. Cox and Assistant Secretary of the Navy Franklin D. Roosevelt, promised to promote Progressive ideals. In contrast, the Republican candidates, Ohio Senator Warren Harding and Massachusetts Governor Calvin Coolidge, promised a return to what Harding called "normalcy."

3. The Republican ticket won a landslide victory winning every state outside of the South. Americans now eagerly began a New Era that promised peace and prosperity.

The Red Scare has generated a significant number of APUSH exam questions. Be prepared for short-answer questions asking you to interpret political cartoons and contrasting primary source passages on the Palmer Raids. Test writers also expect you to compare and contrast the Red Scare in 1919–1920 with the Second Red Scare from 1947 to 1954. ***See Chapter 26 for a detailed discussion of the Second Red Scare and McCarthyism.***

II. THE IMPORTANCE OF THE AUTOMOBILE

A. IMPACT ON MASS PRODUCTION

1. When automobiles first appeared in the late 1890s, they seemed to be a luxury toy for the rich. However, a gifted self-taught engineer named Henry Ford audaciously vowed, "to democratize the automobile. When I'm through," Ford predicted, "everybody will be able to afford one."
2. Ford fulfilled his prediction by applying the principles of assembly line production to the manufacture of automobiles. In the first automobile factories, cars remained in one place while a team of skilled mechanics built the vehicle from the ground up. In contrast, on Ford's new assembly line, overhead conveyer belts and huge turning tables carried moving parts past stationary workers.
3. The moving assembly line enabled Ford to reduce the time it took to build a car from 12.5 hours to just 1.5 hours. As mass production techniques improved, the price of a Model T Ford fell from $850 in 1908 to $290 in 1924.
4. The moving assembly line's precision and efficiency created a new economy based upon mass production. Affordable refrigerators, washing machines, and electric irons rolled off assembly lines across America. The new method of production was not without disadvantages for American workers. Assembly lines created monotonous jobs that eliminated craftsmanship and turned workers into human robots.

B. IMPACT ON DAILY LIFE

1. In the late 1920s, a team of sociologists asked a lifelong resident of Muncie, Indiana, to describe the changes taking place around him. The perceptive but slightly incredulous resident replied, "Why on earth do you need to study what's changing this country? I can tell you what's happening in just four letters: A-U-T-O!"
2. The small-town resident was right. The automobile was indeed a symbol of a new industry transforming American life. Surging car sales stimulated the growth of companies that produced steel, rubber tires, glass, and gasoline. Spurred by the Federal Highway Act of 1916, a growing network of paved roads crisscrossed the country.
3. Automobiles did more than just stimulate the economy; they also changed countless aspects of daily life. During the 1920s the automobile transformed America from a land of isolated small

towns into a nation of interconnected cities and suburbs. Gas stations, road signs, automatic three-color traffic lights, roadside diners, and traffic jams all became ubiquitous parts of the fabric of American life.

C. MAKING CONNECTIONS: TECHNOLOGY AND WORKERS

1. During the 1920s humans interacted with machines on assembly lines based on the principles of "scientific management" developed by Frederick W. Taylor. Taylorism used time-and-motion studies to reduce wasted motion and eliminate unnecessary workers.
2. During the 1980s, automobile companies began to use robots to automate their assembly lines. Manufacturers found that the robots were efficient, cost-effective, and safe. However, worried skeptics argue that an accelerating "automation bomb" has the potential to eliminate millions of jobs. Sophisticated robots programmed by highly trained technicians are rapidly becoming the norm in factories across America.

III. THE ROARING TWENTIES

A. RADIO

1. On November 2, 1920, radio station KDKA in Pittsburgh announced the news that the Republican candidate Warren Harding had won a landslide victory over his Democratic rival James Cox. The broadcast signaled the birth of a new industry. By the end of the decade at least one-third of all American households owned a radio.
2. As the radio mania swept across the country, listeners could enjoy news bulletins, weather reports, sports games, and comedy shows. Families across America listened to the same programs, laughed at the same jokes, and of course heard the same advertisements. By 1929, a growing advertising industry paid radio stations $1 billion to air commercials urging consumers to "buy now and pay later" for an enticing array of products ranging from toothpaste to the latest electric vacuum cleaner.

B. MOVIE STARS

1. In late 1903 American audiences shrieked with shock and delight as the leader of an outlaw band of bandits appeared to point a gun directly at them in a film titled *The Great Train Robbery*. The

popularity of this twelve-minute movie helped launch a new American industry.

2. During the 1920s, moviegoers bought over 80 million tickets a week as Hollywood became the center of America's fifth-largest industry. Feature-length silent films turned Greta Garbo, Charlie Chaplin, and Rudolph Valentino into celebrities earning six-figure salaries.

3. In 1927, enthralled fans watched and listened to the first "talkie," *The Jazz Singer*. Silent films quickly vanished and a new galaxy of stars, including a cartoon mouse named Mickey, reigned over Hollywood.

C. FLAPPERS

1. During the 1920s a rebellious generation of young adults challenged traditional values. Their new independent spirit expressed itself in the changes postwar women were making in their lives. Although most women still followed traditional paths of marriage and family, a growing number of young, well-educated women began choosing a different lifestyle. Influenced by feminists, women wanted greater freedom in their lives. A vanguard of college-educated women sought new careers in medicine, law, and science.

2. Young women called flappers provided the most visible and shocking model of the new American woman. Flappers challenged conventional norms of feminine appearance by wearing short skirts, heavy makeup, and close-cut bobbed hair. They further jolted the traditional guardians of morality by smoking cigarettes, sipping bootleg liquor, and dancing the Charleston.

D. LOST GENERATION WRITERS

1. A group of novelists found much to criticize in America's new mass culture. Known as the Lost Generation, these writers expressed disillusionment with American culture and often moved to Paris.

2. F. Scott Fitzgerald and Sinclair Lewis were the best-known Lost Generation novelists. Fitzgerald captured the unfulfilled promise of the Roaring Twenties in *This Side of Paradise* and in his masterpiece *The Great Gatsby*. Lewis took satiric aim at middle class conformity and materialism in *Main Street* and *Babbitt*.

IV. THE HARLEM RENAISSANCE

A. THE NEW NEGRO

1. During the 1920s, Harlem emerged as a vibrant center of African American culture. A new generation of black writers and artists created an outpouring of literary and artistic works known as the Harlem Renaissance.

2. Langston Hughes, Claude McKay, Jean Toomer, James Weldon Johnson, and Zora Neale Hurston formed a core group of Harlem Renaissance writers. Taken together their works expressed a new spirit of black hope and pride. In an influential anthology of Harlem Renaissance writings, Alain LeRoy Locke argued that Harlem functioned as a creative incubator for a "New Negro" who was seizing the opportunity for an assertion of both individual and collective identity.

B. MARCUS GARVEY

1. In May 1917, a 30-year-old black Jamaican named Marcus Garvey arrived in Harlem. He soon discovered that African Americans could not escape racism simply by moving to northern cities. Garvey promptly organized a chapter of an organization he called the United Negro Improvement Association (UNIA). Though hardly noticed at the time, Garvey's new organization marked a milestone in the growth of black nationalism.

2. Influenced by Woodrow Wilson's concept of self-determination, Garvey preached a message of racial pride and self-help. He exhorted his followers to glorify their African heritage and rejoice in the beauty of their black skin. "We have a beautiful history," Garvey told his listeners, "and we shall create another one in the future."

3. Garvey's vision captured the imagination of black people in America, the Caribbean, and Africa. By the mid-1920s, the UNIA had 700 branches in 38 states and the West Indies. Garvey had become one of the most famous black spokespersons in the world.

4. Garvey's fame proved to be short-lived. In the mid-1920s he was charged with mail fraud, sentenced to jail, and ultimately deported to his native Jamaica. Garvey nonetheless left behind an important legacy. His emphasis upon racial pride and economic self-sufficiency influenced Malcolm X's concept of black nationalism. Dr. King praised Garvey as "the first man on a mass scale and level to give millions of Negroes a sense of dignity and destiny."

V. INTOLERANCE AND NATIVISM

A. UNDERSTANDING CAUSATION: WHAT CAUSED INTOLERANCE AND NATIVISM IN THE 1920s?

1. Flappers, satiric writers, immigrants, and radicals were all aspects of the new urban culture taking root during the 1920s. Historian Robert Divine argues that rural Americans resented these assaults on their traditional values. According to Divine, "Rural Americans saw in the city all that was evil in contemporary life . . . Accordingly, the countryside struck back at the new dominant urban areas, aiming to restore the primacy of the Anglo-Saxon and predominantly Protestant culture they revered."

2. A second group of historians led by Burl L. Noggle do not view the intolerance and nativism during the 1920s as a strictly rural counterattack. Noggle argues that the twin forces of industrialization and urbanization "left many Americans in such a state of disequilibrium that they could not relieve their anxieties and regain their sense of security without taking some sort of action." The Red Scare represented the first postwar manifestation of this national insecurity. Seen from this perspective, Noggle believes that the Red Scare "never really ended." Intolerance and nativism were both deeply rooted and thus enduring characteristics of American society during the 1920s.

B. THE SACCO AND VANZETTI CASE

1. The most celebrated criminal trial of the 1920s involved two Italian-born anarchists, Nicola Sacco and Bartolomeo Vanzetti. The two men were arrested for a payroll robbery and murder.

2. A lack of conclusive evidence convinced many that Sacco and Vanzetti were victims of prejudice against radicals and recent immigrants. Nonetheless, following seven years of litigation both men were executed in the electric chair.

C. THE SCOPES TRIAL

1. In January 1925, the state of Tennessee passed the Butler Act forbidding the teaching of evolution in the public schools. The act expressed the alarm felt by many fundamentalist Christians who opposed Darwin's theory of evolution because it challenged their literal interpretation of the Bible.

2. John T. Scopes, a Tennessee high school science teacher, accepted the American Civil Liberties Union offer to test the constitutionality

of the Butler Act. Clarence Darrow, a well-known champion of civil liberties, agreed to defend Scopes. William Jennings Bryan, a three-time Democratic presidential candidate and well-known religious fundamentalist, represented the state. For a national and international audience the case provided a dramatic illustration of the cultural conflict between fundamentalism represented by Bryan and modernism represented by Darrow.

3. In the end, the court found Scopes guilty and fined him $100.00. The Tennessee Supreme Court overruled the fine on a technicality while upholding the Butler Act.

D. IMMIGRATION RESTRICTION

1. The Sacco and Vanzetti case highlighted the public's fear of recent immigrants. A new postwar wave of arrivals from Southern and Eastern Europe sparked a nationwide movement to limit immigrants from these regions.
2. Congress responded to the nativist push for restrictive measures by passing the National Origins Act of 1924. The law limited annual immigration to 2 percent of a country's population in the United States as of the 1890 census, sharply cutting the flow of immigrants from Southern and Eastern Europe.

E. THE RISE AND FALL OF THE KU KLUX KLAN

1. The original Ku Klux Klan terrorized newly freed blacks in the post–Civil War South before dying out in the 1870s. The post–World War I mood of distrust and intolerance fueled a revival of the KKK. The new Klan directed its hostility toward immigrants, Catholics, Jews, and African Americans. It favored immigration restriction and white supremacy.
2. By the mid-1920s, membership in the Klan swelled to as many as 4 million people. However, passage of the National Origins Act removed the Klan's most popular issue. Divided by recurring leadership quarrels, the Klan once again became a marginal group on the periphery of American society.

VI. THE REPUBLICAN ASCENDANCY

A. HARDING AND THE "RETURN TO NORMALCY"

1. The American public welcomed the end of Wilson's idealistic crusades and enthusiastically endorsed Harding's promise of a "return to normalcy." Harding's economic policies reconfirmed

the traditional partnership between business and government. His Secretary of Treasury Andrew Mellon reduced tax rates for the wealthy, raised tariffs, and ignored antitrust regulations.

2. Although Harding was personally honest, his relaxed leadership enabled venal appointees to profit from their corrupt activities. Visibly troubled by the scandals rocking his administration, Harding suffered a sudden heart attack and died on August 2, 1923.

B. "SILENT CAL"

1. The Harding administration scandals left Vice President Coolidge untouched. A man of few words, Coolidge deserved his popular nickname "Silent Cal."
2. America enjoyed a period of unprecedented prosperity as Coolidge won election to a full term in 1924. The popular president could have easily won reelection in 1928. However, the taciturn Coolidge unexpectedly announced, "I do not choose to run."

C. HERBERT HOOVER

1. The Republicans turned to Secretary of Commerce Herbert Hoover to be their party's standard bearer in the 1928 presidential election. The public respected Hoover as a generous humanitarian and a skilled administrator.
2. Hoover's landslide victory over Al Smith of New York seemed to confirm the public's support for Republican policies. Buoyed by good times, Hoover confidently predicted, "We in America are nearer to the final triumph over poverty than ever before in the history of any land."

APUSH test writers often ask students to compare and contrast economic, cultural, and social conditions in the 1920s with those in the 1950s. See the end of Chapter 27 for a detailed comparison of life in these two key decades.

THE GREAT DEPRESSION AND THE NEW DEAL 1929–1939

Chapter 24

I. UNDERSTANDING CAUSATION: CAUSES OF THE GREAT DEPRESSION

A. THE STOCK MARKET

1. The big bull market reached its peak on September 3, 1929. On that date, the New York Times average price of industrial stocks reached 452. That figure represented a gain of 342 points from January 1921 and 114 points from January 1929.
2. Wall Street's speculative bubble burst on Thursday, October 24, 1929 (which came to be known as "Black Thursday"), as waves of panic selling overwhelmed the New York Stock Exchange. The selling reached a crescendo on Tuesday, October 29. Within less than a week, stocks lost 37 percent of their value.
3. At first the Wall Street crash appeared to have only hurt the roughly 3 million investors who owned stock. The United States' vast industrial and agricultural resources were physically undamaged. But the stock market crash had dealt a severe blow to investors and to banks. It also revealed serious underlying economic weaknesses.

B. OVERPRODUCTION AND UNDERCONSUMPTION

1. In 1929, American factories produced nearly half of the world's industrial goods. Rising productivity generated enormous profits. However, this wealth was unevenly distributed. At the time of the crash, the richest 5 percent of the population earned nearly one-third of all personal income. Meanwhile, fully 60 percent of all American families earned less than the $2,000 a year needed to buy basic necessities. Eighty percent of the nation's families had no savings whatsoever.
2. The U.S. economy was simultaneously experiencing overproduction by business and underconsumption by consumers. As inventories of unsold goods piled up, stores reduced their orders and factories began to cut back production and layoff workers. These actions triggered a downward economic spiral.

C. THE PLIGHT OF THE FARMER

1. Many farmers never shared in the prosperity of the 1920s. Scientific farming methods combined with new trucks and tractors enabled farmers to dramatically increase the yield of crops per acre. At the same time, American farmers faced new competition from grain growers in Australia and Argentina.

2. The global surpluses of agricultural products drove prices and farm incomes down. Between 1929 and 1933 agricultural income plunged by 60 percent. Unable to sell their crops for a profit, many farmers could not pay their mortgages. By early 1933, embittered farm families watched helplessly as banks foreclosed on about 20,000 farms a month.

II. HARD TIMES

A. DOWN! DOWN! DOWN!

1. Between 1929 and 1932, all the major indicators documented the same story of economic collapse. By July 1932 the Dow Jones Industrial Average plummeted to an all-time low of 58 as investors lost $74 billion. During these three years, 86,000 businesses closed their doors and 9,000 banks declared bankruptcy wiping out 9 million savings accounts.

2. The burden of hard times fell most heavily on those least able to afford it. Unemployment rose from just 3.2 percent in 1929 to a staggering 24.9 percent in 1932. Poverty soon became a way of life for one-fourth of the population.

B. THE DUST BOWL

1. Beginning in 1930, a severe drought hit the Great Plains. The lack of rain combined with unusually hot summers created great clouds of dust from what had once been fertile soil. Large areas of Kansas, the Texas panhandle, Oklahoma, and eastern Colorado became known as the Dust Bowl.

2. Agriculture virtually ceased in the hardest hit parts of the Dust Bowl. Over 350,000 desperate people fled the Great Plains. Called "Oakies" because many came from Oklahoma, they loaded their meager belongings into battered cars and headed west along Route 66 to California. John Steinbeck captured the ordeal faced by these proud but impoverished migrants in his powerful novel *The Grapes of Wrath*. Dorothea Lange's poignant photographs portrayed their struggle in California.

III. HERBERT HOOVER AND THE GREAT DEPRESSION

A. HOOVER'S PHILOSOPHY OF GOVERNMENT

1. Hoover believed that America's economy was fundamentally sound. In March 1930 he confidently predicted, "The crisis will be over in 60 days."

2. Despite rising unemployment and falling industrial production, Hoover rejected calls for federal action. He argued that a program of federal relief would violate the Constitution and undermine his cherished values of rugged individualism and local voluntarism.

B. THE RECONSTRUCTION FINANCE CORPORATION

1. While Hoover rejected federal programs to help the poor, he did listen to bank executives who pleaded for federal aid. In early 1932, Congress created the Reconstruction Finance Corporation (RFC) to make emergency loans to distressed banks and businesses. The RFC loaned $1.75 billion to 7,400 banks, insurance companies, and railroads.

2. The RFC went beyond anything the federal government had ever done before. Its emergency loans helped limit the number of bankruptcies. However, indignant critics accused Hoover of insisting on rugged individualism for ordinary people standing in breadlines while supporting a "billion-dollar soup kitchen" for distressed bankers.

C. THE BONUS ARMY

1. In the spring of 1932, about 20,000 World War I veterans converged on Washington, D.C., to lobby Congress to pass a bill providing the immediate payment of their promised bonuses from the First World War.

2. Supported by Hoover, the Senate rejected the bill. Despite this defeat, many veterans and their families encamped in Washington. Embarrassed by the presence of so many unemployed men in the nation's capital, Hoover ordered the army to forcibly remove the Bonus Marchers. His callous treatment of the veterans accelerated Hoover's already sinking popularity.

D. THE ELECTION OF 1932

1. The deepening depression crippled any chance Hoover had of being reelected. Sensing victory, the Democrats nominated

Franklin D. Roosevelt, the popular reform-minded governor of New York. FDR won an overwhelming victory, ushering in a period of Democratic political dominance that lasted 20 years.

2. During the presidential campaign, FDR inspired the Democratic convention by promising cheering delegates, "I pledge you, I pledge myself, to a new deal for the American people."

IV. THE HUNDRED DAYS

A. THE BANKING CRISIS

1. When FDR took the oath of office on March 4, 1933, he boldly declared, "First of all, let me assert my firm belief that the only thing we have to fear is fear itself–nameless, unreasoning, unjustified terror." Despite Roosevelt's calming reassurance, thirty-eight states closed their banks, as America's economy tottered on the brink of collapse.

2. FDR knew he had to restore public confidence in the nation's banking system. While his economic advisors prepared emergency legislation for Congress, Roosevelt proclaimed a four-day bank holiday. On March 9, both houses of Congress passed the Emergency Banking Relief Act. The act provided for reopening the nation's largest and strongest banks while weaker banks first received loans and then later opened under strict Treasury Department supervision.

3. On March 12, FDR addressed the nation by radio in his first fireside chat. The president explained the steps Congress had taken and reassured the public that "it is safer to keep your money in a reopened bank than under the mattress." FDR's strategy restored public confidence as deposits far exceeded withdrawals. A few months later Congress created the Federal Deposit Insurance Corporation (FDIC), insuring bank deposits up to $2,500. The FDIC underscored the government's commitment to protecting deposits and preventing another panic. (Today each depositor is insured to $250,000 per insured bank.)

4. The banking crisis set the tone for the New Deal. FDR opposed making drastic changes. Instead of nationalizing the banks, he strove to reform and revive America's economic institutions.

B. RELIEF MEASURES

1. The banking crisis marked the beginning of a history-making period known as the Hundred Days. From March 9 to June 16,

1933, Congress approved fifteen major pieces of social and economic legislation formulated by a group of presidential advisors known as the "brain trust."

2. Unlike Hoover, Roosevelt recognized that America's millions of unemployed workers needed direct federal relief. The Civilian Conservation Corps (CCC) created a jobs program for unemployed young men aged 18 to 25. The men lived in camps and worked on a variety of conservation projects in the nation's parks and recreation areas. During the nine years of its existence, over 2.5 million workers earned $30 a month cutting trails, building reservoirs, and planting a shelter-belt of 200 million trees stretching from Texas to Canada.
3. The Public Works Administration (PWA) contributed to the New Deal's relief program by financing more than 34,000 construction projects at a cost of more than $6 billion. Between 1933 and 1939, armies of PWA workers constructed about 35 percent of the new hospitals and health facilities in the U.S. and 70 percent of all educational buildings.
4. The New Deal relief programs did not end unemployment. But they did restore a sense of national purpose and energy missing since the depths of the depression.

C. RECOVERY MEASURES

1. FDR asked Congress to take unprecedented action to meet the farm crisis. The Agricultural Adjustment Act (AAA) proposed to increase farm income by paying farmers to leave acres unplanted. For example, the nation's wheat growers removed some 8 million acres of wheat from production. As a result, the average price of wheat rose from 38 cents a bushel in 1932-1933 to 74 cents a bushel in 1933-1934. Despite the initial outcry over reducing crops at a time when people were hungry, the prices of wheat, corn, cotton, and other basic agricultural products began to rise.
2. The brain trust created a bold program to stimulate industrial recovery. The National Recovery Act (NRA)—which was part of the broader National Industrial Recovery Act (NIRA)—encouraged the nation's businesses to draw up codes defining minimum prices, wages, and workers' hours. The NRA codes were supposed to end excess competition and restore profits. Launched with great fanfare, the NRA soon aroused a barrage of criticism from opponents who denounced it as a formula for "creeping socialism."
3. The Tennessee Valley Authority (TVA) contributed to the New Deal's recovery program by authorizing the construction of a

system of dams and hydroelectric plants to provide inexpensive electricity and flood control for residents of the impoverished Tennessee Valley. This ambitious program of regional planning helped to stimulate growth in an area that had been amongst America's most underdeveloped regions.

D. MAKING COMPARISONS: PROGRESSIVE REFORM AND THE NEW DEAL

1. Both the Progressive Era and New Deal reformers supported government action to remedy social and economic problems. However, neither the Progressives nor the New Dealers directly addressed the problems of racial discrimination and segregation faced by African Americans.
2. The Progressive Era reformers favored legislative actions by state and local governments. They did not endorse direct federal relief for the unemployed or the poor. In contrast, the New Dealers favored federal legislation to provide jobs and direct relief.

V. THE NEW DEAL UNDER ATTACK

A. CONTEXT

1. The New Deal helped pull America out of the depths of the Great Depression. Industrial production slowly rose and unemployment fell from about 13 million in 1933 to 9 million in 1936.
2. Despite these gains, full recovery still remained elusive. A contentious group of critics attacked the New Deal and offered radical plans to revive the economy.

B. THREE RADICAL CRITICS

1. Father Charles Coughlin was a Catholic priest from Detroit. Known as the "Radio Priest," Coughlin delivered weekly radio sermons to a nationwide audience estimated at over 30 million people. Like the late nineteenth century Populists, Coughlin supported nationalizing the banks and coining more silver dollars.
2. Francis E. Townsend was a retired physician who argued that the New Deal did not do enough for older Americans. Outraged by the sight of three elderly women looking for food in garbage cans, Townsend proposed giving everyone over the age of 60 a monthly government check for $200.00. The recipient had to promise to spend all the money each month. Townsend Clubs quickly spread across the country as more than 10 million people signed petitions endorsing the doctor's plan.

3. Huey Long was a colorful and controversial governor and U.S. Senator from Louisiana. Known as the "Kingfish," Long broke with the New Deal. He then developed his own "Share Our Wealth" program promising to tax the rich and guarantee each American a $5,000 home and an annual income of $2,500. When a national poll indicated that Long might win strong support on a third-party ticket, he announced his intention to run for President in 1936. Then in September 1935, an assassin shot and killed Long on the steps of the Louisiana capitol in Baton Rouge.

VI. THE SECOND NEW DEAL

A. CONTEXT

1. Father Coughlin, Dr. Townsend, and Senator Long drew support from desperate Americans demanding more dramatic changes. FDR recognized that he had to "steal the thunder" from these outspoken critics by embracing additional reforms.
2. The 1934 mid-term elections gave the Democrats commanding majorities in both the House and the Senate. "Boys, this is our hour," Roosevelt aide Harry Hopkins exalted. "We've got to get everything we want—a works program, social security, wages and hours, everything—now or never." Led by Roosevelt and Hopkins, the Democratic majorities did enact a series of far-reaching programs known as the Second New Deal.

B. THE WORKS PROJECTS ADMINISTRATION

1. Congress enacted the Works Projects Administration (WPA) in April 1935. Initially funded with $5 billion, the WPA launched an ambitious program that included constructing 600,000 miles of highways, repairing 100,000 bridges, and erecting thousands of public parks and recreational facilities.
2. The WPA did more than hire construction workers. It also funded innovative projects designed to utilize the skills of artists, actors, and writers. For example, the Federal Art Project employed artists to paint murals for post offices, libraries, and other public buildings across America.

C. THE SOCIAL SECURITY ACT

1. Signed by President Roosevelt on August 14, 1935, the Social Security Act answered the Townsend Plan by enacting the New Deal's most far-reaching legislative initiative. The act established a pension for retired people over the age of sixty-five. A small

payroll tax paid by both workers and employers financed the fund. In addition, the Social Security Act committed the national government to a broad range of social welfare activities including federal grants-in-aid for old age assistance and aid for dependent children.

2. The Social Security Act had important limitations. It initially excluded farm laborers, domestic servants, and the self-employed. It also took money out of workers' paychecks at a time when low consumer demand remained one of the main causes of the depression.

D. THE NATIONAL LABOR RELATIONS ACT

1. The Second New Deal gave the labor movement a significant victory with the passage of the National Labor Relations Act (NLRA). Often called the Wagner Act for its sponsor, New York Senator Robert Wagner, the NLRA protected the right of workers to join unions and bargain collectively with management.
2. The NLRA also created a National Labor Relations Board to supervise union elections and investigate unfair labor practices by employers.

E. MAKING CONNECTIONS: LABOR UNIONS

1. The NLRA revitalized the union movement in America. When the Great Depression began, trade unions represented only about 3 million workers. John L. Lewis, the head of the United Mine Workers, took the lead in forming the Congress of Industrial Organizations (CIO) to unionize automobile and steel workers. By the end of the 1930s, unions represented 9 million workers, or 28 percent of the nonfarm workforce.
2. Membership in labor unions peaked in 1954 when 35 percent of American workers belonged to a union. However, the twin forces of deindustrialization and automation began to substantially reduce the number of industrial jobs. By 2015, union membership stood at just 11.1 percent of all American workers. The largest and most prominent unions today are public sector employees such as government workers, teachers, and police.

APUSH test writers expect students to be able to compare Roosevelt's New Deal with Lyndon Johnson's Great Society. See Chapter 28 for a detailed comparison of these two programs.

VII. THE SUPREME COURT VERSUS THE NEW DEAL

A. THE SUPREME COURT STRIKES DOWN THE NIRA AND THE AAA

1. In the summer of 1935, the Supreme Court began to deliver a series of decisions overturning key New Deal programs. In *Schechter v. United States*, the Court unanimously struck down the National Industrial Recovery Act (NIRA) because it gave the federal government powers of economic regulation that could not be justified under the interstate commerce clause. A few months later the Court also invalidated the AAA.
2. These decisions alarmed President Roosevelt. New Dealers feared that the Supreme Court would soon strike down the Social Security Act and the Wagner Act.

B. THE COURT-PACKING SCHEME

1. Determined to prevent the Supreme Court from overturning the New Deal, FDR surprised Congress by asking for the authority to appoint a new Supreme Court justice for every member older than 70. This would allow Roosevelt to appoint six new justices more receptive to the New Deal.
2. Both the public and members of Congress opposed Roosevelt's "court-packing" bill as a violation of judicial independence and the separation of powers. Although the Democrats enjoyed large majorities in both houses of Congress, they refused to approve the Court Reform Bill. The rejection marked FDR's first major legislative defeat.
3. Although FDR lost the court-packing battle, he ultimately achieved his goal as the Supreme Court became more receptive to the New Deal. The Court upheld both the Wagner Act and the Social Security Act. In addition, several justices retired and Roosevelt appointed nine new members of the Court.

VIII. UNDERSTANDING CAUSATION: CONSEQUENCES OF THE NEW DEAL

A. THE NEW DEAL AND AFRICAN AMERICANS

1. The New Deal did not directly confront racial injustice. For example, the CCC camps often segregated white and black workers. In addition, FDR did not risk losing the support of

southern Democrats by endorsing legislation banning the poll tax and making lynching a crime.

2. Although the New Deal did not mark a turning point in American race relations, it did mark the beginning of important steps benefitting African Americans. For example, FDR appointed a number of black officials to his administration who became known as the "Black Cabinet."

B. THE NEW DEAL AND AMERICAN POLITICS

1. Herbert Hoover's election in 1928 continued the era of Republican dominance that began with the election of McKinley in 1896. However, just four years later a revitalized Democratic Party led by Franklin Roosevelt brought an abrupt end to the period of Republican dominance. The voting blocs and interest groups that supported FDR are known as the New Deal coalition.
2. The New Deal coalition included urban families, labor unions, Catholics, Jews, white Southerners, and African Americans. These voters formed an electoral majority that enabled the Democratic Party to win the White House in seven of the nine presidential elections between 1932 and 1968.

C. MAKING CONNECTIONS: AFRICAN AMERICANS AND THE DEMOCRATIC PARTY

1. Although the New Deal did not directly confront Jim Crow segregation, it did help African Americans survive the Great Depression. In the 1936 presidential election, over 90 percent of black voters switched their allegiance to FDR and the Democratic Party.
2. The New Deal coalition of black and white Southern voters proved to be fragile. As the Democratic Party began to endorse civil rights legislation in the 1960s, its support among white Southerners steadily eroded. Today, white Southerners are a key component in the Republican Party and African Americans are a key component in the Democratic Party.

D. THE NEW DEAL AND WOMEN

1. Many observers noted that women seemed invisible during the Great Depression. The PWA and other New Deal agencies almost exclusively hired men. The CCC excluded women entirely, prompting critics to ask, "Where is the she-she-she?"

2. Although the New Deal did not directly challenge gender inequality, First Lady Eleanor Roosevelt did play an important role in promoting equal treatment for women and African Americans. In one highly publicized incident, Eleanor Roosevelt resigned from the Daughters of the American Revolution to protest the organization's decision to ban Marian Anderson, a world-renowned African American singer, from performing at Constitution Hall in Washington, D.C. With Eleanor Roosevelt's support, Anderson gave an Easter Sunday concert on the steps of the Lincoln Memorial attended by an integrated audience of 75,000 people.

E. THE NEW DEAL AND THE NATIONAL ECONOMY

1. As 1937 opened, FDR optimistically pointed to several promising signs of economic recovery. Unemployment fell to 14 percent and industrial output returned to pre-crash levels. Confident that the economic crisis was receding, Roosevelt reduced funding for New Deal programs. These cuts triggered a sudden downturn known as the "Roosevelt Recession" of 1937–38.
2. Historian William Leuchtenburg described the New Deal as a "halfway revolution." He argued that conservative Democrats prevented FDR from fully implementing a program of deficit spending. Advocated by the British economist John Maynard Keynes, this strategy called for the government to stimulate the economy by spending more money than it received in taxes.
3. The New Deal did not bring about the full economic recovery Roosevelt promised. The United States finally emerged from the Great Depression when the federal government sharply increased military spending as the nation prepared for World War II.

F. THE NEW DEAL AND THE ROLE OF THE FEDERAL GOVERNMENT

1. The New Deal accelerated the process of expanding the role of the federal government begun during the Progressive Era. Under the New Deal, the federal government assumed the responsibility for ensuring the health of the nation's economy and the welfare of its citizens.
2. New Deal programs provided tangible examples of the importance of the federal government. For example, the New Deal provided legal protection for labor unions, price stability for farmers, electricity for rural Americans, and old age insurance for the elderly.

3. As the federal government's role expanded, so did the power of the presidency. Under FDR, the presidency became the center of power in the federal government.

APUSH test questions often ask students to evaluate the legacy of the New Deal. Be prepared for a long-essay or DBQ question asking you how the New Deal changed the role of the federal government.

THE UNITED STATES AND THE WORLD 1921–1945

Chapter 25

I. AMERICA'S ROLE IN THE WORLD, 1921–1933

A. CONTEXT

1. America fought World War I as an idealistic crusade to "make the world safe for democracy." However, the war left many Americans feeling bitterly disillusioned. Led by Henry Cabot Lodge, the Senate rejected the League of Nations and Wilson's vision of a new world order based upon the principle of collective security.
2. Although the United States rejected the League of Nations, it nonetheless emerged from the war as the world's richest and most powerful nation. As a result, the United States could not avoid playing an active role in international affairs.

B. THE WASHINGTON NAVAL CONFERENCE, 1921

1. The United States could not ignore Japan's growing threat to American interests in Asia. In 1921, the Harding administration invited Japan, Great Britain, and representatives from other European nations to Washington to discuss a range of Asian problems.
2. The expensive naval arms race among the United States, Great Britain, and Japan posed the most pressing problem. After intense negotiations, the powers agreed to limit battleship and aircraft carrier production. The Japanese also signed a treaty agreeing to respect China's independence and America's Open Door policy.

C. THE DAWES PLAN

1. Germany's new democratic government faced a catastrophic period of hyperinflation as the value of the mark fell with terrifying speed. By the summer of 1923, a glass of beer cost 2 million marks and a loaf of bread 4 million marks.
2. The United States alone had the economic resources to rescue Germany. An international committee of financial experts led by

Charles Dawes, an American banker and statesman, devised a plan to prevent the German economy from collapsing. The Dawes Plan provided an initial $200 million loan from American banks to stabilize Germany's currency. The plan also created a more realistic schedule for German reparation payments.

3. Implemented in 1924, the Dawes Plan appeared to work. As the German economy revived, it attracted additional American loans that totaled over $3 billion. By 1929, Germany industrial output matched its prewar production.

D. THE "SPIRIT OF LOCARNO"

1. In 1925, the French and German foreign ministers met in the Swiss town of Locarno where they signed a treaty promising that their two countries would never again resort to war against each other. World leaders praised the "spirit of Locarno" and admitted Germany into the League of Nations.
2. The "spirit of Locarno" soon led to the Kellogg-Briand Pact. In 1928, the American Secretary of State Frank Kellogg used a foot-long gold pen to join the French Foreign Minister Aristide Briand in signing a pledge "to renounce war as an instrument of national policy." Within a short time, almost every country in the world, including the Soviet Union, signed the Kellogg-Briand Pact.
3. The Kellogg-Briand Pact symbolized the world's hope for a period of peace and prosperity. But this hope rested upon a belief that the late 1920s economic boom would continue.

II. THE RETREAT FROM RESPONSIBILITY, 1933–1939

A. CONTEXT

1. The Wall Street crash and the ensuing Great Depression sent shock waves across the industrialized world. Between 1929 and 1932, global manufacturing fell by 38 percent while international trade dropped by 65 percent. Unemployment rates skyrocketed causing angry, jobless workers to demand sweeping economic and political changes.
2. Millions of frightened people lost faith in their democratic governments and turned to fascism, a new political movement that denied individual rights and glorified rule by a militaristic dictator. Fascist leaders in Italy, Germany, and Japan seized power promising

to revive economic growth, punish traitorous minorities, and restore national pride.

B. THE MARCH OF FASCIST AGGRESSION

1. The Italian dictator Benito Mussolini dreamed of resurrecting the glories of ancient Rome by building a colonial empire in Africa. In October 1935, Mussolini ordered a massive invasion of Ethiopia. His unprovoked attack represented a crucial test of the League of Nations' commitment to collective security. Although the League condemned the violation of its charter, its members did nothing to stop Mussolini.
2. The League's failure to deter Mussolini encouraged the German dictator Adolf Hitler to defy the Versailles Treaty. In March 1936, he boldly ordered 35,000 German troops into the Rhineland, a 30-mile-wide demilitarized zone on either side of the Rhine River that formed a strategic buffer between Germany and France. Hitler's unexpected action stunned the British and French. Despite having sufficient military resources to repel the Germans, the French failed to act, fearing the risk of beginning a new war.
3. The Japanese also took advantage of the League's failure to stop aggression. By 1936, Japan's new militaristic government renounced its Washington Conference agreements and withdrew from the League of Nations. In 1937, Japan invaded northern China touching off a full-scale war that marked the beginning of World War II in Asia.

C. AMERICAN NEUTRALITY

1. American isolationists argued that the United States should follow George Washington's advice to avoid becoming politically involved in European affairs.
2. In 1934, Senator Gerald P. Nye chaired a special committee investigating American munitions dealers. After two years, the Nye Committee concluded that avaricious "merchants of death" duped America into entering World War I in order to earn enormous profits.
3. The Nye Committee's accusations led isolationists to demand that Congress pass laws to prevent a repeat of the mistakes that pushed the United States into the First World War. Between 1935 and 1937, Congress passed a series of three Neutrality Acts banning both loans and the sale of weapons to nations at war. The acts also warned Americans to avoid sailing on the ships of countries at war.

D. ROOSEVELT'S QUARANTINE SPEECH

1. President Roosevelt recognized that the United States could not isolate itself from the spreading fascist aggression. In his 1937 Quarantine Speech, FDR warned "[t]he peace-loving nations must make a concerted effort in opposition to those violations of treaties . . . which today are creating a state of international anarchy and instability from which there is no escape through mere isolation or neutrality."
2. FDR's argument that the United States should expand its role in global affairs failed to persuade the isolationists. Their muted response to his plea to "quarantine" the disease of fascist aggression convinced Roosevelt that he could not successfully challenge the prevailing public support for neutrality.

Be prepared to discuss how the First World War affected American diplomacy during the 1920s and 1930s. Note how Washington's Farewell Address continued to influence American foreign policy.

III. THE ROAD TO PEARL HARBOR, 1939–1941

A. THE WAR IN EUROPE

1. While America tried to remain at peace, Hitler plunged Europe into war. On September 1, 1939, Germany launched a massive blitzkrieg or "lightning war" against Poland. France and Britain immediately declared war on Germany.
2. After a six-month lull in fighting, devastating German blitzkriegs led to the fall of Denmark, Norway, Belgium, and France. Only Great Britain, now led by Winston Churchill, held out against Hitler.
3. The alarming events in Europe persuaded Congress to increase the defense budget and approve a Selective Service Act providing for the country's first military draft during peacetime.

B. THE LEND-LEASE ACT

1. On December 8, 1940, President Roosevelt received an urgent message from Winston Churchill. The British Prime Minister bluntly warned that Great Britain was running out of supplies and money to continue its desperate fight against Nazi Germany.

2. FDR recognized that a Nazi-dominated Europe would be a moral abomination and a direct threat to America's national security. Aware of the public's continuing strong isolationist sentiment, FDR resolved that America had to adopt a policy of "all aid short of war."

3. In a fireside chat on December 29, 1940, the president explained that America must become an "arsenal of democracy" by providing war materials to Great Britain. He then asked Congress to approve a Lend-Lease Act allowing him to send war materials to any country whose defense he considered vital to the United States.

4. After months of acrimonious debates, Congress passed the Lend-Lease Act on March 11, 1941. America's depression-ridden industries now roared to life producing weapons to fight Hitler and Mussolini. Polls, however, still showed that 80 percent of the American people wanted to stay out of World War II.

C. PEARL HARBOR

1. The debate over the Lend-Lease Act overshadowed ominous events taking place in Asia. Japan's militaristic rulers became members of the Axis Powers along with Germany and Italy. Meanwhile, the long-standing rivalry between the United States and Japan for Pacific supremacy further escalated when Japanese forces overran French Indochina in July 1941. Recognizing Japan's reliance upon imported American oil and scrap iron, FDR ordered a total embargo on trade with Japan.

2. The embargo forced Japanese leaders to make a fateful decision. They could give in to the American demand that they withdraw from Indochina or they could attack the U.S. fleet at Pearl Harbor and then seize the rich oil fields in the Dutch East Indies. When negotiations with the Roosevelt administration reached an impasse, the Japanese decided to launch a surprise attack on Pearl Harbor.

3. In late November 1941, a Japanese fleet that included 6 aircraft carriers and over 400 warplanes secretly headed into the vast and empty waters of the North Pacific. At 7:55 AM on December 7, 1941, the first of three waves of planes attacked the U.S. Pacific Fleet. Within two hours, Japanese warplanes sank or damaged 18 ships and killed 2,403 men.

4. The next day President Roosevelt asked Congress for a declaration of war against Japan. Four days later, Germany and Italy declared war on the United States. The Axis leaders confidently predicted that the United States would lack the will to fight a prolonged war.

They were wrong. An angry and united America entered World War II determined to crush the Axis Powers.

IV. THE INTERNMENT OF JAPANESE AMERICANS

A. CONTEXT

1. Revenge and fear can fuel a very explosive combination of emotions. When the Japanese fleet struck Pearl Harbor, furious Americans demanded revenge. But revenge against Japan would have to wait for American factories to build a mighty armada of ships and planes.
2. As fear swept across America, it was easy to believe that the West Coast would be Japan's next target. It was all too easy to displace anger and fear against Japan to the approximately 110,000 people of Japanese birth and descent who lived on the West Coast.

B. EXECUTIVE ORDER 9066

1. Japanese Americans at no time posed a military or security threat to the United States. Nonetheless, key California military and political officials and journalists agreed that "military necessity" demanded a forceful and immediate action.
2. On February 19, 1942, President Roosevelt responded to the public outcry by signing Executive Order 9066 authorizing the military to evacuate all people of Japanese ancestry from the West Coast. Japanese Americans had just 48 hours to dispose of their businesses and property before reporting to Army assembly centers.

C. *KOREMATSU v. UNITED STATES*

1. The government interred, or kept confined, about 110,000 Japanese Americans in ten detention camps located in desolate western lands owned by the federal government. The internment constituted the most serious violation of civil liberties during wartime in American history.
2. Fred Korematsu was a Japanese American who knowingly refused to obey the internment order. In *Korematsu v. United States* he argued that Executive Order 9066 deprived Japanese Americans of life, liberty, and property without due process of law. In a controversial decision, the Supreme Court upheld the constitutionality of the government's evacuation policy citing the existence of "the gravest imminent danger to the public safety."

3. In 1988, Congress issued a formal apology to Japanese Americans and offered each individual camp survivor $20,000 in reparation. The legislation admitted that government actions were based on "race prejudice, war hysteria, and a failure of political leadership."

V. VICTORY IN EUROPE

A. GET GERMANY FIRST

1. Americans initially directed their anger at Japan. Roosevelt, however, realized that Hitler posed the greater threat to America's long-term security. If the Nazis succeeded in defeating both Great Britain and the Soviet Union, they could transform Europe into an unconquerable fortress.
2. Given these strategic considerations, FDR and Churchill agreed upon a military strategy of defeating Hitler first. Churchill confidently predicted, "Hitler's fate is sealed, Mussolini's fate is sealed."

B. BIG THREE DIPLOMACY

1. Known as the Big Three, Roosevelt, Churchill, and the Soviet leader Joseph Stalin first met in November 1943 at Tehran, Iran. The meeting confirmed that the United States and Great Britain would open a second front by invading France.
2. Known as D-Day, the Allied invasion of France began on June 6, 1944. Commanded by General Dwight D. Eisenhower, American, British, and Canadian troops successfully stormed the Normandy beaches and then liberated Paris less than three months later. Faced with American and British forces advancing from the west and Russian forces advancing from the east, Hitler took his own life on April 30, 1945.
3. The Big Three held their second and final meeting at Yalta in February 1945. Roosevelt and Churchill agreed to a temporary division of Germany. In return, Stalin agreed to join the war against Japan three months after the Nazis surrendered. Stalin also agreed that Poland should have a representative government based on free elections.

C. THE PRODUCTION MIRACLE

1. When Stalin met Roosevelt at Tehran, the Soviet dictator offered this admiring toast: "To American production, without which this war would have been lost." Stalin was right. American industry

crushed the Axis powers beneath an overwhelming weight of weaponry.

2. Prior to World War II, airplanes and ships had been built one at a time. Led by Henry Ford and Henry Kaiser, American factories used assembly line techniques to mass-produce weapons. By 1944, round-the-clock shifts turned out a new bomber every hour and a cargo ship every 17 days. Between 1940 and 1945, American workers built a staggering total of 296,429 warplanes, 5,425 cargo ships, and 102,351 tanks and self-propelled guns.

VI. THE HOMEFRONT: WOMEN

A. WOMEN AND THE WAR EFFORT

1. Nearly 350,000 American women served in uniform, volunteering for the newly formed Women's Army Corps (WACs) and other service branches. The women freed men for combat by performing 200 non-combat jobs stateside and in every theatre of the war. For example, women drove trucks, repaired planes, rigged parachutes, and served as radio and telephone operators. In addition, over 70,000 women provided vital service as army and navy nurses.
2. World War II created new job opportunities for women. Between 1940 and 1945, almost 6 million additional female workers entered the labor force as the female percentage of the U.S. workforce rose from 27 percent to nearly 37 percent.
3. The iconic "Rosie the Riveter" poster celebrated the women who worked in the nation's munitions factories. The Rosie poster was more than just a patriotic symbol. Over 310,000 women worked in the aircraft industry in 1943 where they represented two-thirds of the total workforce. In addition, women welders, crane operators, and electricians performed heavy industrial jobs long considered "men's work."

B. MAKING CONNECTIONS: WOMEN AND THE WORKFORCE

1. World War II opened new opportunities for many American women. However, the war did not erode the traditional view that a woman's primary role was still that of a wife and mother. *The New York Times* underscored this view of gender roles by confidently predicting, "The most important postwar plans of the majority of women in the WAC include just what all women want—their own homes and families."

2. Although World War II did not alter the widespread belief that women defense workers were playing a temporary role, it did serve as a vehicle for accelerating the ongoing process of increasing female participation in the labor force. World War II thus foreshadowed the dramatic expansion of women's workforce participation that accompanied the second wave of feminism launched by the publication of *The Feminine Mystique* in 1963.

VII. THE HOMEFRONT: AFRICAN AMERICANS

A. CONTEXT

1. The Great Depression slowed the historic exodus of African Americans from the rural South to northern and western cities. However, booming defense industries reignited the Great Migration, luring 700,000 blacks to leave the South.
2. Racial prejudice limited the social and economic gains African Americans hoped to achieve. In 1940, the president of North American Aviation reflected the prevailing prejudice among corporate managers when he explained, "While we are in complete sympathy with the Negro, it is against company policy to employ them as aircraft workers or mechanics . . . regardless of their training . . . there will be some jobs as janitors for Negroes."

B. EXECUTIVE ORDER 8802

1. Policies like the one announced by the aviation executive, outraged A. Philip Randolph. As the president of the all-black Brotherhood of Sleeping Car Porters, Randolph organized the March on Washington Movement to demand an end to racial discrimination in government and defense industries.
2. President Roosevelt wanted to prevent a highly visible and divisive protest march by as many as 100,000 black Americans. Supported by First Lady Eleanor Roosevelt, the president issued Executive Order 8802, providing for "the full and equitable participation of all workers in defense industries, without discrimination because of race, creed, color, or national origin." The order created the Fair Employment Practices Committee to monitor and enforce the presidential directive.
3. Executive Order 8802 is often described as an economic Emancipation Proclamation because it marked the first time since the end of Reconstruction that the federal government openly committed itself to opposing racial discrimination.

C. THE "DOUBLE V" CAMPAIGN

1. Black leaders pointed out that World War II provided a constant and painful daily reminder of the inequities faced by African Americans. For example, America's 1.2 million black soldiers and sailors fought in strictly segregated units.

2. African Americans were keenly aware of the contradiction between fighting for democracy abroad while enduring racial discrimination at home. Blacks enthusiastically supported a "Double V" campaign to win victory over fascism in Europe and victory over discrimination in the United States.

D. MAKING CONNECTIONS: THE MARCH ON WASHINGTON

1. The March on Washington Movement and the "Double V" campaign expressed the new mood of militancy among African Americans. During the war, membership in the National Association for the Advancement of Colored People (NAACP) surged from 50,000 to 450,000. In 1944, picketers outside a segregated restaurant in Washington, D.C., carried a placard that succinctly summarized America's racial dilemma: "We Die Together. Let's Eat Together."

2. The March on Washington Movement did not end with the declaration of Executive Order 8802. A. Philip Randolph's strategy of taking the struggle for civil rights to the streets inspired Dr. King and other civil rights activists. In 1963, Randolph served as the head of the March on Washington at which Dr. King delivered his historic "I Have a Dream" speech. The march played a key role in mobilizing public support for the landmark Civil Rights Act of 1964.

APUSH test questions often ask students to evaluate change and continuity on the home front during World War II. Be prepared for a long-essay or DBQ question asking you to evaluate how World War II affected changes and continuities in the experiences of American women and African Americans.

VIII. MAKING COMPARISONS: THE DECISION TO USE THE ATOMIC BOMB

A. CONTEXT

1. Franklin Roosevelt died on April 12, 1945. Two weeks later Secretary of War Henry L. Stimson informed President Truman about the top secret Manhattan Project to develop an atomic bomb.
2. Truman learned about the Manhattan Project as American forces closed in on the Japanese home islands. On July 16, 1945, American scientists successfully tested an atomic weapon at a desolate stretch of desert in New Mexico. The blast created a fireball with a core temperature three times hotter than the sun.

B. ARGUMENTS FOR USING THE ATOMIC BOMB AGAINST JAPAN

1. The atomic bomb would avoid a costly invasion of Japan that would inflict heavy casualties on both the American forces and Japanese civilians.
2. The atomic bomb would convince the Japanese government to immediately surrender.
3. The atomic bomb would prevent the Soviet Union from gaining any influence over the postwar settlement with Japan.
4. The atomic bomb would demonstrate America's overwhelming power and convince Stalin to be more cooperative in formulating postwar plans.

C. ARGUMENTS FOR NOT USING THE ATOMIC BOMB AGAINST JAPAN

1. The atomic bomb would utterly destroy Japanese cities and cause horrible human suffering.
2. The atomic bomb would become unnecessary since Japan was already very close to surrendering.
3. The atomic bomb would become unnecessary because the United States could have demonstrated its awesome power by detonating the weapon over an uninhabited island.
4. The atomic bomb would trigger an expensive and dangerous nuclear arms race with the Soviet Union.

D. TRIUMPH AND TRAGEDY

1. President Truman chose to use America's nuclear weapons. Two atomic bombs destroyed both Hiroshima and Nagasaki. Aghast at the horrible loss of life, Emperor Hirohito told his war council, "I cannot bear to see my innocent people suffer any longer."
2. The formal Japanese surrender took place on September 2, 1945, on the deck of the battleship *Missouri* in Tokyo Bay. World War II was now over, but the atomic age and the Cold War were about to begin.

UNIT 8 PERIOD 8 1945–1980

KEY CONCEPTS

KEY CONCEPT 8.1
The United States responded to an uncertain and unstable postwar world by asserting and working to maintain a position of global leadership, with far-reaching domestic and international consequences.

KEY CONCEPT 8.2
New movements for civil rights and liberal efforts to expand the role of government generated a range of political and cultural responses.

KEY CONCEPT 8.3
Postwar economic and demographic changes had far-reaching consequences for American society, politics, and culture.

TRUMAN, THE COLD WAR, AND THE SECOND RED SCARE 1946–1952

Chapter 26

I. THE BEGINNING OF THE COLD WAR

A. CONTEXT

1. The United States emerged from the Second World War as the world's most powerful and prosperous country. In 1947, America produced half of the world's manufactured goods, 57 percent of its steel, 43 percent of its electricity, and 62 percent of its oil.
2. In contrast, the Soviet Union suffered heavy losses during the war. The Nazi invasion destroyed many Russian cities and claimed as many as 20 million lives.
3. The contrasting impact of World War II helps to explain why the United States and the Soviet Union acted differently after the war. While American leaders focused on building a peaceful and prosperous world order, Soviet leaders focused on building a buffer zone in Eastern Europe to protect their country from a future invasion.

B. THE IRON CURTAIN

1. The Soviet Union steadily tightened its grip on Eastern Europe. Directed by Stalin, the Red Army installed new pro-Russian governments. Across Eastern Europe, communist officials imprisoned opponents, censored newspapers, and established state-controlled radio stations. Guards patrolled the borders to prevent people from escaping.
2. The Soviet actions alarmed Winston Churchill. In a 1946 speech in Fulton, Missouri, he warned Americans that, "An Iron Curtain has descended across the continent." No longer independent, the nations of Eastern Europe were fast becoming satellites controlled by the Soviet Union.

C. CONTAINMENT

1. Each report about the loss of freedom in Eastern Europe exacerbated tensions between the United States and the Soviet Union. As the initial postwar spirit of optimism vanished, the two former allies became increasingly suspicious rivals.

2. Secretary of Commerce Henry Wallace urged a policy of restraint. He argued that the Soviet Union had a legitimate right to control a sphere of influence along its western border. "Getting tough," Wallace said, "never bought anything real and lasting—whether for schoolyard bullies or world powers. The tougher we get, the tougher the Russians will get."

3. George Kennan, a leading expert on Soviet affairs, disagreed with Wallace. He predicted that the United States and the Soviet Union would remain antagonists for many years. Kennan pointed out that Soviet leaders espoused a communist ideology, or system of beliefs, convincing the Soviet people that "the outside world was hostile and that it was their duty eventually to overthrow the political forces beyond their borders."

4. In an influential 1947 article published in *Foreign Affairs*, Kennan recommended that the United States adopt a policy of "long-term, patient but firm and vigilant containment." By containment, he meant adopting a strategic policy of blocking the expansion of Soviet influence.

Don't neglect Henry Wallace's call for a foreign policy of conciliation and restraint. Be prepared to compare and contrast how Wallace and Kennan viewed Soviet conduct.

D. THE TRUMAN DOCTRINE

1. The threat of Soviet expansion was not limited to Eastern Europe. In early 1947, Russian pressure threatened the independence of Greece and Turkey. Since World War II, these two nations had depended upon Great Britain for financial support. However, on February 21, 1947, the British delivered two notes to the U.S. State Department acknowledging that they lacked the resources to aid Greece and Turkey. An American official later noted, "Great Britain had within the hour handed the job of world leadership with all its burden and all its glory to the United States."

2. President Truman accepted America's new responsibility. On March 12, 1947, he addressed a joint session of Congress and asked for

$400 million in military and economic aid to help Greece and Turkey.

3. Truman did not stop his address with a request for money. In what historian John Spanier calls "one of the most important speeches in American history," Truman articulated a new foreign policy that became known as the Truman Doctrine. The president confidently announced, "I believe that it must be the policy of the United States to support free peoples who are resisting attempted subjugations by armed minorities or by outside pressure."

E. UNDERSTANDING CAUSATION: CONSEQUENCES OF THE TRUMAN DOCTRINE

1. Congress overwhelmingly approved Truman's request for funds to assist Greece and Turkey. American aid played a vital role in helping these two countries successfully resist Soviet pressure.

2. The Truman Doctrine marked the beginning of the Cold War, a prolonged era of economic, political, technological, and ideological competition between the United States and the Soviet Union. As the leader of the Free World, the United States pledged to use its strength to limit the spread of communism throughout the world. This commitment to a policy of containment dominated American foreign policy from 1947 to the collapse of the Soviet Union in 1991.

II. CONTAINMENT IN EUROPE

A. THE MARSHALL PLAN

1. Greece and Turkey were not the only countries that needed aid. World War II left Western Europe in ruins. Homeless families struggled to survive in shattered cities. Devastated factories could not provide employment or produce badly needed goods.

2. Secretary of State George Marshall convinced President Truman that the United States had to act quickly. Speaking at Harvard University in June 1947, he proposed a bold plan to offer massive economic aid to help reconstruct Europe.

3. The Marshall Plan committed $13 billion to help rebuild sixteen Western European countries. These desperately needed funds helped Western Europe stage a remarkable economic recovery. Within four years, industrial production within the region was 41 percent higher than it had been on the eve of World War II. The

Marshall Plan thus accomplished its twin goals of reconstructing Western Europe and containing communism.

B. THE NATO ALLIANCE

1. The Truman Doctrine and the Marshall Plan represented the first two phases of America's new containment policy. The third phase came in 1949 when the United States, Canada, and ten Western European nations formed the North Atlantic Treaty Organization (NATO).
2. Article 5 of the North Atlantic Treaty commits each member state to consider an attack against one member state to be an armed attack against them all. America's decision to join an alliance based upon collective security marked a decisive break from its rejection of the League of Nations and its prewar policy of isolationism.
3. The NATO alliance escalated the Cold War. Stalin retaliated by forming the Warsaw Pact, an alliance linking the Soviet Union and seven Eastern European countries. Two hostile alliances now confronted each other across a divided continent.

C. THE BERLIN AIRLIFT

1. In 1945, the Allies divided Germany into four occupation zones, one each for the United States, Great Britain, France, and the Soviet Union. The city of Berlin lay 110 miles inside the Soviet occupation zone. Like Germany, it was divided into four occupation zones.
2. In June 1948, the United States, Great Britain, and France agreed to merge their occupation zones into a new German republic. Fearing a resurgent Germany, Stalin cut off Western highway and rail access to West Berlin. The 2.2 million people living in West Berlin had coal supplies for 45 days and enough food for just 36 days.
3. The Berlin blockade represented the first great Cold War test of wills between the United States and the Soviet Union. If Truman withdrew from West Berlin, he would lose the city and undermine confidence in America's policy of containment.
4. Truman refused to withdraw, declaring, "We are going to stay, period." He surprised Stalin by ordering a massive airlift to supply the 4,500 tons of food and fuel Berliners needed each day. Recognizing that the blockade was failing, Stalin reopened access into West Berlin.
5. The Berlin Airlift had a number of important consequences. The constant roar of planes over Berlin provided a convincing

demonstration of American power and will. The crisis changed the relationship between Germany and the Western Allies from that of occupiers and occupied, to partners in a joint struggle to defend the Free World. Following the Berlin Airlift, the Western Allies created the Federal Republic of Germany, or West Germany. Stalin responded by establishing the East German state, the German Democratic Republic.

D. MAKING CONNECTIONS: THE IMPORTANCE OF BERLIN

1. The success of the Berlin Airlift magnified West Berlin's importance. As Germany's largest city and former capital, Berlin had tremendous political and psychological significance. The stalemate over the status of West Berlin continued. In 1961, the Soviets surrounded the city with a 28-mile concrete wall designed to prevent East Germans from escaping to freedom in West Berlin. The Berlin Wall quickly became a symbol of the Cold War and Soviet oppression.
2. On November 9, 1989, the East German government yielded to popular pressure and opened the Berlin Wall. As the incredible news spread, the long-divided city erupted into joyous celebration. Jubilant Berliners danced, sang, and chanted, "The Wall is gone! The Wall is gone!" The fall of the Berlin Wall was a watershed event marking the end of the Cold War in Europe.

III. CONTAINMENT IN ASIA: JAPAN AND CHINA

A. A NEW JAPAN

1. President Truman placed General Douglas MacArthur in charge of the Japanese occupation. Under MacArthur's direction, Japan adopted a new constitution that created a democratic government. At the same time, American aid helped Japan rebuild factories, launch new electronic industries, and implement a program of land reform. By 1953, the Japanese economy was performing at prewar levels.
2. MacArthur's display of firm but fair leadership won the respect of the Japanese people. The United States and Japan gradually came to view each other as allies.

B. THE FALL OF CHINA

1. While the Japanese recovered, a civil war divided China. As World War II ended, conflict between the Nationalists led by Chiang

Kai-shek and the Communists led by Mao Zedong spread across the country.

2. Despite massive American aid, Chiang's forces steadily lost ground. An American military advisor reported that the Nationalist losses were due to "the world's worst leadership" and "a complete loss of will to fight."
3. On October 1, 1949, Mao triumphantly announced the birth of the People's Republic of China. Meanwhile, Chiang and the remnants of his defeated army fled to Taiwan, an island 110 miles from the Chinese mainland.
4. In early 1950, Mao signed a treaty of friendship with the Soviet Union. Alarmed Americans viewed the Chinese Revolution as part of a menacing Communist monolith. The fall of China represented a bitter defeat for American Cold War diplomacy. The U.S. refused to establish diplomatic relations with Mao's new government. Instead, Truman recognized the government of Taiwan as the representative of all China.

IV. CONTAINMENT IN ASIA: THE KOREAN WAR

A. A DIVIDED PENINSULA

1. Korea occupies a strategic peninsula that borders China and Russia and extends to within 100 miles of Japan. After World War II, the United States and the Soviet Union agreed to temporarily divide Korea at the 38th parallel.
2. As Cold War tensions increased, the 38th parallel hardened into a permanent demarcation line. The Soviet Union supported a communist government in the north, while the United States supported a pro-Western government in the south.

B. FROM INVASION TO STALEMATE

1. On June 25, 1950, the North Korean army suddenly attacked South Korea. Supported by artillery and heavy tanks, about 90,000 North Korean soldiers smashed through the South Korean defenses and rolled south.
2. Truman saw the invasion as a test of containment and an opportunity to prove that Democrats were not "soft" on Communism. Rather than ask Congress for a declaration of war, Truman appealed to the United Nations to intervene. Taking advantage of a temporary Soviet boycott, the UN Security Council

passed a resolution calling upon international assistance to aid South Korea. This marked the first time in history that a world organization mobilized to stop aggression.

C. THE TRUMAN-MacARTHUR CONTROVERSY

1. Led by General Douglas MacArthur, the UN forces recaptured all of South Korea. In October 1950, MacArthur confidently crossed the 38th parallel in a bid to reunite the entire Korean peninsula.
2. The Chinese repeatedly warned that they would not "stand idly by" and permit a North Korean defeat, thus allowing an American military presence near China's key industrial area in Manchuria. On November 25, China launched a massive counterattack catching MacArthur by surprise and driving the UN forces back into South Korea.
3. Truman now decided to abandon the goal of unifying Korea and instead adopted a policy of fighting a limited war to save South Korea. MacArthur indicated his disagreement in a public letter to the House Republican leader that concluded: "There is no substitute for victory."
4. MacArthur's open act of insubordination forced Truman to remove the general from all of his commands. This decisive action protected the principle of civilian control of the military.
5. MacArthur's dismissal did not prevent the Korean War from continuing for more than two years. The North Koreans finally signed an armistice providing for a cease-fire that left the border between the two Koreas at the 38th parallel.

D. UNDERSTANDING CAUSATION: CONSEQUENCES OF THE KOREAN WAR

1. Prior to the Korean War, U.S. policy had been limited to containing Soviet power in Western Europe and the Mediterranean. The Korean War expanded American involvement in Asia, transforming containment into a global struggle.
2. Truman's decision to commit American troops without Congressional approval set a precedent for U.S. involvement in the Vietnam War.
3. The Korean War fueled a massive American rearmament program. The defense budget soared from $13 billion in 1950 to $50 billion in 1953. These expenditures boosted economic growth. However, they also led to an informal alliance of America's military

and defense industries that President Eisenhower later called the "military-industrial complex."

4. Prior to the Korean War, African Americans fought in segregated units. In July 1948, President Truman ordered the racial desegregation of the U.S. armed forces. The Korean War marked the first time American forces fought in integrated units.

5. The Korean War began and ended at the 38th parallel. Korea continues to be a tense and divided peninsula with no formal peace treaty. Approximately 30,000 American troops remain stationed at the 38th parallel to deter North Korean aggression.

V. THE SECOND RED SCARE

A. MAKING CONNECTIONS: FEAR OF RADICALISM

1. A fear of radicalism has been a recurrent characteristic of American life and politics. During the 1790s, the Federalists exploited public distrust of aliens who supported France and criticized President Adams. During the 1850s, the Know-Nothings vehemently protested that Catholics posed a danger to America's republican institutions. And following World War I, a Red Scare directed public frustration at radical labor unions, communist sympathizers, and alleged subversives.

2. This pattern of fear and anxiety directed at scapegoats erupted again during the late 1940s and early 1950s. The "loss" of China followed by a military stalemate in Korea shocked the country. Public apprehension deepened when the Soviet Union exploded its first atomic bomb ending America's nuclear monopoly. These stunning reversals triggered a wave of anxiety and fear known as the Second Red Scare.

B. THE LOYALTY PROGRAM

1. President Truman vigorously rejected Republican charges that his administration was "soft" on communism. In March 1947, Truman issued an executive order creating a Federal Employee Loyalty program.

2. During the next four years, government loyalty boards investigated over 3 million federal employees. The boards dismissed 490 government workers, but failed to uncover any cases of espionage. Reckless allegations of misconduct nonetheless ruined many once-promising careers.

C. THE HOUSE UN-AMERICAN ACTIVITIES COMMITTEE

1. Congress created the House Un-American Activities Committee in 1938 to investigate foreign subversives. During the Second Red Scare, HUAC turned its attention from Nazis to possible communist influence in Hollywood.

2. In 1947, HUAC held two weeks of hearings designed to investigate the film industry. Scores of Hollywood executives and actors were forced to answer this accusatory question: "Are you now or have you ever been a member of the Communist Party?" A group of ten writers and directors—the so-called Hollywood Ten—were cited for contempt of Congress for refusing to testify. In addition, motion picture executives drew up a "blacklist" of about 500 screenwriters, directors, and writers who were suspended from work for their supposed political beliefs and associations.

3. HUAC next turned its attention to the State Department. Prodded by the relentless investigation of Richard Nixon, a freshman congressman from California, the committee discovered that a prominent State Department official named Alger Hiss had been a Soviet spy in the 1930s. Even more disquieting news surfaced when the government discovered that a British-American spy network transmitted atomic secrets to the Soviet Union.

D. THE RISE OF McCARTHYISM

1. The HUAC revelations touched a sensitive public nerve. The American people believed they were locked in a life-or-death struggle with the Soviet Union. Angry and bewildered citizens wanted to know why America appeared to be losing the Cold War.

2. Joseph McCarthy, a previously obscure Senator from Wisconsin, skillfully exploited the political climate of paranoia. On February 9, 1950, McCarthy told an audience in Wheeling, West Virginia, that America's foreign policy failures could be traced to communist influence in the State Department. He menacingly declared, "I have in my hand a list of 205—a list of names known to the Secretary of State as being members of the Communist Party and who nevertheless are still working and shaping policy in the State Department."

3. McCarthy failed to uncover a single communist. His practice of making unsubstantiated accusations of disloyalty without evidence became known as *McCarthyism*.

E. THE FALL OF McCARTHY

1. McCarthy's campaign of innuendo and half-truths continued into the Eisenhower administration. Many presidential advisors urged Ike to use his own great prestige to confront McCarthy. But Eisenhower refused, saying, "I will not get in the gutter with that guy."
2. McCarthy finally caused his own downfall when he launched a televised investigation of the U.S. Army. During the spring of 1954, a national audience of more than 20 million people watched as McCarthy bullied witnesses, twisted testimony, and introduced phony evidence. The Army-McCarthy hearings turned public sentiment against McCarthy, revealing him to be an unscrupulous demagogue.
3. In December 1954, the full Senate formally censured McCarthy for his dishonorable conduct. Flashing his famous grin, Ike asked his cabinet, "Have you heard the latest? McCarthyism is McCarthywasm."

VI. MAKING COMPARISONS: THE FIRST AND SECOND RED SCARES

A. THE FIRST RED SCARE

1. The First Red Scare lasted from 1919 to 1920. Millions of victorious soldiers returned from Europe only to find unemployment, labor unrest, and widespread racial tensions. Meanwhile, the Bolshevik Revolution and the ensuing creation of a communist dictatorship in the Soviet Union seemed to pose a threat to American society. This fear of revolutionary unrest at home and abroad led to the First Red Scare.
2. Attorney General A. Mitchell Palmer led the fight against radical subversion. Palmer mobilized an army of government agents who raided the homes, offices, and meeting places of radical labor unions, alleged socialists, recent immigrants, and aliens. The Palmer Raids constituted a serious violation of civil liberties as the government deported about 500 aliens without hearings or trials.
3. The paranoia inspired by the First Red Scare broke after the ill-conceived Palmer Raids aroused widespread protests from defenders of American civil liberties. America then turned to enjoy a New Era of carefree prosperity symbolized by jazz, flappers, and the Model T.

B. THE SECOND RED SCARE

1. The fear of radicalism reasserted itself in the late 1940s and early 1950s. The Second Red Scare was a response to rising Cold War tensions with the Soviet Union. The threat of nuclear war and the evidence that communist spies had infiltrated the Manhattan Project and the State Department triggered a wave of anticommunist fear and suspicion.

2. The House Un-American Activities Committee (HUAC) and Senator Joseph McCarthy led the fight to uncover spies infiltrating government agencies. HUAC investigated the Hollywood film industry and the State Department. Their investigation of Hollywood led to unfounded accusations and ruined careers. However, their investigation of the State Department led to surprising revelations of suspicious conduct by Alger Hiss. Intoxicated by his power, McCarthy ignored civil liberties while failing to discover a single communist agent.

3. The paranoia inspired by the Second Red Scare broke after the Army-McCarthy hearings fully revealed McCarthy's vicious campaign of smear and innuendo. Americans then turned to enjoy a period of unprecedented prosperity symbolized by suburban neighborhoods, shopping centers, and sleek new cars.

APUSH test writers have devoted particular attention to the causes and consequences of the First and Second Red Scares. Be prepared to compare and contrast these two events.

THE EISENHOWER ERA 1952–1960

I. UNDERSTANDING CAUSATION: CAUSES OF THE ECONOMIC BOOM

A. CONTEXT

1. The 1950s witnessed the beginning of an unprecedented quarter century of sustained economic growth. In just one generation, the American people moved from the depths of the Great Depression to enjoying the highest standard of living the world had ever known.
2. Historian James T. Patterson asserts that America's booming economy was "the most decisive force in shaping attitudes and experiences in the postwar era."

B. COLD WAR DEFENSE SPENDING

1. The military budget provided the single most important stimulus for postwar economic expansion. America's commitment to contain the Soviet Union in Europe and fight the Korean War in Asia pushed the defense budget from $13 billion in 1949 to over $50 billion in 1953.
2. Defense spending played an important role in spurring economic growth in parts of the South and West Coast.

C. THE BABY BOOM

1. America's thriving economy provided jobs and income renewing people's faith in the future. More and more Americans married at younger ages. By 1956, the average age of marriage for men dropped to 22 and to 20 for women.
2. The marriage boom triggered a postwar surge in the birth rate known as the baby boom. More than 40 million babies were born in the 1950s, with 4.3 million in the peak year of 1957.
3. Dozens of industries profited from the baby boom. In 1958, *Life* magazine calculated that during its first year a baby was "a

potential market for $800.00 worth of products." For example, the legions of new babies annually consumed 1.5 billion cans of baby food.

D. CONSUMER SPENDING

1. Rising affluence promoted a zeal for consumer products. The widespread use of credit cards created a powerful stimulus for shopping and borrowing. In 1945, the entire country contained just 8 shopping centers. Fifteen years later, 3,840 shopping centers lined the nation's highways.
2. Suburban homeowners equipped their kitchens with new refrigerators, washing machines, and dishwashers—but television sets dominated their living rooms. Using techniques pioneered on radio, advertisers sponsored popular programs such as *I Love Lucy* and *Father Knows Best* so they could broadcast commercials designed to stimulate demand for products ranging from cars to toothpaste.

E. MAKING CONNECTIONS: POVERTY IN AMERICA

1. During the 1950s, most commentators focused on describing the familiar lifestyle of middle-class Americans. As a result, they ignored the continuing persistence of pockets of poverty in the rural South, Appalachia, the inner cities, and among agricultural workers in the West.
2. This lack of public attention changed when Michael Harrington published *The Other America* in 1962. Harrington described what other social observers had missed—that about 25 percent of the nation's 176 million people lived in poverty. "How long," he asked, "shall we ignore this underdeveloped nation in our midst?" Harrington's compelling description of the plight of impoverished Americans played an important role in inspiring President Johnson's War on Poverty.

II. SUBURBIA

A. MASS PRODUCTION OF HOMES

1. William Levitt successfully applied assembly line production techniques learned in the automobile and shipping industries to building homes in Long Island, New York, New Jersey, and Pennsylvania. Levitt's affordable mass-produced homes provided a model for builders across the country.

2. The G.I. Bill enabled World War II veterans to buy new homes with little or no down payments and low long-term interest rates. It also allowed over one million men to go to college and therefore become white-collar workers who boosted economic growth.

3. Much of the suburban growth occurred in an arc of states stretching from the Carolinas to Florida and on to Texas and Southern California. Known as the Sun Belt, this region steadily gained political, economic, and cultural influence.

B. INTERSTATE HIGHWAYS

1. Promoted by President Eisenhower, the landmark Federal Highway Act of 1956 created a 42,000-mile system of multiple-lane interstate highways.

2. The new interstates enabled suburbanites to commute from their homes to their jobs in the cities. At the same time they sparked sustained growth in the automobile, petroleum, and trucking industries, while also fostering an on-the-road culture featuring motels like Holiday Inn and fast-food restaurants like McDonald's.

C. THE REVIVAL OF THE CULT OF DOMESTICITY

1. The 1950s witnessed a dramatic revival of the cult of domesticity. By the end of the decade, nearly three-fourths of all American women between the ages of 20 and 24 were married. Youthful marriages and a soaring birth rate encouraged a return to traditional gender roles in which men pursued careers and women devoted themselves to housework and raising their children.

2. The mass media reinforced and idealized the new cult of domesticity. Television programs featured suburban homes filled with happy moms who maintained immaculate kitchens while their husbands commuted to relatively stress-free white-collar jobs.

D. MAKING CONNECTIONS: WHAT ARE MOTHERS FOR?

1. In the popular television series *Leave It to Beaver*, young Beaver Cleaver admired his mom's ability to resolve problems saying, "When we're in a mess, you kind of make things seem not so messy." Beaver's mom, June Cleaver, knowingly replied, "Well isn't that sort of what mothers are for?"

2. The endless routine of shopping, cooking, and chauffeuring kids frustrated many college-educated women. Bored and isolated, they searched for a very different answer to June Cleaver's question. In 1963, a suburban mom named Betty Friedan struck a nerve when

she opened her book *The Feminine Mystique* by asking, "Is this all?" The question and Friedan's call for women to pursue fulfilling work outside their homes touched a sense of restless dissatisfaction that helped ignite a second wave of feminism in the United States.

III. CRITICS AND REBELS

A. CONTEXT

1. The new suburban lifestyle did not enjoy unanimous approval. Social critics decried mass-produced Levittowns packed with endless rows of identical box houses.
2. By 1959, 200 corporations controlled 50 percent of the nation's business assets. A growing number of social scientists worried that many white-collar employees were becoming nameless, interchangeable cogs in vast impersonal corporations.

B. SOCIAL CRITICS

1. William H. Whyte's book *The Organization Man* described how the corporate emphasis upon "the Team" created a stifling conformity that squelched personal identity. *The Lonely Crowd* by Harvard sociologist David Riesman extended Whyte's critique by arguing that America's corporate culture produced "other-directed" employees who prized getting along above taking individual risks.
2. Novelists also joined the chorus of critics who found flaws in an economy dominated by impersonal corporations. For example, Sloan Wilson's novel *The Man in the Gray Flannel Suit* tells the story of a young couple, Tom and Betsy Rath, who struggle against the pervasive pressures of middle-class conformity. The book's title comes from Tom's sudden realization that "all I could see was a lot of bright young men in gray flannel suits rushing around New York in a frantic parade to nowhere." Tom then looks at himself and is aghast to discover that he too is wearing a gray flannel suit.

C. THE BEAT GENERATION

1. During the 1950s, a small but culturally influential group of self-described "Beats" rejected suburban America's carefree consumption and mindless conformity. Easily identified by their unconventional long hair and distaste for "square" suburban lifestyles, the Beats preferred to live in urban enclaves in New York City and San Francisco.

2. Beat generation writers and poets such as Allen Ginsberg and Jack Kerouac scorned middle-class suburban life. Kerouac linked happiness with personal freedom. Like other Beats he celebrated impulsive actions and the pursuit of immediate pleasure. In his autobiographical novel *On the Road*, Kerouac wrote "spontaneous prose" describing how he found adventure and renewal while traveling across the country. The Beats pioneered a nonconformist lifestyle foreshadowing the emergence of the hippies in the 1960s.

D. ARTISTIC REBELS

1. Like contemporary Beat writers, Modern artists pursued a personal quest for radical freedom of expression. Instead of attempting to portray the world around them, mid-century Modernists stressed private concerns and personal experiences as the sources of their art. During the 1950s, New York City became the center of the Western art world.
2. Jackson Pollock, Willem de Kooning, and Mark Rothko emerged as the acknowledged leaders of the New York School of Abstract Expressionism. Pollock created Abstract Expressionist paintings by spontaneously dripping paint on a canvas spread across the floor. He believed this artistic style emphasized individuality and freedom from traditional constraints.

E. ROCK AND ROLL

1. Relatively few Americans read Beat Generation poems or visited trendy art galleries to see Abstract Expressionist paintings. However, most Americans did listen to music on their radios. In 1951, a Cleveland disc jockey named Alan Freed discarded bland popular music and instead began to play black rhythm and blues artists. Freed renamed the new sound "rock and roll."
2. Elvis Presley embodied the new rock and roll sound and its rebellious attitude. His hit songs and sexually suggestive onstage gyrations thrilled teenagers and horrified their parents. Like Beat Generation writers, rock and roll singers challenged accepted beliefs about sex, race, and work. Rock and roll soon became the sound that helped shape and define the new teenage culture.

Be prepared to discuss how intellectuals, artists, youth, and black activists challenged the Eisenhower-era status quo.

IV. TURNING POINTS IN AMERICAN HISTORY: *BROWN v. BOARD OF EDUCATION*, 1954

A. CONTEXT

1. In the 1896 *Plessy v. Ferguson* decision, the U.S. Supreme Court ruled that racially separate facilities, if equal, did not violate the Constitution. According to the Court, segregation was not discrimination.
2. Despite the Double V Campaign and the desegregation of the Army, Jim Crow segregation remained entrenched throughout the South. Ubiquitous "Colored Only" signs provided African Americans with humiliating reminders of their second-class status.
3. Since its founding in 1909, the NAACP had adopted the strategy of filing legal cases to gain justice and civil rights for African Americans. Led by Thurgood Marshall, the NAACP's Legal Defense and Education Fund won important Supreme Court victories ruling against "separate but equal" facilities in graduate and professional schools.

B. "THE DOCTRINE OF 'SEPARATE BUT EQUAL' HAS NO PLACE"

1. When the 1953–54 school year opened, 2.5 million African American children attended all-black public schools in twenty-one states, ten of them outside the Old South. The facilities in these segregated schools were far from equal to those in white schools. In 1954, Southern states spent an average of $165.00 for their white students and $115.00 for their black students.
2. Thurgood Marshall and the NAACP legal team chose five test cases to challenge state laws mandating segregation in the public schools. The *Brown* case took its name from the first name on the list—Oliver Brown of Topeka, Kansas. Brown wanted his eight-year-old daughter Linda to attend a nearby all-white elementary school instead of the all-black school twenty-five blocks from their home.
3. Marshall argued that segregated schools violated the "equal protection of the laws" guaranteed by the Fourteenth Amendment. Speaking for a unanimous Court, Chief Justice Earl Warren declared, "We conclude that in the field of public education, the doctrine of separate but equal has no place. Separate educational facilities are inherently unequal."
4. The *Brown* decision opened a new era in the African American struggle for equal rights. The Court's landmark ruling galvanized

the nation's 15 million black citizens to begin demanding "Freedom Now!"

C. MASSIVE RESISTANCE AND LITTLE ROCK

1. Outraged leaders across the South called for "massive resistance" to the Court's desegregation ruling. In Congress, 82 representatives and 19 senators signed a Southern Manifesto accusing the Supreme Court of "a clear abuse of judicial power."
2. Massive resistance became a reality in Little Rock, Arkansas. The local school board adopted a desegregation plan calling for nine black students to integrate Little Rock's Central High School. The crisis began when an angry white mob surrounded the school and threatened the safety of the nine black students.
3. This blatant display of resistance convinced President Eisenhower that he had a constitutional duty to enforce the *Brown* decision. Ike ordered 1,100 paratroopers to Little Rock to protect the black students and enforce the Supreme Court's desegregation order. Eisenhower thus became the first president since Reconstruction to use federal troops to enforce the rights of African Americans.

D. MAKING CONNECTIONS: THE IMPACT OF THE *BROWN* DECISION

1. Although the *Brown* decision initially faced "massive resistance" in the South, it provided irresistible moral legitimacy to the struggle for legal equality. Sparked by *Brown*, the modern civil rights movement began a crucial decade of mass protests culminating with the passage of the historic 1964 Civil Rights Act.
2. *Brown*'s original goal of achieving school desegregation became part of a larger campaign for social justice. The African American civil rights movement inspired women, people with disabilities, and other minority groups to also demand "equal protection of the laws."

Brown v. Board of Education *is one of the most frequent APUSH topics. Be prepared to write a long-essay discussing how the Court's decision marked a turning point in American history.*

V. THE CIVIL RIGHTS MOVEMENT, 1956–1960

A. THE MONTGOMERY BUS BOYCOTT

1. On December 1, 1955, a white Montgomery City Lines bus driver ordered a 42-year-old black seamstress named Rosa Parks to give up her seat to a white passenger. Parks refused by firmly saying one fateful word, "No."

2. Rosa Parks' refusal to give up her seat sparked the Montgomery Bus Boycott. Led by her young minister, the 26-year-old Dr. Martin Luther King, Jr., the black community supported Parks by boycotting the city buses. The boycott ended 15 months later when the Supreme Court ruled that segregation on public buses was unconstitutional.

B. DR. KING AND NONVIOLENT CIVIL DISOBEDIENCE

1. The Montgomery Bus Boycott catapulted Dr. King to national prominence. He soon emerged as America's foremost civil rights leader.

2. Dr. King inspired his followers with a message of nonviolent civil disobedience derived from Henry David Thoreau's essay "Resistance to Civil Government." In this seminal work, Thoreau wrote that if a law requires a person "to be an agent of injustice to another, then, I say, break the law." Dr. King founded the Southern Christian Leadership Conference (SCLC) to apply this moral principle of civil disobedience in test cases throughout the South.

C. THE SIT-IN MOVEMENT

1. Despite the victories in Montgomery and Little Rock, segregation continued to be a humiliating fact of daily life throughout the South. Jim Crow laws still segregated public bathrooms, drinking fountains, and lunch counters.

2. Dr. King's philosophy of nonviolent civil disobedience inspired four black college students in Greensboro, North Carolina, to take action. Calling segregation "evil pure and simple," the Greensboro Four sat down at a "whites only" Woolworth lunch counter on February 1, 1960, and ordered cups of coffee and slices of apple pie. When the waitress refused to take their order, the students remained seated. Their "sit-in" tactic worked. After losing over $200,000 in business, the Greensboro Woolworth desegregated its lunch counter.

3. The Greensboro sit-in energized a wave of student protests across the South. An estimated 70,000 demonstrators held "read-ins" in libraries, "watch-ins" at movie theaters, and "wade-ins" at beaches. Encouraged by Ella Baker, black and white students formed the Student Nonviolent Coordinating Committee (SNCC) to facilitate student activism.

VI. THE COLD WAR

A. "A MULTIPLICITY OF FEARS"

1. On the surface, a majority of Americans seemed to enjoy a good life in the mid-fifties. The country liked Ike because his administration brought a material prosperity unequalled in American history.
2. The surface appearance of calm belied the reality of an underlying sense of anxiety and even fear. In a press conference in 1954, Eisenhower noted that Americans were "suffering from a multiplicity of fears." The president was right. The fear of international communism, the fear of domestic subversion, and, most of all, the fear of nuclear annihilation all produced a deep sense of anxiety.

B. MASSIVE RETALIATION AND BRINKSMANSHIP

1. The fear of war was not imaginary. By 1954, both the United States and the Soviet Union had exploded hydrogen bombs. What Winston Churchill called the "balance of terror" seemed frighteningly real.
2. President Eisenhower and his Secretary of State John Foster Dulles added to public anxiety by announcing the United States would no longer become involved in expensive limited wars. Instead, Dulles declared a new strategy called massive retaliation. This meant the United States would consider using its arsenal of nuclear weapons to halt Soviet aggression.
3. Threatening to use nuclear weapons would require nerves of steel. "If you are scared to go to the brink," Dulles warned, "you are lost." Journalists promptly labeled this policy of going to the brink of nuclear war without going over the edge "brinksmanship."

C. VIETNAM

1. Most Americans knew very little about Vietnam. Yet, events in this remote Asian country would transform it and the United States.

2. Following World War II, France attempted to regain control over its valuable colonies in what had been known as French Indochina. However, the French soon became entangled in a costly war with communist forces led by Ho Chi Minh.

3. In 1954, the French suffered a disastrous defeat at the Battle of Dien Bien Phu. The exhausted French and the victorious Vietnamese reached an agreement known as the Geneva Accords. Both sides agreed to divide Vietnam at the 17th parallel. Ho Chi Minh would rule north of the parallel, while a French-backed government would rule south of it. A final agreement specified that free elections would be held in 1956 to unify Vietnam under one government.

D. THE DOMINO THEORY

1. The French defeat forced Eisenhower to make a fateful decision. Ike refused to abandon South Vietnam to Ho Chi Minh. At a news conference he explained, "When you have a row of dominoes set up, you knock over the first one, and what happens to the last one is the certainty that it will go over very quickly. So you could have the beginning of a disintegration that will have the most profound consequences." Called the domino theory, this belief became the justification for America's involvement in Vietnam.

2. The election called for in the Geneva Accords never took place. Instead, the U.S. sponsored a new South Vietnamese government headed by Ngo Dinh Diem. Within a short time, South Vietnamese communists called Viet Cong began a guerilla war to overthrow Diem. Eisenhower's decision to protect South Vietnam left his successors a dangerous problem.

E. *SPUTNIK*

1. On October 4, 1957, millions of Americans turned on their television sets and heard a newscaster tell them, "Listen now for the sound which forever separates the old from the new." The beeping sound they heard came from a 184-pound satellite called *Sputnik* (Russian for "traveling companion") that the Russians had shot into orbit earlier that day.

2. *Sputnik* jolted America's self-confidence. A stunned public concluded that the Russians had surpassed the United States in science and technology.

3. In July 1958, an alarmed Congress created the National Aeronautics and Space Administration (NASA) to compete with the Soviet space program. Congress also passed the National Defense

Education Act to fund accelerated science and math programs in the nation's public schools and universities.

VII. MAKING COMPARISONS: THE 1920s AND THE 1950s

A. TECHNOLOGY

1. The 1920s witnessed remarkable advances in silent and synchronized-sound movies, airplanes, telephones, and consumer appliances. The decade also marked the beginning of the radio age. At the same time, Henry Ford pioneered mass production techniques for the automobile. The automobile sparked the beginning of highway construction while also spurring the growth of the petroleum, glass, and rubber industries.
2. The 1950s witnessed remarkable advances in jet aircraft, improved kitchen appliances, and lifesaving antibiotics and vaccines. The decade also marked the beginning of the television age. At the same time, William Levitt pioneered mass production techniques for homes. Widespread ownership of cars and the construction of the new interstate highway system contributed to the growth of suburbs around American cities.

B. INTOLERANCE

1. The 1920s witnessed widespread intolerance. The decade opened with a Red Scare directed against alleged radicals and communist sympathizers. Jim Crow laws remained entrenched in the South as African Americans attended segregated schools and faced formidable obstacles to exercising their right to vote. A resurgent Klan promoted racism while also fueling a movement that successfully persuaded Congress to pass the highly restrictive Immigration Act of 1924.
2. The 1950s witnessed widespread intolerance. The decade opened with a Second Red Scare sparked by Senator McCarthy's unfounded accusations that communist sympathizers were working in the State Department. "McCarthyism" inspired loyalty oaths and Hollywood blacklists intended to suppress dissent. Although Jim Crow segregation remained entrenched, a growing Civil Rights movement achieved major victories in the *Brown v. Board of Education* decision and the Montgomery Bus Boycott.

C. LITERATURE

1. The 1920s witnessed a remarkable outburst of literary activity. Harlem Renaissance writers such as Langston Hughes and Zora

Neale Hurston expressed pride in their African American culture. At the same time, Lost Generation writers such as F. Scott Fitzgerald and Sinclair Lewis expressed a critical view of American society and the materialistic spirit dominating the decade.

2. The 1950s witnessed the publication of popular academic and literary works challenging the banality and conformity of the decade. David Riesman's *The Lonely Crowd* and William Whyte's *The Organization Man* criticized the oppressive conformity found in the suburbs and in America's large corporations. Meanwhile, Beat writers such as Jack Kerouac and Allen Ginsburg protested the era's excessive materialism while also calling for greater individualism.

THE 1960s

Chapter 28

I. JFK PROCLAIMS A NEW FRONTIER

A. "THE TORCH HAS PASSED TO A NEW GENERATION"

1. John F. Kennedy defeated Richard Nixon by a razor-thin popular margin of 116,000 votes. "The margin is narrow," Kennedy admitted, "but the responsibility is clear."
2. On January 20, 1961, Dwight Eisenhower, then the oldest man ever to serve as President, watched as his successor, John F. Kennedy, took the oath of office as the youngest man to hold the nation's highest office. As a brilliant winter sun sparkled on a layer of newly fallen snow, the 43-year-old president proudly announced, "The torch has passed to a new generation of Americans."

B. THE NEW FRONTIER

1. JFK inspired America with his pledge to boldly lead the country into a "New Frontier." Hoping to become an activist President in the tradition of Franklin Roosevelt, Kennedy's New Frontier included plans to fight poverty, support civil rights for African Americans, aid education, and provide health insurance for the elderly.
2. Once in office, Kennedy began enacting a number of innovative programs. For example, the Peace Corps sent thousands of idealistic volunteers to battle hunger, disease, and illiteracy in developing nations in Africa, Asia, and Latin America. The Alliance for Progress proposed to use America's economic strength to fight poverty in Latin America. And in the space race with the Soviets, Kennedy committed the United States to put the first man on the moon.

II. JFK AND THE COLD WAR

A. BERLIN

1. During the presidential campaign, Kennedy predicted that communist expansion posed the most important threat to the Free

World. "To be an American in the next decade," he warned, "will be a hazardous experience. We will live on the edge of danger."

2. Kennedy's first Cold War confrontation came in Berlin. At a summit meeting in Vienna in June 1961, Soviet Premier Nikita Khrushchev threatened to isolate West Berlin by placing it under the control of East Germany. When Kennedy refused to surrender Western occupation rights, Khrushchev angrily declared, "If you want war, that is your problem."

3. Aware of America's formidable nuclear arsenal, Khrushchev did not want to provoke a war. But he did want to stop the stream of 3 million refugees who fled from East Germany to West Berlin. On August 13, 1961, Khrushchev ordered East German troops to begin constructing a concrete wall topped with barbed wire along the border between East and West Berlin. Known as the Berlin Wall, the barrier cut the flow of refugees, thus ending the Berlin crisis. However, the superpower stalemate continued as Berlin, like all of Europe, remained divided.

B. THE BAY OF PIGS INVASION

1. In the late 1950s, Fidel Castro led a popular revolution that overthrew Cuba's corrupt dictator Fulgencio Batista. Although he promised to turn Cuba into a democratic nation, Castro seized American-owned businesses, nationalized the country's major industries, and established close ties with the Soviet Union.

2. When he became president, Kennedy learned that the Central Intelligence Agency (CIA) was preparing an army of 1,400 Cuban exiles to invade Cuba at the Bay of Pigs on the island's southern coast. The CIA confidently predicted the invaders would spark a popular uprising that would overthrow Castro. Despite serious doubts, Kennedy allowed the invasion to take place on April 17, 1961.

3. The dream of overthrowing Castro quickly turned into a nightmare when a powerful Cuban army overwhelmed the exile force. The fiasco handed JFK an embarrassing defeat damaging his credibility and inviting further provocations from Castro and Khrushchev.

C. THE CUBAN MISSILE CRISIS

1. Tempted by Kennedy's inexperience and apparent lack of resolve, an emboldened Khrushchev secretly allowed Russian technicians to build 42 ballistic missile sites in Cuba. The missiles could be fitted with nuclear warheads 20 to 30 times more powerful than the bomb that destroyed Hiroshima.

2. A high-flying U-2 spy plane discovered the missile sites on October 14, 1962. Kennedy and his advisors recognized that these weapons posed a serious threat to America's national security and the global balance of power. After days of secret deliberations, Kennedy publicly announced a "quarantine" or naval blockade of Cuba and demanded the removal of the missiles already in place. If the Soviet Union refused, the United States would launch a massive invasion force to destroy the missiles.

3. The world now faced the terrifying possibility of a nuclear war. Confronted with America's firm determination and overwhelming military superiority, Khrushchev agreed to remove the missiles in return for an American pledge not to invade Cuba.

D. UNDERSTANDING CAUSATION: CONSEQUENCES OF THE CUBAN MISSILE CRISIS

1. The Cuban Missile Crisis enhanced Kennedy's popularity and global prestige. In contrast, it weakened Khrushchev and played a key role in his fall from power two years later.

2. Having approached the brink of nuclear catastrophe, Kennedy and Khrushchev worked to improve relations and prevent a recurrence of such a dangerous confrontation. They agreed to install a "hotline" allowing direct communication between Washington and Moscow in a crisis.

3. The successful resolution of the Cuban Missile Crisis gave Kennedy a new confidence. In an important speech delivered on June 10, 1963, JFK shifted from confrontational Cold War rhetoric by reminding his listeners, "We all breathe the same air. We all cherish our children's futures." Three months later the United States and the Soviet Union signed the Partial Test Ban Treaty banning nuclear tests in the atmosphere.

III. "WE SHALL OVERCOME"

A. CONTEXT

1. During the 1960 presidential campaign Kennedy pledged to actively work for African American civil rights. However, as president he failed to launch an attack on segregation in the South.

2. While JFK wavered, black activists turned to direct action to confront Jim Crow segregation. For example, mob violence did not deter the Freedom Riders from winning an order from the Interstate Commerce Commission banning segregation in

interstate bus terminals. Across the country, more and more blacks marched against segregation as they sang the civil rights anthem, "We shall overcome."

B. BIRMINGHAM

1. In April 1963, the focus of the civil rights struggle shifted to Birmingham, Alabama. At that time, Birmingham was the largest segregated city in the United States. Eugene "Bull" Connor, the city's Commissioner of Public Safety, promptly arrested over 3,000 demonstrators, including Dr. King.
2. While in jail, Dr. King wrote his famous "Letter from Birmingham City Jail" in which he defended civil disobedience as a justified response to unjust segregation laws. Dr. King called upon white clergymen to join him in being "extremists for the cause of justice."
3. Bull Connor did not read Dr. King's letter. On May 3, his men used clubs, snarling police attack dogs, and high-pressure fire hoses to disperse a peaceful demonstration. Connor's strategy backfired when outraged Americans watched news broadcasts of what one journalist called "a visual demonstration of sin, vivid enough to rouse the conscience of the entire nation."

C. PRESIDENT KENNEDY SPEAKS OUT

1. The events in Birmingham forced President Kennedy to act. In a televised address on June 11, 1963, he forcefully argued for racial justice: "We are confronted primarily with a moral issue . . . The heart of the question is whether all Americans are to be afforded equal rights and equal opportunities, whether we are going to treat our fellow Americans as we want to be treated."
2. Kennedy's speech marked a major turning point in the civil rights movement. Eight days later, the president called upon Congress to pass a sweeping civil rights bill that would prohibit segregation in public places, speed up school integration, and ban discrimination in hiring practices.

D. THE MARCH ON WASHINGTON

1. Dr. King recognized the importance of building a nationwide alliance of what he called a "coalition of conscience" to support President Kennedy's civil rights bill. Dr. King and other black leaders called for a massive March on Washington to demonstrate public support for the bill.

2. The climax of the day came when Dr. King addressed a crowd of over 200,000 black and white civil rights supporters. His famous "I Have a Dream" speech left an indelible memory on everyone who heard it. Inspired by Dr. King, the unified crowd sang "We shall overcome" and repeatedly chanted "Pass the bill!"

E. MAKING COMPARISONS: DR. KING AND MALCOLM X

1. Dr. King advocated non-violent protests to challenge Jim Crow segregation. He worked to create a racially integrated society in which people "will not be judged by the color of their skin but by the content of their character." Dr. King opposed violence arguing, "It destroys community and makes brotherhood impossible."

2. During the early 1960s, Malcolm X emerged as a leading voice of an increasingly militant wing of the civil rights movement. He embraced black nationalism as an alternative to Dr. King's vision of a racially integrated society achieved by peaceful means. Malcolm X exhorted blacks to cast off the shackles of racism "by any means necessary" including violence: "When I say fight for independence right here, I don't mean any nonviolent fight, or turn-the-other-cheek fight. Those days are gone, those days are over."

IV. NOVEMBER 22, 1963

A. DALLAS

1. In the fall of 1963, President Kennedy appeared to be fulfilling his promise as a leader. He met the Soviet challenge in Cuba, took the first steps toward reducing Cold War tensions, and launched a moral and legislative attack on segregation. About 60 percent of the public approved his performance.

2. No one foresaw that a terrible national tragedy lay just ahead. On November 22, 1963, Lee Harvey Oswald shot and killed President Kennedy in Dallas, Texas. The tragic news flashed instantly across the nation and then around the world. Television became what one reporter called "the window on the world." Shocked viewers watched a somber Vice President Lyndon Johnson take the oath of office while a grief-stricken Jacqueline Kennedy stood by his side.

B. MAKING CONNECTIONS: THE KENNEDY LEGACY

1. President Kennedy achieved a mixed record of successes and failures. Cold War historians condemn his rash decision to approve the Bay of Pigs invasion while praising his adept handling of the

Cuban Missile Crisis. Social historians fault Kennedy for initially moving slowly on civil rights, but laud his strong moral leadership toward the end of his presidency. Overall, presidential scholars rank JFK as a good, but not great, president.

2. Unlike professional historians, the American public consistently awards Kennedy the highest approval rating of any president since Franklin Roosevelt. JFK's youth and vitality embodied the aspirations of a new generation. Historian Alan Brinkley concludes, "He remains a powerful symbol of a lost moment, of a soaring idealism and hopefulness that subsequent generations still try to recover."

V. THE GREAT SOCIETY

A. "LET US CONTINUE"

1. Lyndon Johnson took office under tragic and demanding circumstances. No previous vice president had ever witnessed the assassination of a president.
2. Johnson reminded a joint session of Congress that when listing his goals President Kennedy had said, "Let us begin." The new president solemnly declared, "Let us continue."

B. LANDMARK CIVIL RIGHTS LEGISLATION

1. Johnson understood that civil rights remained America's most urgent social problem. Demonstrating his legendary ability to persuade Senators to support his bills, LBJ overcame strong Southern opposition and won passage of the 1964 Civil Rights Act.
2. The landmark act gave all citizens the right to use public facilities such as hotels, restaurants, and theatres. The law authorized the attorney general to bring suits to speed school desegregation. In addition, it created the Equal Employment Opportunity Commission to prevent job discrimination. Finally, Title VII barred discrimination based on sex. Women's groups successfully used this provision to secure government support for greater equality in education and employment.
3. President Johnson and civil rights leaders now turned to the issue of voting rights. A combination of literacy tests and poll taxes effectively nullified the Fifteenth and Nineteenth amendments giving black men and women the right to vote. The Voting Rights Act of 1965 abolished literacy tests and other tactics used to

prevent blacks from voting. At the same time, the Twenty-fourth Amendment outlawed the poll tax in federal elections. Together the Voting Rights Act and the Twenty-fourth Amendment enabled millions of African American citizens to vote for the first time.

C. THE WAR ON POVERTY

1. President Johnson believed his landslide victory over Barry Goldwater in the 1964 presidential election gave him a mandate to pursue his dream of creating a Great Society that would use America's great prosperity to help improve the quality of life for everyone.
2. Despite America's great wealth, about one-fifth of the nation's families earned less than $3,000 a year. Shocked by this jarring fact, LBJ declared an "unconditional War on Poverty."
3. Congress passed a host of new federal programs to help the poor. For example, high school dropouts learned new skills in over 50 Job Corps camps, while half-a-million pre-school children attended special Head Start programs to help them prepare for school. Although many criticized the War on Poverty for waste, it gave hope to millions and helped reduce the number of poor by nearly 10 million people from 1964 to 1967.

D. MAKING CONNECTIONS: CHANGING PATTERNS OF IMMIGRATION

1. The Immigration Act of 1965 abolished the system of national quotas instituted during the 1920s. The act established a ceiling of 120,000 on immigrants from the Western Hemisphere and 170,000 from the rest of the world. The law established preferences for close relatives as well as for those with needed occupational skills.
2. The Immigration Act of 1965 has had a profound impact on America's demographic character. The family unification preference led to the phenomenon of chain immigration in which the naturalization of a single immigrant from Asia, Africa, or Hispanic background opened the door to his or her brothers and sisters and their spouses.
3. These provisions have triggered a major new wave of immigration. Between 1990 and 2010 about 20 million immigrants entered the United States. The largest number of these immigrants came from Latin America and Asia.

E. MAKING COMPARISONS: THE NEW DEAL AND THE GREAT SOCIETY

1. Both the New Deal and the Great Society used the power of the federal government to promote social justice, fight poverty, and solve social problems. As a result, both programs led to an increase in federal spending for social services. And finally, both the New Deal and the Great Society supported the arts, encouraged housing construction, helped the elderly, and instituted government-sponsored employment programs.

2. The New Deal responded to an economic depression while the Great Society was enacted during a period of economic prosperity. Unlike the New Deal, the Great Society included landmark legislation protecting the civil liberties and voting rights of African Americans. While both programs fought poverty, the Great Society included a program providing preschool education for disadvantaged children.

VI. THE VIETNAM WAR, 1964–1967

A. CONTEXT

1. When Kennedy took the oath of office, about 900 American military advisers aided the South Vietnamese army. This minimal military presence failed to deter Viet Cong attacks designed to destabilize the South Vietnam government.

2. Distracted by Cold War crises in Berlin and Cuba, Kennedy hoped an additional 15,000 military advisors would buttress the South Vietnamese government. He planned to conduct a thorough review of America's commitment to South Vietnam when he returned from Dallas.

B. THE GULF OF TONKIN RESOLUTION

1. President Johnson inherited an increasingly dangerous situation in South Vietnam. On August 4, 1964, he received unsubstantiated reports that North Vietnamese gunboats had fired on two American destroyers patrolling in the Gulf of Tonkin. The next day, Johnson asked Congress to pass a resolution authorizing him to take "all necessary measures to repel any armed attack against the forces of the United States and to prevent further aggression." The House of Representatives unanimously supported the Gulf of Tonkin Resolution while just two Senators opposed it.

2. Johnson's handling of the Gulf of Tonkin affair seemed to be a major political success. Opinion polls showed that 72 percent of the American public supported his handling of the war in Vietnam. Very few people listened when Senator Wayne Morris, who voted against the resolution, warned: "We are in effect giving the President war-making powers in the absence of a declaration of war. I believe that to be a historic mistake."

C. ESCALATION

1. While LBJ focused on his Great Society legislation, the situation in South Vietnam continued to deteriorate. By the beginning of 1965, the Viet Cong controlled almost three-fourths of South Vietnam's land and over half its population. American observers all agreed that the nation would collapse within a short time.
2. LBJ vowed, "I am not going to be the President who saw Southeast Asia go the way China went." He therefore rejected the options of withdrawing the U.S. advisors or negotiating a peace settlement. Instead, in March 1965 he took the fateful step of choosing to dramatically escalate America's military commitment by sending combat troops to Vietnam.
3. When it became clear that North Vietnam could not be quickly defeated, Johnson poured more men and money into the war effort. By the end of 1967, about 500,000 American soldiers guarded South Vietnam's cities and patrolled its rice paddies. Search-and-destroy missions killed over 200,000 enemy soldiers, but left one-fourth of the people in South Vietnam homeless. The Viet Cong struck back with deadly ambushes and hidden booby-traps. About 16,000 American soldiers lost their lives between 1965 and 1967.

D. HAWKS VERSUS DOVES

1. When President Johnson escalated the war about two-thirds of the public approved his decision. Known as "hawks," they argued that America was fighting a just cause to defend freedom in South Vietnam. Without American help, South Vietnam would collapse and communist oppression would spread across all of Southeast Asia.
2. When the war did not end quickly, a growing number of people began to question the rationale for the Vietnam War. Known as "doves," critics argued the U.S. could not win a guerilla war in Asia. The tragic loss of life was too great. Instead of saving South Vietnam, American bombers were destroying it. The dollars spent

in Vietnam would be better spent funding Great Society programs to rebuild American cities and help the poor.

3. The increasingly bitter debate between the hawks and the doves divided America. A deeply ambivalent housewife expressed the public's mood of frustration when she told an interviewer, "I want to get out, but I don't want to give up."

APUSH test writers often use political cartoons to test your knowledge of the debate between the hawks and the doves. In addition, be prepared for a cartoon illustrating how the cost of the Vietnam War deprived Great Society programs of needed funding.

VII. TURNING POINTS IN AMERICAN HISTORY: THE COUNTERCULTURE

A. THE NEW LEFT

1. The civil rights movement inspired activist students at elite Big Ten and Ivy League universities. In 1962, members of the Students for a Democratic Society (SDS) held a national convention at Port Huron, Michigan. Tom Hayden wrote the "Port Huron Statement" expressing the group's disillusionment with materialistic values and Cold War policies.

2. The founders of the SDS referred to their movement as the New Left to distinguish themselves from "Old Left" communists and socialists during the 1930s. The New Left claimed liberals were doing too little to address racial and economic inequality.

B. ANTIWAR PROTESTS

1. Although most college students did not share the New Left's radical political views, they did participate in the national debate between the hawks and the doves.

2. As the Vietnam War escalated, college professors organized teach-ins to discuss American policy in Vietnam. The teach-ins convinced many students that the Vietnam War was immoral. Soon thousands of students began to organize antiwar demonstrations across America.

C. THE HIPPIES

1. The students' most significant impact occurred outside their university campuses and antiwar protests. A number of young people called hippies believed love, not war, provided the real solution to America's problems. Hippies argued that this could only be accomplished by creating a new alternative lifestyle or counterculture.

2. Raised in the most prosperous society the world had ever known, hippies nonetheless rejected the values of hard work, neat appearance, and economic success taught by their parents. Instead, the new counterculture emphasized the importance of being "groovy" by "doing your own thing." Being groovy meant wearing long hair, jeans, sandals, and love beads instead of business suits and dresses.

3. Hippies believed they were leading America into a new age of harmony and understanding. A "summer of love" in San Francisco's Haight-Ashbury district in 1967 attracted thousands of "flower children" to a "love-in" featuring sexual freedom, drugs, and communal living.

4. Arlo Guthrie, a popular hippie singer, confidently predicted, "Peace is on the way. People are simply gonna learn that they can get more by being groovy than by being greedy." In fact, the struggle between flower power in San Francisco and firepower in Vietnam had only just begun.

D. THE IMPACT OF THE COUNTERCULTURE

1. The counterculture challenged traditional values boasting that it represented a new generation with a new explanation. In many ways the counterculture became the culture as the hippies' rejection of traditional values and lack of trust of authority figures became important strands in the national mind. In addition, the counterculture's commitment to liberation inspired both the women's movement and the gay rights movement.

2. The counterculture stunned and repelled Americans who embraced the nation's traditional values. Soon to be called "the great silent majority," these Americans became part of a cultural and political backlash that rejuvenated the conservative movement and ultimately played a key role in the election of Ronald Reagan in 1980.

Don't neglect the counterculture. The APUSH Framework specifically identifies it as a key movement in the 1960s. The counterculture could generate a challenging continuity-and-change-over-time long-essay question.

VIII. BLACK POWER

A. THE LONG HOT SUMMERS

1. While the hippies preached love and peace, inner cities across America burst into flames. During the long hot summers from 1965 to 1967, civil unrest scarred cities and towns across America. The riots in 1967 claimed 43 lives in Detroit and 26 in Newark, New Jersey while leaving 1,800 injured people in 23 other cities.
2. The riots focused attention on African Americans living in inner city ghettoes in the North and on the West Coast. The civil rights movement and the War on Poverty raised hopes that could not be quickly fulfilled. The Civil Rights and Voting Rights Acts addressed Jim Crow discrimination in the South, but failed to improve the daily lives of unemployed inner-city residents in the North who lived in deteriorating housing while their children attended failing schools.

B. THE KERNER COMMISSION REPORT

1. The mounting civil unrest alarmed the nation and prompted President Johnson to appoint a special commission to investigate the causes of the 1967 riots and provide recommendations for future actions. Led by Governor Otto Kerner of Illinois, the 11-member commission released its report on February 29, 1968.
2. The Kerner Commission concluded that the migration of middle-class families to suburbs left impoverished inner city neighborhoods. The commission bluntly warned that, "Our nation is moving toward two societies, one black, one white—separate and unequal." It called for massive government spending programs to fight poverty by building new housing, improving schools, and training unemployed workers for new jobs.
3. The Kerner Commission failed to achieve its objectives. Unwilling to shift scarce resources from the Vietnam War to social reform, President Johnson chose to ignore the report. At the same time, conservatives called for a renewed emphasis upon restoring law and order.

C. STOKELY CARMICHAEL

1. The riots shook the civil rights movement's confidence in peaceful reform. Following the assassination of Malcolm X in 1965, Stokely Carmichael became the best-known militant black leader. Carmichael expressed growing impatience with Dr. King's nonviolent marches when he boldly called for "black power." Carmichael's transition from a leader of SNCC to the black power movement represents an important change over time as part of the civil rights movement and highlights the historical complexity of the era.

2. As expressed by Carmichael, black power meant that African Americans should control their own communities by developing black-owned businesses and electing black public officials. Carmichael's call for black power captured the imagination of inner city black youths while alarming the general public.

IX. 1968

A. THE TET OFFENSIVE

1. On January 31, 1968, the first day of the Vietnamese New Year (Tet), Viet Cong and North Vietnamese forces attacked over one hundred cities, villages, and military bases across Vietnam. Although U.S. and South Vietnamese forces regained the initiative and won a military victory, the heavy fighting undermined President Johnson's confident prediction that "victory was just around the corner."

2. As LBJ's credibility and popularity sank, senators Eugene McCarthy and Robert Kennedy launched campaigns to challenge him for the Democratic presidential nomination. Their campaigns inspired antiwar activists and placed enormous pressure on the beleaguered president.

B. JOHNSON'S SURPRISE ANNOUNCEMENTS

1. President Johnson felt increasingly bitter and isolated. On March 31, 1968, he announced a series of shocking decisions. He rejected General Westmoreland's request for 206,000 more troops and instead ordered a halt to the bombing of North Vietnam. He also called upon the leaders of North Vietnam to begin peace talks.

2. Johnson then paused and told the nation his final decision: "I have decided that I shall not seek, and will not accept the nomination of my party for another term as your President."

C. TWO ASSASSINATIONS

1. Four days after President Johnson's speech, a man later identified as James Earl Ray shot and killed Dr. King as the civil rights leader stood on a balcony near his motel room in Memphis, Tennessee. Ray's motives for the crime remain unknown.
2. The news of Dr. King's death touched off a wave of violent riots. Many African Americans, Hispanics, and working-class Americans looked to Robert Kennedy for leadership. Backed by these groups, Kennedy defeated McCarthy in the crucial California primary.
3. On June 5, 1968, an already shaken nation watched in stunned disbelief as Kennedy was shot and killed after he thanked his triumphant supporters for their help. The assassin was an Arab nationalist named Sirhan Sirhan who opposed Kennedy's support for Israel.

D. THE DIVIDED DEMOCRATS

1. The deeply divided Democratic Party met in Chicago where they nominated Vice President Hubert Humphrey for President. However, violent antiwar demonstrations marred Humphrey's nomination. The spectacle of police firing tear gas at demonstrators badly tarnished the Humphrey campaign.
2. The Democrats faced another divisive challenge when Alabama Governor George C. Wallace ran as a third-party candidate. Wallace threatened to take away many traditional Democratic votes by appealing to working-class Americans who were upset by the urban riots and antiwar demonstrations.

E. AND THEN THERE WAS NIXON

1. While the shocking events of 1968 dominated the news, Richard Nixon staged a remarkable political comeback. Nixon believed that most Americans were tired of hippies, antiwar demonstrators, and urban rioters. He carefully avoided controversy while promising he had a plan to find an honorable end to the Vietnam War.
2. Nixon easily won the Republican Party's presidential nomination. On Election Day, Nixon won a solid majority of the electoral votes while winning a narrow margin of the popular votes. Richard Nixon now assumed the burden of ending the Vietnam War and reuniting a badly divided country.

THE 1970s

I. MINORITY LIBERATION MOVEMENTS

A. CONTEXT

1. The civil rights movement created a climate of protest that inspired other discontented minority groups.
2. During the late 1960s and throughout the 1970s, Native Americans, Hispanics, and gays all formed movements demanding that America address their grievances.

B. NATIVE AMERICANS

1. In 1970, the Native American population numbered about 800,000 people. Largely ignored by the rest of the country, Native Americans comprised the nation's least prosperous and least healthy group. For example, they suffered from an unemployment rate ten times the national average and had an average lifespan of just forty-six, twenty years less than the national average.
2. In 1968, a group of young militant Native Americans embraced the concept of "Red Power" by forming the American Indian Movement (AIM). Inspired by the Black Power movement, AIM activists staged protests designed to draw attention to tribal grievances. For example, in November 1969 a group of American Indians began a 19-month occupation of the abandoned federal prison on Alcatraz Island in San Francisco Bay. The prolonged occupation demonstrated a resurgence of Native American pride.
3. In February 1973, AIM staged a dramatic and symbolic takeover of the village of Wounded Knee, site of the infamous 1890 massacre of Sioux by federal troops. AIM used the 71-day standoff with federal authorities to demand changes in the administration of the Pine Ridge Reservation.
4. The Native American demonstrations gained publicity and achieved concrete results. For example, the Nixon administration supported the Indian Education Act providing federal funds for new schools that would be under tribal control.

C. HISPANIC AMERICANS

1. Hispanics are a large and diverse group that includes migrants from Puerto Rico, Cuba, Central America, and Mexico. The 1960 census reported 3 million Hispanics living in the United States, the great majority of whom were Mexican Americans. This number grew to 9.6 million in 1970 and to 14.5 million in 1980.
2. Delano, California, is a major agricultural community where growers produce half the world's supply of table grapes. In 1962, Cesar Chavez and Dolores Huerta co-founded the National Farm Workers Association (NFWA), which later became better known as the United Farm Workers (UFW), to represent the thousands of vineyard workers. Three years later, they began the Delano Grape Strike against growers who refused to recognize the UFW.
3. Chavez vowed "to resist with every ounce of human endurance and spirit." Inspired by Dr. King's nonviolent tactics, Chavez staged a 28-day hunger strike, led peaceful protest marches, and appealed for a nationwide boycott of grapes. Pressured by a boycott that grew to include 17 million consumers, growers signed a contract recognizing the UFW.
4. Like their Native American and African American counterparts, young Mexican Americans became more militant. In 1969, fifteen hundred Mexican students met in Denver to formulate a more aggressive political and cultural agenda. They proclaimed a new term, *Chicano*, to replace *Mexican American*, and later organized a political party, La Raza Unita (The United Race), to promote such Chicano goals as bilingual education and Chicano studies programs.

D. GAY AMERICANS

1. During the 1960s, most states defined homosexuality as an immoral and illegal activity. Police used vice laws to harass and arrest gay men and lesbians.
2. The Stonewall Inn was a popular gay bar in New York City's Greenwich Village. Police officers raided the inn during the early morning hours of June 28, 1969. The raids provoked spontaneous demonstrations calling for an end to police harassment.
3. The Stonewall Riots played a key role in sparking the modern Gay Liberation Movement. One year later, thousands of people marched in New York City's Gay Pride Parade. By 1973 there were about 800 gay organizations across the country.

4. The Gay Liberation Movement won a number of significant victories during the 1970s. For example, in 1973 the board of the American Psychiatric Association voted to remove homosexuality from its list of mental illnesses. Four years later, Harvey Milk became the first openly gay person elected to public office in California, when he won a seat on the San Francisco Board of Supervisors.

The APUSH Framework specifically identifies the American Indian, Hispanic, and gay movements as key developments during the 1970s. Be sure to carefully review the leaders, goals, and achievements of each of these movements.

II. THE WOMEN'S RIGHTS MOVEMENT: THE SECOND WAVE

A. CONTEXT

1. During the early 1960s, the average housewife spent 55 hours a week on domestic chores. Betty Friedan's research indicated that this endless routine of housework deeply frustrated college-educated housewives. Friedan expressed this frustration in her book *The Feminine Mystique.*

2. *The Feminine Mystique* sold 3 million copies and helped spark a "second wave" of the American feminist movement. Inspired by Friedan, a new generation of women took up the call for gender equality.

3. The public's response to *The Feminine Mystique* was not the only factor responsible for the revival of the feminist movement. The spirit of protest that energized the civil rights, anti-war, and minority liberation movements also served as a catalyst for discontented women.

B. THE NATIONAL ORGANIZATION FOR WOMEN (NOW)

1. Title VII of the 1964 Civil Rights Act outlawed sexual discrimination in employment, but much work remained to be done. Employers routinely paid women lower salaries than men and often denied them opportunities to advance.

2. In 1966, twenty-eight women's rights activists created the National Organization for Women (NOW) "to bring American women into full participation in the mainstream of American society NOW."

3. With Friedan as its first president, NOW challenged sexual discrimination in the workplace, funded suits for equal wages, lobbied companies to provide day care for infant children, and demanded an end to want ads appearing in sex-segregated newspaper columns.

C. RADICAL FEMINISM

1. A younger, more radical group of feminists challenged NOW's leadership. Radical feminists argued "assumptions of male supremacy are as . . . crippling to women as assumptions of white supremacy are to the Negro."
2. Radical feminists vowed to eradicate sexism and promote "women's liberation." Militant feminists focused on personal issues such as reproductive rights, domestic violence, and the objectification of women as sexual objects.

D. FEMINIST SUCCESSES

1. Title IX of the 1972 Higher Education Act required schools to give equal opportunities to women in admissions and athletics. In 1970, just 15 percent of women participated in intercollegiate sports. Ten years later the rate of participation doubled to 30 percent.
2. In its landmark 1973 decision in *Roe v. Wade,* the Supreme Court ruled that abortion is protected by the right to privacy implied by the Bill of Rights.
3. Women broke through a number of employment barriers. For example, America saw its first female firefighters, railroad engineers, airline pilots, and construction workers. In politics, Connecticut's Ella Grasso became the first elected woman governor of a state.
4. During the 1970s all five military academies enrolled women. By 1980, very few all-male colleges remained. One student accurately reflected the shift in attitudes when he concluded, "Life is coed, school should be also."

E. THE EQUAL RIGHTS AMENDMENT

1. In 1972, Congress passed the Equal Rights Amendment (ERA) and then sent it on to the states for ratification. The amendment stated that, "Equality of rights under the law shall not be denied or abridged by the United States or by any State on account of sex."
2. The ERA quickly passed in 35 of the 38 state legislatures needed for ratification. However, opponents led by Phyllis Schlafly mounted

a successful campaign to block the ERA. The defeat of the ERA marked a significant setback for the women's rights movement.

F. MAKING CONNECTIONS: WOMEN'S RIGHTS MOVEMENTS, 1890–1920 AND 1960–1980

1. Middle-class white women dominated the women's movements in both periods. Women in both eras formed organizations to promote feminist agendas. For example, both the National American Woman Suffrage Association (NAWSA) and the National Organization for Women (NOW) worked to increase women's access to higher education and to professional schools.
2. During the period from 1890 to 1920, the women's rights movement successfully focused its energies on winning passage of the Nineteenth Amendment granting women suffrage. In contrast, during the 1960s and 1970s the women's rights movement failed to achieve passage of the Equal Rights Amendment.

III. THE ENVIRONMENTAL MOVEMENT

A. *SILENT SPRING*, 1962

1. During the 1950s, most biologists accepted the prevailing view that DDT and other chemical pesticides were useful tools to eradicate mosquitoes and other harmful insect pests. However, an American marine biologist named Rachel Carson conducted research indicating that DDT and other chemicals were in fact having an inimical effect upon the nation's wildlife.
2. Carson published her findings in *Silent Spring*, a groundbreaking book that helped launch the environmental movement.

B. ENVIRONMENTAL DISASTERS

1. In January 1969, an oil rig explosion in the Santa Barbara Channel turned miles of pristine Southern California beaches into an environmental nightmare killing thousands of seabirds and marine animals. Just six months later an oil slick on the Cuyahoga River in Cleveland, Ohio, caught fire and burned two railroad bridges.
2. These two highly publicized disasters alarmed the public. On April 22, 1970, over 20 million concerned citizens participated in the nation's first annual Earth Day. Fully 70 percent of the public ranked the environment as America's most pressing problem.

C. CONGRESS RESPONDS

1. Congress responded to the public outcry by enacting a far-reaching program of environmental legislation. The Clean Air Act set strict standards to reduce automobile and factory emissions. The Water Pollution Control Act provided funds to protect America's sea coasts and clean up its neglected rivers and lakes. The Endangered Species Act protected rare plants and animals from extinction.
2. In addition to these measures the Nixon administration banned the use of DDT and created the Environmental Protection Agency (EPA) to enforce a range of environmental guidelines.

The debate over natural resources and environmental policies has generated a number of test questions. Be prepared for a possible long-essay or DBQ testing your knowledge of environmental issues during the 1970s.

IV. THE VIETNAM WAR, 1969–1975

A. VIETNAMIZATION

1. Nixon inherited a difficult situation in Vietnam. He found himself squeezed between an impatient public at home and an intransigent enemy abroad.
2. Nixon and his National Security Advisor, Dr. Henry Kissinger, developed a "two-track" strategy to end American involvement and prevent the North Vietnamese from conquering South Vietnam. First, they would continue peace negotiations. Second, they began a policy called Vietnamization whereby Nixon gradually withdrew American troops, leaving the burden of fighting to the South Vietnamese.
3. Nixon appealed to "the great silent majority" of Americans to support his policies. The silent majority included "non-shouters and non-demonstrators" who often lived in Sun Belt states. This conservative group formed the core of a new Republican coalition of voters.

B. CAMBODIA AND KENT STATE

1. Nixon's strategy of Vietnamization appeared to be working. Then, on April 30, 1970, Nixon surprised the nation by sending American

ground troops into Cambodia. The president explained that enemy forces used bases inside Cambodia to launch raids on South Vietnam. Nixon insisted the bases had to be destroyed to enable more American forces to leave Vietnam.

2. Nixon's announcement stunned the nation. Outraged doves questioned the President's strategy of shortening the war by escalating it. Skepticism turned to anger as indignant college students protested the Cambodian invasion.

3. Police and the National Guard were called upon to maintain order on some college campuses. Then, on March 4, 1970, tragedy struck at Kent State University in Ohio. Frightened National Guard soldiers opened fire on demonstrators, killing four student bystanders.

4. News of the Kent State shootings ignited a tidal wave of protests as over 400 colleges closed or suspended exams and almost 100,000 antiwar demonstrators staged a protest march in Washington. Nixon later wrote, "Those few days after Kent State were among the darkest of my presidency."

C. THE PARIS PEACE ACCORDS

1. After three more years of bloody fighting and intense U.S. bombing, the peace negotiations between Henry Kissinger and the North Vietnamese reached a conclusion. On January 23, 1973, President Nixon announced that an agreement had been reached "to end the war and bring peace with honor to Vietnam and Southeast Asia."

2. The Paris Peace Accords called for the U.S. to withdraw its remaining 23,700 troops and advisors within 60 days. In return, the North Vietnamese would release almost 600 American prisoners of war. The agreement left the South Vietnamese government in power, but permitted almost 150,000 North Vietnamese troops to remain in South Vietnam.

D. THE FALL OF SAIGON

1. Nixon assured the South Vietnamese government that the United States would "respond with full force should the settlement be violated by North Vietnam." But the 1973 War Powers Act prevented Nixon from keeping his promise. Passed over Nixon's veto, the legislation requires the President to notify Congress within 48 hours of committing armed forces to military action and forbids American troops from remaining for more than 60 days without Congressional authorization. At the same time,

the ongoing Watergate scandal weakened Nixon and led to his resignation.

2. The North Vietnamese recognized that America would no longer take forceful action to protect South Vietnam. In March 1975, they launched a powerful armored invasion of South Vietnam. As the North Vietnamese advanced upon Saigon, helicopters rescued the last remaining Americans. The South Vietnamese government surrendered on April 30, 1975.

E. UNDERSTANDING CAUSATION: CONSEQUENCES OF THE VIETNAM WAR

1. The Vietnam War claimed a staggering death toll. More than 58,000 U.S. troops died and another 300,000 were wounded. The war killed an estimated 2 million Vietnamese civilians, 1.1 million North Vietnamese troops, and 200,000 South Vietnamese soldiers.
2. The war played a key role in the Nixon administration's decision to replace the draft with an all-volunteer military force.
3. The massive bombing campaigns left both North and South Vietnam in ruins. The U.S. Army's use of herbicides such as Agent Orange devastated Vietnam's natural environment.
4. The war created widespread public distrust of the U.S. government. For example, the publication of the *Pentagon Papers* in 1971 confirmed suspicions that the Johnson administration had deliberately misled the public about America's reasons for escalating the war.
5. The polarizing public debate over the war divided families, friends, and eventually the entire nation. It shattered the liberal consensus supporting the Great Society. In addition, the Vietnam War helped fuel the conservative resurgence supported by the rising influence of the silent majority.
6. The Vietnam War created skepticism about international involvements called the "Vietnam Syndrome." Many Americans questioned foreign entanglements that might lead to "another Vietnam."

V. NIXON AND THE COLD WAR

A. CONTEXT

1. During the years after World War II, American leaders divided the world into two rival blocks of nations—the Communist World and

the Free World. As the leader of the Free World, the U.S. attempted to contain Soviet expansion and isolate the People's Republic of China (PRC).

2. Nixon and Kissinger believed that time had come to pursue bold foreign policy initiatives that would reshape global politics. On July 15, 1971, Nixon stunned the world by announcing he would accept an invitation to visit the PRC in February 1972.

B. OPENING TIES TO CHINA

1. Nixon's historic trip marked the first time a U.S. president had visited the PRC. For eight days and nights, enthralled American television audiences watched as Nixon met with Chairman Mao Zedong, exchanged toasts with Premier Zhou Enlai, and visited the Great Wall.
2. At the end of his visit Nixon proudly proclaimed, "This was the week that changed the world." His visit ended a quarter of a century of separation between the U.S. and China. In a joint statement known as the Shanghai Communiqué, the two countries promised to begin new relations in trade, travel, and cultural exchanges.

C. MAKING CONNECTIONS: U.S.–CHINESE RELATIONS

1. As Nixon's visit ended, Premier Zhou Enlai predicted, "The gates of friendship have been opened." Subsequent years did witness a growth and widening of ties between the U.S. and China. For example, the two countries established full diplomatic relations in 1979.
2. Today America's relationship with China is characterized by the simultaneous existence of friendship and friction. Cultural ties include 235,000 Chinese students currently studying in American colleges and universities. Economic ties have dramatically expanded as China is now the largest foreign holder of U.S. debt. Nonetheless, tensions still exist on issues such as cybersecurity, tariffs, human rights, and Chinese military ambitions in the South China Sea.

D. ESTABLISHING DÉTENTE WITH THE SOVIET UNION

1. Three months after returning from China, Nixon stunned the world again by becoming the first American president to visit Moscow. During the seven-day summit, Nixon and Soviet Premier Leonid Brezhnev agreed upon a joint space mission and signed a Strategic Arms Limitation Treaty. Although the SALT I agreement did not end

the nuclear arms race, it did place limitations on both the number of intercontinental ballistic missiles and the construction of anti-ballistic missile systems.

2. The SALT I treaty signaled the beginning of a new period of détente or relaxed tensions between the two rival superpowers.

VI. ECONOMIC AND POLITICAL SHOCKS

A. THE ARAB OIL EMBARGO

1. On October 6, 1973, Egypt and Syria attacked Israel on Yom Kippur, the holiest day of the Jewish year. Although American military aid enabled Israel to prevail, the effects of the war continued.
2. Nixon's decision to help Israel angered many oil-rich nations. As the most important members of the Organization of Petroleum Exporting Countries (OPEC), they had the power to reduce the supply of oil and raise prices. On October 20,1973, they chose to do both.
3. The Arab oil embargo quickly disrupted daily life across the United States. Motorists who had assumed that gasoline would always be cheap and plentiful found themselves waiting in long gas lines, forming carpools, and watching helplessly as gas prices nearly doubled.
4. The effects of the energy crisis did not end with the resumption of oil shipments in April 1974. The oil embargo marked the end of the post–World War II economic boom and the beginning of an inflationary spiral that plagued the U.S. economy during the rest of the 1970s and into the early 1980s.

B. WATERGATE SCANDAL

1. On June 17, 1972, police arrested five burglars who had broken into the headquarters of the Democratic National Committee at the Watergate apartment and office complex in Washington, D.C.
2. President Nixon was never directly implicated in the Watergate break-in. However, instead of firing the corrupt officials responsible for the crime, he chose to "play it tough" and attempt to cover up the scandal. Two months after the break-in, Nixon announced that a "complete investigation" found "no one in the White House staff, no one in this administration, presently employed, was involved in this very bizarre incident." Nixon was lying. Evidence from

secret White House tapes later revealed a "smoking gun" proving that Nixon ordered the CIA to stop the FBI from investigating the Watergate break-in. This constituted a clear example of deliberate obstruction of justice.

3. The House Judiciary Committee ultimately voted to recommend that Nixon be impeached. On August 9, 1974, Richard Nixon became the first president to resign from office. Vice President Gerald Ford then became the nation's 38th president. "My fellow Americans," Ford reassured, "our long national nightmare is over." Ford later pardoned Nixon to great public uproar.

C. UNDERSTANDING CAUSATION: CONSEQUENCES OF WATERGATE

1. The Watergate crisis demonstrated that the Constitution's system of checks and balances worked!
2. But Watergate also undermined public confidence in America's political leadership. Many questioned the government's ability to solve pressing economic and social problems.
3. In the short run, Nixon's resignation created a national desire for new leadership that helped elect Jimmy Carter in 1976.
4. Nixon's resignation also created a power vacuum in the Republican Party that a revitalized conservative movement, led by Ronald Reagan, soon filled.

VII. THE CARTER PRESIDENCY, 1977–1981

A. STAGFLATION

1. Carter began his presidency with high hopes. However, he soon faced a seemingly intractable economic problem. The American economy was simultaneously experiencing a combination of double-digit inflation and rising unemployment. Economists called this unusual phenomenon stagflation.
2. Stagflation had at least two deep-rooted causes. First, President Johnson attempted to pay for both the Vietnam War and the Great Society without raising taxes, thus creating strong inflationary pressures. Second, the U.S. economy had become dangerously dependent upon inexpensive imported oil. The OPEC price increases played a significant role in driving up the cost of everything from gasoline to groceries.

B. THE CAMP DAVID ACCORDS

1. President Carter pursued an idealistic foreign policy. He promised to defend human rights, pledging that his actions would be guided by "fairness not force."

2. Carter's commitment to patient negotiating achieved a dramatic breakthrough in Middle East diplomacy. In September 1978, he invited Egyptian President Anwar Sadat and Israeli Prime Minister Menachem Begin to meet with him at Camp David, the presidential retreat in Maryland. After 13 days of tense negotiations, a beaming Carter announced that the two sides had reached a historic peace agreement. Under the terms of the Camp David Accords, Israel agreed to return the Sinai Peninsula to Egypt and the two nations pledged to sign a peace treaty ending thirty years of hostility.

C. THE IRAN HOSTAGE CRISIS

1. The Camp David Accords marked Carter's greatest triumph. Within a year, events in Iran plunged the Carter presidency into a crisis it was unable to successfully resolve. On November 4, 1979, a mob stormed the American embassy in Tehran and took more than 50 Americans hostage. After months of futile negotiations, Carter authorized a secret rescue mission that failed.

2. The Iranian hostage crisis, double-digit inflation, and the continued rise in energy prices seriously weakened Carter's popularity. Opinion polls reported less than 25 percent of the public approved his leadership.

D. THE ELECTION OF 1980

1. During the 1980 presidential campaign, the Republican candidate Ronald Reagan repeatedly asked the American people to answer one question: "Are you better off now than you were four years ago?"

2. On Election Day, voters overwhelmingly answered "no." Reagan and his running mate, George H. W. Bush, won a landslide victory.

UNIT 9 PERIOD 9
1980–PRESENT

KEY CONCEPTS

KEY CONCEPT 9.1
A newly ascendant conservative movement achieved several political and policy goals during the 1980s and continued to strongly influence public discourse in the following decades.

KEY CONCEPT 9.2
Moving into the 21st century, the nation experienced significant technological, economic, and demographic changes.

KEY CONCEPT 9.3
The end of the Cold War and new challenges to U.S. leadership forced the nation to redefine its foreign policy and role in the world.

THE REAGAN–BUSH ERA 1980–1992

Chapter 30

I. REAGAN AND THE CONSERVATIVE RESURGENCE

A. CONTEXT

1. Lyndon Johnson crushed Barry Goldwater in the 1964 presidential election. LBJ's overwhelming victory seemed to usher in a new age of liberal dominance and conservative retreat.

2. Despite surface appearances, an unanticipated series of historic events and demographic forces revived the conservative movement. By the 1980 presidential election, a previously unconnected coalition of Sun Belt conservatives, evangelical Christians, and blue-collar "Reagan Democrats" converged to elect Ronald Reagan.

B. THE RISE OF THE SUN BELT

1. First recognized during the 1950s and '60s, the population and influence of the Sun Belt continued to grow during the 1970s. Led by California, Florida, and Texas, the Sun Belt's population surged past the older industrial regions in the North and East.

2. The Sun Belt states included a prosperous suburban population voicing increasingly strong opposition to intrusive government regulations and rising taxes. The Sun Belt conservatives formed what historian Lisa McGirr calls "the ground forces of the conservative revival."

3. The Electoral College reflected the Sun Belt's rising political power. For example, California's number of electoral votes rose from 32 in 1960 to 45 in 1980, the most of any state.

C. THE RISE OF THE NEW RIGHT

1. During the 1964 presidential campaign, Barry Goldwater argued that the liberal welfare state created by the New Deal should be reversed. Goldwater's message survived his defeat. While New Left activists criticized the Great Society for not being bold enough,

conservative political activists decried the program for enlarging the welfare state.

2. Political observers called the growing conservative movement the New Right. By 1980, New Right political operatives honed a message calling for states' rights, a more limited federal government, and free-market economic policies.

D. THE RISE OF THE RELIGIOUS RIGHT

1. The counterculture's attack on traditional values, the newly vocal gay rights movement, and the assertiveness of radical feminists all alarmed evangelical Christians. In addition to these concerns, two key Supreme Court decisions mobilized what became known as the Religious Right. In *Engel v. Vitale* (1962), the Court ruled that local officials violated the separation of church and state by composing a school prayer and encouraging its recitation in the public schools. Eleven years later, in *Roe v. Wade,* the Court guaranteed women the right to an abortion.
2. By the mid-1970s, over a quarter of adult Americans identified themselves as born-again Christians. Led by Jerry Falwell and Pat Robertson, a new generation of evangelical ministers used popular television programs to voice the growing perception that the erosion of traditional values was causing a serious moral decline. In 1979, Falwell formed the Moral Majority to advance the conservative agenda and defeat liberal politicians.

E. THE RISE OF REAGAN

1. Ronald Reagan was born in 1911 in rural Illinois. He graduated from Eureka College and then worked as a radio announcer and sportscaster before beginning a Hollywood movie career. Although never a major star, Reagan did perform in fifty-three movies between 1937 and 1953. These years in front of a camera helped Reagan develop a comfortable stage presence that would become a political asset during the age of television.
2. When Reagan's movie career ended, he became the genial host of the popular television program *The General Electric Theater.* As the voice of the General Electric Company, Reagan's political views shifted to the right.
3. In 1964, Reagan delivered a forceful television speech on behalf of Barry Goldwater. The speech established Reagan as a rising leader in the conservative movement. In 1966, he won the first of two terms as governor of California. Reagan's promise to restore order

at the Berkeley University campus placed him in the forefront of the reaction against the counterculture.

4. In the 1980 presidential campaign, Reagan offered voters an optimistic vision of America's future. His self-assurance and solid conservative credentials united a victorious coalition that swept him to an overwhelming victory. The new president confidently called upon America to "begin an era of national renewal."

The conservative resurgence has already generated multiple-choice questions and a DBQ. Be prepared to answer a short-answer or long-essay question on this important Framework topic.

II. REAGAN'S ECONOMIC PROGRAM

A. CONTEXT

1. President Reagan inherited a combination of rising unemployment and inflation known as stagflation. Less then three weeks after taking office, he told the nation, "We're in the worst economic mess since the Great Depression."

2. Reagan opposed the use of a New Deal-type program to revive the economy. Instead, he reversed generations of progressive thought by declaring, "Government is not the solution to our problems. Government is the problem."

B. REAGANOMICS

1. Reagan called upon Congress to sharply reduce government funding of social and welfare programs. He argued that these cuts would help curb federal spending and fight inflation. Reagan also asked Congress to enact a three-year 25 percent cut in personal and corporate tax rates.

2. Reagan believed these tax cuts would stimulate economic growth. According to supply-side economic theory, falling tax rates would encourage consumers to buy more goods and corporations to hire more workers.

3. Reporters promptly labeled the president's supply-side economic program Reaganomics. Reagan skillfully used television speeches to build public support for his program. The president's success

earned him the nickname the "Great Communicator." Within a few months, Congress passed Reagan's budget and tax cuts.

C. UNDERSTANDING CAUSATION: CONSEQUENCES OF REAGANOMICS

1. Reaganomics failed to produce immediate results. Instead of reviving, the economy sank into a steep recession as unemployment climbed to over 10 percent. Despite the difficult beginning, Reagan urged the public "to stay the course."
2. Reagan's confidence proved to be justified. America enjoyed a sustained period of economic growth from 1982 to 1988. During this time the economy added more than 17 million jobs and inflation dropped to single digits.
3. However, Reaganomics also produced troubling long-term problems. Despite deep cuts in social programs, federal spending continued to escalate as the defense budget soared to new heights to counter the perceived Soviet threat. Because of Reagan's massive tax cuts, the government took in less money and had to borrow heavily to pay its bills. Under Reagan, the national debt of the United States tripled from about $900 billion to $2.6 trillion. Once the world's biggest lender, the United States had become its largest debtor.

III. REAGAN AND THE COLD WAR

A. CONTEXT

1. Reagan became president at a particularly pivotal time in the Cold War. Détente failed to deter Soviet aggression. In late 1979, the Red Army invaded Afghanistan to support a pro-Soviet puppet government. The following year, Polish workers formed an independent labor union called Solidarity. Led by Lech Walesa, Solidarity demanded greater freedom for the Polish people. Instead of permitting a more open society, Polish authorities, backed by Moscow, arrested Walesa and abolished Solidarity.
2. Reagan refused to accept the widespread belief that the Cold War was a permanent geopolitical reality and that the Soviet Union was an indestructible adversary. He had a deep aversion for communism, believing it denied basic human rights. Even more importantly, Reagan had a life-long conviction that the United States was an exceptional nation with a mission to use its power and influence to advance the cause of freedom.

B. THE "EVIL EMPIRE"

1. The collapse of détente chilled relations between the United States and the Soviet Union. Shortly after taking office, President Reagan charged that the Soviets were aggressors who "reserve unto themselves the right to commit any crime, to lie, and to cheat." Using a well-known term from the popular *Star Wars* movie series, he later called the Soviet Union "an evil empire" responsible for the renewal of Cold War tensions.

2. The Soviet actions in Afghanistan and Poland convinced many Americans that the United States needed a much more aggressive approach in the Cold War. The Reagan Doctrine met this need by pledging the United States would oppose the global influence of the Soviet Union by supporting anti-communist movements. For example, the Reagan administration supplied Afghan fighters with sophisticated anti-aircraft Stinger missiles. The president also sent U.S. troops into the small Caribbean island nation of Grenada to oust a pro-Marxist government that appeared to be forging ties with Russian and Cuba.

3. The Reagan Doctrine led to a massive military buildup. Between 1980 and 1985, U.S. defense budgets increased from $144 billion to $295 billion. In 1983, President Reagan proposed a Strategic Defense Initiative as an added check on Soviet nuclear capability. Reagan envisioned creating a space-based missile defense system capable of striking down nuclear missiles before they could reach the United States. The press promptly called Reagan's plan "Star Wars," by then a popular cultural reference point.

C. "NEW THINKING"

1. Reagan's military buildup forced the Soviets into an expensive arms race they could not afford. Mikhail Gorbachev, the new Soviet leader, concluded his country's troubled economy could no longer bear the cost of an accelerating arms race with the United States. Shortly after taking power in 1985, he announced his intention to pursue a foreign policy based on "new thinking."

2. Reagan's assertive policies did not rule out tactical flexibility. He tested Gorbachev's commitment to stressing diplomacy over force in a series of five summit meetings. In December 1987, Gorbachev became the first Soviet leader in 14 years to visit the United States. The two leaders opened a new era in superpower relations by signing the Intermediate Nuclear Forces (INF) Treaty banning nuclear missiles with ranges of 300 to 3,400 miles. This marked the first time Washington and Moscow agreed to eliminate an entire class of nuclear weapons.

D. MAKING CONNECTIONS: PRESIDENTIAL SPEECHES AT THE BERLIN WALL

1. On June 26, 1963, President Kennedy delivered a speech in West Berlin in which he resolutely proclaimed, "All free men, wherever they may live, are citizens of Berlin, and therefore, as a free man, I take pride in the words, 'Ich bin ein Berliner.'" Kennedy's speech underscored America's support for West Berlin just 22 months after the construction of the Berlin Wall.

2. On June 12, 1987, President Reagan delivered a speech in West Berlin in which he resolutely proclaimed, "Mr. Gorbachev, tear down this wall!" Reagan's speech underscored America's support for freedom and human rights. Later in his speech, Reagan predicted the "[wall] cannot withstand faith; it cannot withstand truth. The wall cannot withstand freedom."

IV. BUSH AND THE END OF THE COLD WAR

A. CONTEXT

1. Vice President George H. W. Bush proved to be a strong presidential candidate. Supported by Sun Belt voters, he easily defeated Massachusetts Governor Michael Dukakis.

2. As Bush took office, the winds of change continued to sweep across Eastern Europe. The Polish government legalized Solidarity in April 1989. Just four months later, Polish voters elected a non-communist prime minister, marking the first time since the Russian Revolution a communist regime had been peacefully turned out of office.

B. "THE WALL IS GONE!"

1. A stunning series of historic events quickly followed the Polish elections. Emboldened by Gorbachev's refusal to use military force to support repressive Eastern European regimes, East Germans began holding huge protest demonstrations to demand freedom and democracy.

2. The unthinkable occurred on November 9, 1989, when a new East German leader opened the Berlin Wall. As an amazed world watched on television, jubilant Berliners slammed hammers into the wall, smashing the despised symbol of communist oppression into small concrete souvenirs. Less than one year later, the United States, Soviet Union, and the nations of Europe accepted German reunification.

C. THE COLLAPSE OF THE SOVIET UNION

1. The winds of change soon battered the Soviet Union. As central controls loosened, nationalist groups in the fourteen republics surrounding the Russian Republic demanded greater control over their internal affairs. Gorbachev watched helplessly as his authority weakened and his popularity plummeted.

2. On December 25, 1991, Gorbachev resigned his position as the leader of a country that ceased to exist. Fifteen independent republics, the largest of which was Russia, replaced the now defunct Soviet Union.

D. THE NEW WORLD ORDER

1. President Bush hailed the collapse of the Soviet Union as the beginning of what he called a "new world order."

2. Bush echoed ideas expressed by President Wilson during the First World War when he pledged to work for "a world in which freedom and respect for human rights find a home among all nations."

V. CRISIS IN THE PERSIAN GULF

A. CONTEXT

1. Cold War relations between the United States and the Soviet Union were often tense, but nonetheless stable. The Soviet Union left the United States as the world's only superpower. It also left the United States searching for a new foreign policy

2. President Bush wanted America to support a "new world order" based upon international cooperation. A crisis in the Persian Gulf tested this goal.

B. SADDAM HUSSEIN AND KUWAIT

1. On August 2, 1990, Iraqi President Saddam Hussein shocked the world by ordering his army to invade neighboring Kuwait. Catching the oil-rich emirate by surprise, Iraq's army easily overran Kuwait.

2. Conquering Kuwait was part of a much larger plan. Hussein dreamed of becoming the Middle East's most powerful Arab leader. Kuwait owned almost 10 percent of the world's proven oil reserves. Since Iraq also had 10 percent, taking Kuwait would double its oil

reserves. Hussein would then be in a position to intimidate Saudi Arabia and dominate the global oil market.

C. BUSH RESPONDS

1. President Bush recognized that the United States could not allow any nation to dominate the Persian Gulf and thus control the world's oil supply. He also argued that the United States had to stand up to Iraq to deter other would-be aggressors.
2. Bush successfully forged an international coalition to stop Hussein. The UN Security Council passed a resolution demanding that Iraq withdraw its forces by January 15, 1991. When Hussein refused, Bush ordered a massive air offensive called Operation Desert Storm that destroyed Iraq's air defense centers and cut its supply lines.
3. The ground assault began on February 24, 1991. In the largest land operation since World War II, coalition forces smashed through Iraqi defenses and liberated Kuwait.

D. AFTERMATH OF THE PERSIAN GULF WAR

1. Despite winning an overwhelming military victory, President Bush chose not to press for Hussein's removal from power. This decision would have fateful consequences a dozen years later.
2. Victory in the Persian Gulf War lifted Bush's approval rating to nearly 90 percent. However, Bush could not maintain this lofty level as dissatisfaction with his decision to raise taxes eroded public support. Helped along by a brief but sharp recession in 1990-91, Bill Clinton ended the Reagan-Bush era in the 1992 presidential election, returning the Democrats to the White House.

The Reagan presidency has generated questions on every APUSH exam. However, don't neglect to study the end of the Cold War and the beginning of a new world order under President George H.W. Bush.

KEY EVENTS AND TRENDS IN POST–COLD WAR AMERICA

1993–2001

I. THE CLINTON PRESIDENCY

A. NAFTA

1. President Clinton was a strong proponent of free trade. He successfully lobbied Congress to approve the North American Free Trade Agreement (NAFTA). The agreement united the U.S., Mexico, and Canada in a common market without trade barriers.
2. NAFTA critics warned that free trade would cost American workers their jobs as companies moved factories to Mexico. Once in Mexico, the factories hired inexpensive workers, imported duty-free materials and equipment and then exported finished products back to the United States. American labor leaders vehemently protested, arguing that NAFTA sent 700,000 American jobs to Mexico between 1993 and 2011.

B. HEALTH-CARE REFORM

1. President Clinton hoped to extend the nation's social safety net to the forty million Americans who lacked health insurance.
2. A task force led by First Lady Hillary Rodham Clinton produced a 1,300-page plan guaranteeing coverage to every American. Congressional opponents defeated the plan arguing that it was too bureaucratic, complex, and costly.

C. WELFARE REFORM

1. Led by Newt Gingrich, the Republicans regained control of both houses of Congress in 1994. President Clinton recognized the electorate's increasingly conservative outlook. In a 1996 radio address to the nation, he echoed President Reagan's opposition to the growth of federal regulations by declaring, "The era of big government is over . . . "

2. The Welfare Reform Bill reflected Clinton's willingness to work with Republican leaders in Congress. The bill ended the fifty-year federal guarantee of assistance to families with dependent children by making deep cuts in welfare grants and requiring able-bodied welfare recipients to find employment.

D. PEACEKEEPING IN BOSNIA AND KOSOVO

1. Clinton was the first American president since Truman who did not have to face Cold War tensions with the Soviet Union.
2. Post–Cold War problems in the former Yugoslavia tested American diplomacy. Following the fall of its communist government, Yugoslavia fragmented into ethnically diverse and increasingly hostile regions. Muslims, Croatians, and Serbians in Bosnia fought a bloody civil war. President Clinton ordered American air strikes to prevent the Serbs from continuing their campaign of ethnic cleansing. The air campaign led to a cease-fire followed by a peace agreement secured by American mediation.
3. The end of the civil war in Bosnia did not prevent violence from continuing in the former Yugoslavia. In 1999, Serbian leader Slobodan Milošević launched a vicious campaign of ethnic cleansing to purge Kosovo of its Albanian inhabitants. Responding to global outrage, the United States and its NATO allies launched a successful aerial assault on Serbia. An agreement signed in June 1999 placed Kosovo under UN supervision, with NATO troops acting as peacekeepers.

E. AN ECONOMIC BOOM

1. Sparked by the computer and Internet revolutions, the American economy roared to life during the late 1990s. As unemployment fell to 4.8 percent, approval ratings for President Clinton soared to nearly 60 percent.
2. America's booming economy produced surging tax revenues and a budget surplus. Americans confidently looked forward to continued peace and prosperity.

II. TURNING POINTS IN AMERICAN HISTORY: THE 9/11 ATTACKS

A. CONTEXT

1. Governor George W. Bush of Texas, the son of the former president, won a razor-thin victory over Vice President Gore

in the 2000 election. Bush promised to be "a compassionate conservative" who would focus on domestic issues such as educational reform.

2. On Monday, September 10, 2001, air travel in the United States was still relatively stress-free. Passengers could share greetings or goodbyes with friends and families at the boarding gate. Neither the Transportation Security Administration (TSA) nor full-body scanners existed. Very few Americans could identify the Taliban, Al-Qaeda, or Osama bin Laden. All of this and much more would change the next day.

B. SEPTEMBER 11, 2001

1. On the morning of September 11, 2001, nineteen Islamic militant terrorists hijacked four U.S. airliners. The terrorists slammed two planes into the twin towers of the World Trade Center in New York City and a third into the Pentagon. The fourth plane crashed on a field in southern Pennsylvania after heroic passengers attacked the hijackers. The attacks claimed the lives of almost 3,000 innocent victims and first responders.

2. The tragic events on 9/11 stunned the country and shaped new realities for America's foreign policy and domestic life.

C. THE WAR ON TERROR: AFGHANISTAN

1. President Bush vowed the United States would "hunt down and punish those responsible for these cowardly acts." Bush did not have to wait long to learn who was responsible for the 9/11 attacks. Within a short time, Osama bin Laden released videotapes claiming responsibility on behalf of his terrorist organization Al-Qaeda.

2. President Bush's promised "war on terrorism" began in Afghanistan where the Taliban regime protected bin Laden and his Al-Qaeda terrorists. In early October 2001, the United States launched a massive military assault, driving the Taliban from power but failing to capture bin Laden.

3. Despite its auspicious beginning, the war in Afghanistan continued as Taliban and other insurgent groups waged guerrilla war against American forces and the new Afghan government. On May 2, 2011, Navy SEALs killed bin Laden in Abbottabad, Pakistan.

D. THE WAR ON TERROR: IRAQ

1. On January 29, 2002, President Bush gave a State of the Union address identifying Iraq as part of an "axis of evil" that included

Iran and North Korea. The president later claimed that Saddam Hussein had been secretly amassing weapons of mass destruction. After some debate, both houses of Congress voted to authorize the use of military force in Iraq.

2. On March 29, 2003, U.S. forces launched a powerful "shock and awe" air assault that crippled Iraq's air defenses and command-and-control centers. Less than three weeks later, American-led ground forces marched unopposed into Baghdad as Saddam Hussein fled the capital. The Iraqi dictator was captured 9 months later and executed by hanging on December 30, 2006.
3. Restoring order and rebuilding Iraq's shattered economy proved to be far more difficult than the Bush administration anticipated. Within a short time, sectarian violence between Shiite and Sunni Muslims threatened the American goal of creating a stable Iraqi government.
4. The United States deployed approximately 2 million men and women to fight in Afghanistan and Iraq. The wars in these two countries claimed the lives of more than 6,000 American soldiers and left over 44,000 wounded.

E. MAKING CONNECTIONS: OUTSPOKEN CRITICS OF AMERICAN WARS

1. America has had a long line of outspoken critics who opposed the nation's wars. For example, Abraham Lincoln and Henry David Thoreau criticized the Mexican-American War, Jane Addams and Mark Twain denounced the annexation of the Philippines, and Senators Wayne Morse and Ernest Gruening voted against the Tonkin Gulf Resolution.
2. Although the public and Congress strongly supported the invasion of Afghanistan, many questioned the wisdom of invading Iraq. West Virginia Senator Robert Byrd warned that while the United States could win a decisive military victory, it would then face a long and costly "second war" to "win the peace in Iraq." Although Byrd failed to persuade a majority of his colleagues, his prediction proved to be prescient.

Be prepared for a possible short-answer question asking you to compare and contrast primary source views supporting and opposing the Iraq War.

F. THE WAR ON TERROR: IMPACT ON AMERICAN LIFE

1. President Bush signed the USA PATRIOT Act into law on October 26, 2001. Designed to strengthen national security, the law gave the federal government broad powers to combat terrorism by making it easier for law enforcement agencies to search the medical, telephone, financial, and even library records of suspected terrorists. Critics argued that the law's new security measures often conflicted with America's traditional respect for civil liberties.

2. The Homeland Security Act of 2002 combined or created over 200 government agencies into a new cabinet-level department. For example, the Transportation Security Administration (TSA), National Guard, and Secret Service were now all part of the new department.

3. Emergency broadcast tests, full-body scans at airports, sleeper cells, and lone-wolf attacks have all become part of the post-9/11 American psyche. Long accustomed to living in a secure homeland, Americans now know that despite their general happiness, the United States is no longer completely safe.

III. TRANSFORMATION OF THE AMERICAN ECONOMY

A. MILESTONES IN THE DIGITAL REVOLUTION

1. The computer age began in 1946 at the University of Pennsylvania when scientists demonstrated the computing power of ENIAC—the Electronic Numerical Integrator and Computer. Heralded by the press as a "Giant Brain," ENIAC contained 17,460 vacuum tubes and filled a large room. It astounded observers by calculating the trajectory of an artillery shell in just 30 seconds, a speed 2,400 times faster than the 20 hours required for human computations. Mainframe computers soon became a common presence in American military bases, universities, and corporate research centers.

2. The personal computer age began in June 1977 when the newly formed Apple Company first marketed its Apple II computer. Four years later, IBM launched its first PC or personal computer. Led by Apple and IBM, the new generation of computers used microprocessors that drastically reduced computer size while enabling users to read, write, and calculate at unprecedented speeds.

3. Prior to the early 1990s, individual computer operators could not make electronic connections with other users. Introduced during

the mid-1990s, the Internet created a system of interconnected computers allowing individual users to share, seek, and compile information. Today, over 80 percent of Americans and almost 50 percent of the global population have access to an Internet connection.

4. The smartphone revolution began on January 9, 2007, when Steve Jobs boldly proclaimed, "Today Apple is going to reinvent the phone." Jobs wasn't exaggerating. Apple's new iPhone began a revolution in mobile technology that is still transforming daily life throughout the world.

B. GLOBALIZATON

1. The digital revolution dramatically accelerated the global movement of goods, workers, and investment capital. The process by which the world's economies are becoming more integrated and interdependent is known as globalization.
2. Fast-food restaurants provide a widely recognized example of globalization. For example, Subway has 43,985 stores in 112 countries while KFC serves customers in 20,500 locations in 125 countries.
3. Globalization has fostered a new era of global cooperation and cultural diffusion. For example, in 2014 McDonald's opened its first restaurant in Ho Chi Minh City, Vietnam. However, globalization has also intensified worldwide competition for low-cost sources of labor. As a result, 5 million manufacturing jobs have left the United States since 1999. For example, although Nike is headquartered in Beaverton, Oregon, it nonetheless contracts with factories in China, Vietnam, Indonesia, and Mexico.

C. INCOME INEQUALITY

1. In his January 2012 State of the Union message, President Obama argued that a widening gap between the nation's top income earners and "a growing number of Americans [who] barely get by" poses "the defining issue of our time."
2. Government statistics document a widening income inequality. Between 1980 and 2012, the share of aggregate income earned by the top 1 percent rose from 8.2 percent to 19.3 percent. During the same time, middle-class incomes stagnated, while the share of aggregate income earned by the lowest fifth fell from 4.2 percent to 3.2 percent.

3. Economists point to a number of possible causes of this expanding income gap. The increasing integration of the United States into the world economy has led to a declining number of high-paying manufacturing jobs. As a result, wages have stagnated for most Americans. In addition, these trends have led to a decline in union membership and thus the ability of unions to negotiate for higher wages.

D. MAKING CONNECTIONS: THE ROBOTICS REVOLUTION

1. The robotics revolution began during the 1980s when automobile companies first used industrial robots to automate their assembly lines. The robots performed repetitive and sometimes dangerous tasks with speed and precision. Their use enabled companies to lower costs and pass savings on to consumers.
2. The robotics revolution is now becoming a growing part of our everyday life. For example, ATM machines have transformed the banking experience while voice recognition technology enables travelers to make plane, car, and hotel reservations without the help of a human representative. However, the robotics revolution is also eliminating millions of jobs without providing a safety net for displaced workers.

Be prepared for a possible short-answer question asking you to describe three causes of the transformation of the American economy between 1980 and the present.

IV. MAJOR DEMOGRAPHIC TRENDS

A. THE "GRAYING" BABY BOOMERS

1. Approximately one-fourth of all Americans are Baby Boomers born between 1946 and 1964. America's aging boomers are placing increasing pressure on the nation's health care programs and facilities. The growing number of retirees poses a threat to the long-term viability of Social Security.
2. Since the 1980s, many older citizens have chosen to retire to Sun Belt states in the South and West. A majority of Americans now live in the Sun Belt, with California, Texas, and Florida now ranking as America's three most populous states. The region's surging population growth has given Sun Belt states a greater voice in presidential elections and national political issues.

B. THE GROWING IMPORTANCE OF THE MILLENNIALS

1. Millennials comprise a demographic cohort of approximately 80 million people born between 1982 and 2002. In January 2016, the Pew Research Center announced that Millennials had surpassed Baby Boomers to become the nation's largest living generation.
2. Millennials are America's most highly educated, computer literate, and diverse group. Their generally tolerant views on issues ranging from gay marriage to multicultural education are reshaping American life.

C. THE SURGING IMMIGRANT POPULATION

1. Immigration trends have always played an important role in American life. The present era is no exception. Between 1990 and 2010, over 20 million immigrants entered the United States, more than in any previous 20-year period.
2. America's foreign-born population has surged from less than 5 percent in 1970 to nearly 13 percent today. The largest number of immigrants are arriving from Latin America and Asia. Immigration policy has emerged as a contentious issue that includes calls for new laws and even a wall along the Mexican border.

Chapter 32

STRATEGIES FOR THE MULTIPLE-CHOICE QUESTIONS

Your exam will have between 16 and 18 sets of multiple-choice questions. Each set will contain a stimulus prompt followed by 2, 3, or 4 questions. There are no sets with 1 or 5 questions. The majority of the stimulus prompts will use primary source passages and accounts written by modern historians. In addition, you will often be asked to evaluate a political cartoon, map, or graph.

Each of the 55 multiple-choice questions is worth 1 point. The multiple-choice section thus comprises 40 percent of 140 points on an APUSH exam. There is no guessing penalty, so be sure to answer each question.

The multiple-choice questions are not designed to test your ability to recall information from long lists of names, dates, and places. Instead, test writers focus on asking you to demonstrate your ability to use historical thinking skills such as contextualization, causation, change and continuity over time, comparison, and argumentation. As a result, answers focus on your ability to identify key historic trends, patterns, and influential ideas.

A SAMPLE SET OF QUESTIONS BASED ON A PRIMARY SOURCE PASSAGE

"I long to hear that you have declared an independency—and by the way in the new Code of Laws which I suppose it will be necessary for you to make I desire you would Remember the Ladies, and be more generous and favorable to them than your ancestors. Do not put such unlimited power into the hands of the Husbands. Remember, all Men would be tyrants if they could. If particular care and attention is not paid to the Ladies, we are determined to foment a rebellion, and will not hold ourselves bound by any laws in which we have no voice or Representation."

Abigail Adams, Letter to her husband
John Adams, March 31, 1776

1. Which of the following issues of the period was Abigail Adams most directly concerned with in the excerpt?

   (A) Widespread colonial opposition to the Stamp Act

   (B) Growing colonial opposition to Paine's arguments in *Common Sense*

   (C) Growing colonial support for the principle of virtual representation

   (D) The need to address the legal rights of married women

2. An implication of Adams' argument is that

   (A) colonial women would demand a new "Code of Laws" that would include universal suffrage for all American women

   (B) colonial women sought to benefit from republican ideals of equality and individual rights

   (C) colonial women would support a compromise with Great Britain to avoid a bloody war

   (D) colonial women would support a strict interpretation of the Constitution

3. Which of the following best represents a logical extension of the ideas about government expressed in the excerpt?

   (A) A weak federal government is needed to ensure the rights of the states.

   (B) A strong Supreme Court is needed to regulate interstate commerce.

   (C) A system of checks and balances is needed to prevent the abuse of power.

   (D) An Electoral College is needed to prevent the direct election of the chief executive.

4. The ideas expressed in the excerpt have the most in common with ideas later expressed by

   (A) supporters of Andrew Jackson

   (B) proponents of the Wilmot Proviso

   (C) signers of the Seneca Falls Declaration of Sentiments

   (D) opponents of the League of Nations

A STEP-BY-STEP APPROACH

STEP ONE: Carefully read the attribution line at the end of the excerpt.

Most students begin by carefully reading the passage. Resist this temptation. Instead begin by focusing on the information in the attribution line at the end of the passage. The brief but vital information contained in the attribution provides the historic context for the passage. For example, the attribution line in the example on page 299 tells you three key facts. First, the passage is from a letter written by Abigail Adams to her husband John Adams. Second, Abigail wrote the letter at the end of March 1776, just 3 months before the signing of the Declaration of Independence. And third, Abigail is remembered as an advocate for the rights of colonial women.

These three facts are important historic clues that should focus your thinking. For example, what comes to mind when you think of Abigail Adams, women's rights, and the year 1776? Your thoughts could include the impending Declaration of Independence and the potential role of women in the soon-to-be declared American republic.

STEP TWO: Read the passage looking for the main ideas.

The passage is called a stimulus for a reason. Don't overanalyze the passage. Instead read the passage noting how the author uses key words and facts to support a main idea. In this passage, Abigail Adams urges her husband to "Remember the Ladies." Adams' admonition to "be more generous to them than your ancestors" is a reference to the fact that colonial women had few legal rights independent of their husbands. For example, a colonial woman usually lost control of her property when she married.

STEP THREE: Use the process of elimination.

Many times your knowledge of the topic will enable you to quickly spot the correct answer. However, there are questions in which the correct answer will not jump out and say, "Here I am!" When this happens, don't panic. Each APUSH multiple-choice question will contain answers that are clearly historically incorrect. For example, in Question 1 on page 300, you can eliminate answer choice (A) because the furor over the Stamp Act ended in 1766, ten years before Adams' letter. You can eliminate choice (B) because *Common Sense* enjoyed widespread popular support for its defense of republican principles and call for political independence. And finally, you can eliminate choice (C) because the colonies rejected the principle of virtual representation. Using the process of elimination, the correct answer to Question 1 is clearly (D).

It is important to remember that eliminating at least two answer choices means that you will have a 50-50 chance of correctly answering the question. With an educated guess, you should be able to answer at least 30 to 32 multiple-choice questions, thus earning half of the 63 to 65 points you need to score a 3.

STEP FOUR: Answer each question in the set.

You should now be ready to answer each question in the set. Here are the answers to questions 1–4:

Question 1: This question is based on the historical thinking skill of contextualization. Choices (A), (B), and (C) are all wrong because they are factually incorrect. Choice (D) is correct because Adams wanted her husband to write a new "Code of Laws" that would "Remember the Ladies."

Question 2: This question is based on the historical thinking skill of argumentation. Choice (A) is incorrect because women did not demand the suffrage until the Seneca Falls Convention over 70 years later. Choice (C) is incorrect because Adams clearly states that she longs "to hear that you have declared an independency." Choice (D) is incorrect because the Constitution had not yet been written. Choice (B) is correct because Adams' statement shows an understanding of the connection between proclaiming a revolution based upon republican principles and extending them to **women.**

Question 3: This question is based on the historical thinking skill of continuity and change over time. Choices (A), (B), and (D) are incorrect because the passage contains no evidence to support these answers. Choice (C) is correct because Adams asserts "all Men would be tyrants if they could." Adams would support a system of checks and balances as a continuation of her apprehension of giving anyone "unlimited power."

Question 4: This question is based on the historical thinking skill of comparison. Adams is focused on a new "Code of Laws" that would include greater rights for women. Choice (A) is incorrect because

Jackson's supporters favored the suffrage for only white men. Choice (B) is incorrect because proponents of the Wilmot Proviso opposed the extension of slavery into the Western territories. Choice (D) is incorrect because the opponents of the League of Nations opposed entering into international organizations that would limit American autonomy. Choice (C) is correct because the signers of the Seneca Falls Declaration of Sentiments agreed with Adams' conviction that America needed new laws recognizing the rights of women.

A SAMPLE SET OF QUESTIONS BASED ON A POLITICAL CARTOON

Courtesy of the Library of Congress

The Only Way to Handle It

1. The image most clearly references which of the following conditions in America's political climate in 1921?

   (A) A growing commitment to Wilson's policy of moral diplomacy

   (B) A growing resurgence of nativist sentiment

   (C) A growing public opposition to the Ku Klux Klan

   (D) A growing public support for women's suffrage

2. Which of the following developments is the most direct effect of the situation portrayed in the image?

   (A) An increase in the proportion of Chinese immigrants

   (B) A decrease in the proportion of Mexican immigrants

   (C) A decrease in the proportion of immigrants from Northern Europe

   (D) A decrease in the proportion of America's foreign-born population

3. The cartoonist would most likely support

   (A) the execution of Sacco and Vanzetti

   (B) the strict enforcement of prohibition

   (C) the National Origins Act of 1924

   (D) the decision in the Scopes Trial

A STEP-BY-STEP APPROACH

STEP ONE: Carefully examine the cartoon's pictorial and textual elements.

Begin your analysis in the cartoon's upper left corner where a huge mass of Europeans are clamoring to enter a large funnel that will take them to a new land labeled "U.S.A." Now look at the figure of Uncle Sam standing on American soil at the funnel's narrow end. Uncle Sam is inserting a gate labeled "3%" into the funnel. This action is curtailing the flood of people to a mere trickle.

STEP TWO: Consider the cartoon's historic context.

The cartoon was not published in a historic vacuum. During the 30 years before the cartoon was published, a massive wave of immigrants left Europe for America. These so-called New Immigrants came from small towns and villages in Southern and Eastern Europe. Nativists opposed the New Immigrants because they were heavily Catholic and Jewish and because they threatened to take away jobs by working for low wages. Note the papers in Uncle Sam's left hand. They are probably the newly enacted Emergency Quota Act of 1921. The law restricted the number of immigrants admitted from any country to just 3 percent of the number of residents from that same country living in the United States as of the 1910 census.

STEP THREE: Determine the cartoonist's point of view.

Does the cartoonist support or oppose the Emergency Quota Act? The cartoon's title, "The Only Way to Handle It," clearly indicates that the cartoonist supports the new law as a prudent way to prevent unlimited immigration from overwhelming American culture.

STEP FOUR: Answer each question in the set.

You should now be ready to answer each question in the set. Here are the answers to questions 1–3:

Question 1: This question is based on the historical thinking skill of contextualization. Choice (A) is incorrect because as America embraced Harding's policy of "normalcy," the nation turned its back on Wilson's idealistic commitment to moral diplomacy. Choice (C) is incorrect because the Klan enjoyed growing public support in the early 1920s. Choice (D) is incorrect because the states ratified the Nineteenth Amendment granting women the suffrage before Congress passed the Emergency Quota Act of 1921. Choice (B) is correct because the massive wave of European immigration portrayed in the cartoon was generating a strong nativist movement.

Question 2: This question is based on the historical thinking skill of causation. Choice (A) is incorrect because the Chinese Exclusion Act of 1882 prohibited immigration from China, thus preventing an increase in the proportion of Chinese immigrants. Choice (B) is incorrect because the new immigration quotas did not apply to Mexico, thus allowing Mexican immigration to increase. Choice (C) is incorrect because the new quotas favored immigration from *Northern* Europe, thus allowing the proportion of immigrants from this region to increase. Choice (D) is correct because the quotas sharply reduced the overall immigration into the United States, thus reducing the proportion of America's foreign-born population.

Question 3: This question is based on the historical thinking skill of comparison. Choices (A), (B), and (D) are all incorrect because the cartoon provides no direct evidence to support how the cartoonist would view the execution of Sacco and Vanzetti, the enforcement of prohibition, and the decision in the Scopes Trial. Choice (C) is correct because the cartoonist clearly favored the Emergency Quota Act of 1921. Given his support for immigration quotas, the cartoonist would most likely support the even more restrictive quotas in the National Origins Act of 1924.

Chapter 33

PRACTICE MULTIPLE-CHOICE QUESTIONS

Practice with the following AP®-style questions. Then go online to access our timed, full-length practice exam at *www.rea.com/studycenter*.

Questions 1 and 2 refer to the excerpt below.

"For all the calamities that came in the long run, European contact at first offered American Indian peoples many opportunities and advantages. Old World technologies provided a range of trade goods that brought vast improvements to everyday life. . . . What was arguably the greatest contribution, however, was not made of metal but of flesh and blood—the horse. Its effects, especially on western tribes, were truly revolutionary. It altered their material lives, rearranged their relations with their environments, and fed a burst of power and affluence."

— Elliott West, historian, 2009

1. The developments described by West most directly illustrate which of the following major historic trends in the Atlantic world?

   (A) The impact of the Columbian Exchange

   (B) The spread of maize agriculture across North America

   (C) The increasing conflict among European powers over access to New World trade routes

   (D) The use of the *encomienda* system to organize and regulate Native American labor

2. Which of the following most directly contributed to "the calamities" referenced in the excerpt?

(A) Significant population growth and economic development in many parts of Europe

(B) The growing dependence of Native American upon European goods

(C) Widespread epidemics of deadly diseases among New World peoples

(D) The emergence of a racially mixed population in Spanish American colonies

Questions 3 to 5 refer to the excerpt below.

"We appeal to the country itself. . . . by what cabal . . . the designs of many of those whom we call great men have been transacted and carried on, but let us trace these men in authority and favor to whose hands the dispensation of the country's wealth has been committed; let us observe the sudden rise of their estates [compared] with the quality in which they first entered this country. . . . Now let us . . . see what sponges have sucked up the public treasure and wither it has not been privately contrived away by unworthy favorites and juggling parasites whose tottering fortunes have been repaired and supported at the public charge. . . .

— Nathaniel Bacon, "Manifesto," 1676

3. Which of the following types of evidence would best be used to support Bacon's argument in the excerpt?

(A) Records documenting the increased use of enslaved Africans on Virginia tobacco plantations

(B) Debates in the House of Burgesses discussing the expansion of women's property rights

(C) Correspondence between indentured servants and their families in England

(D) Tax records showing the changes in the average incomes of Virginia planters between 1650 and 1675

4. The events described in the excerpt contributed most directly to

(A) intensified efforts to discover gold and other precious metals

(B) the decision to replace indentured servants with enslaved Africans

(C) a shift from tobacco production to an economy based on shipbuilding and trade

(D) the expansion of the suffrage to all white males

5. Bacon most likely wrote his account in order to

(A) justify and explain his actions

(B) promote an alliance between colonists in Virginia and colonists in New England

(C) endorse the cultivation of sugar as a new cash crop

(D) propose a treaty of reconciliation with the Native American tribes

Questions 6 to 8 refer to the excerpt below.

"DEAR SIR: I am in receipt of your letter of the 22d of July . . . giving an account of the late barbarous massacre {of six freedmen] at the town of Hamburgh, S.C. . . . The scene at Hamburgh, as cruel, blood-thirsty, wanton, unprovoked, and uncalled for as it was, is only a repetition of the course which has been pursued in other Southern states within the last few years, notably in Mississippi and Louisiana. . . . There has never been a desire on the part of the North to humiliate the South. Nothing is claimed for one State that is not fully accorded to all others, unless it may be the right to kill Negroes and Republicans without fear of punishment and without loss of caste or reputation. . . . I will give every aid for which I can find law or constitutional power. A government that cannot give protection to life, property, and all guaranteed civil right (in this country, the greatest is an untrammeled ballot) to the citizen, is, in so far, a failure, and every energy of the oppressed should be exerted, always within the law and by constitutional means, to regain lost privileges and protection."

— President Ulysses S. Grant, Reply to the governor of South Carolina, July 26, 1876

6. Efforts by Republicans to establish a base for their party in the South after the Civil War failed because of

(A) the emergence of the sharecropping system

(B) the U.S. Supreme Court decision in *Plessy v. Ferguson*

(C) the allocation of scarce resources to building transcontinental railroads

(D) the South's determined resistance and the North's waning resolve

7. The opinions expressed by President Grant would most likely have been endorsed by

(A) Southern Redeemers

(B) Southern Democrats

(C) Radical Republicans

(D) West Coast nativists

8. Which of the following was NOT a technique used in Southern states to disenfranchise African American voters?

(A) Poll taxes

(B) Literacy tests

(C) White primaries

(D) Loyalty oaths

Questions 9 to 11 refer to the following image from 1901.

Columbia's Easter Bonnet

Courtesy of the Library of Congress

9. The cartoonist most likely supported

(A) United States acquisition of overseas territories

(B) a treaty limiting the naval arms race

(C) government policies favoring corporations

(D) public relations campaigns encouraging women to join the armed forces

10. The image was created most directly in response to the

(A) outbreak of World War I

(B) transformation of the United States into an industrial society

(C) the election of large numbers of women to political offices

(D) United States victory in the Spanish-American War

11. The situation depicted in the image contributed most directly to

(A) the United States decision to suppress an independence movement in the Philippines

(B) public opposition to United States imperialism

(C) the belief that the federal government should play a more active role in promoting economic growth

(D) the women's suffrage movement

Questions 12 to 15 refer to the excerpt below.

"While much is said about moneymaking, not enough is said about efficient, self-sacrificing toil of head and hand. Are not all these things worth striving for? The Niagara Movement proposes to gain these ends. . . . If we expect to gain our rights by nerveless acquiescence in wrong, then we expect to do what no other nation ever did. What must we do then? We must complain. Yes, plain, blunt complain, ceaseless agitation, unfailing exposure of dishonesty and wrong—this is the ancient, unerring way to liberty, and we must follow it."

— W.E.B. Du Bois, "The Niagara Movement," 1905

12. The beliefs expressed in the excerpt most directly challenged the prevailing idea in early twentieth century America that

(A) African Americans should migrate from the South to cities in the North and West

(B) separate but equal public facilities for African Americans were appropriate

(C) sharecropping was the best route to economic advancement

(D) African American voters should shift their allegiance to the Democratic Party

13. Which of the following developments in the second half of the twentieth century best represented the continuation of the ideas expressed in this excerpt?

(A) An environmental movement focused on banning chemical insecticides

(B) A religious movement focused on personal conversion and family values

(C) A women's rights movement focused on challenging sex discrimination in the workplace

(D) A peace movement focused on ending the Vietnam War

14. The excerpt was a direct response to

(A) Ida B. Wells' campaign against lynching

(B) Booker T. Washington's accommodationist policies

(C) Theodore Roosevelt's Square Deal programs

(D) Susan B. Anthony's campaign for women's suffrage

15. Du Bois' ideas about "ceaseless agitation" are most consistent with which of the following?

(A) The controversy over flappers during the 1920s

(B) The migration of Oakies to California during the 1930s

(C) The wave of sit-in demonstrations during the early 1960s

(D) The Best Generation critique of American culture during the 1950s

Questions 16 and 17 refer to the excerpt below.

Little boxes on the hillside,
Little boxes made of ticky tacky
Little boxes on the hillside,
Little boxes all the same. . . .

And the people in the houses
All went to the university.
Where they were put in boxes
And they came out all the same. . . .

And they all play on the golf course
And drink their martinis dry
And they all have pretty children
And the children go to school,

And the children go to summer camp
And then to the university
Where they are put in boxes
And they come out all the same.

— Malvina Reynolds, "Little Boxes," 1962

16. Which of the following movements expressed ideas most similar to the ideas expressed in the excerpt?

(A) "Luck and pluck" novelists in the Gilded Age

(B) Muckrakers in the early 1900s

(C) Harlem Renaissance writers in the 1920s

(D) Beat writers in the 1950s

17. The patterns described by Malvina Reynolds most directly illustrate which of the following major historic developments during the 1950s?

(A) The growing impact of immigration from Latin America and Asia

(B) The rise of McCarthyism

(C) The impact of Great Society urban renewal programs

(D) The conformity and materialism of American culture

Questions 18 and 19 refer to the excerpt below.

"The problem lay buried, unspoken for many years in the minds of American women . . . The suburban wife struggled with it alone. As she made the beds, shopped for groceries, matched slipcover material, ate peanut butter sandwiches with her children, chauffeured Cub Scouts and Brownies, lay beside her husband at night—she was afraid to ask even of herself the silent question—'Is this all?'

— Betty Friedan, *The Feminine Mystique,* 1963

18. The sentiments expressed in the excerpt most directly challenge the prevailing ideal in the 1950s and early 1960s that women should

(A) focus their energies on the domestic sphere

(B) receive equal pay for equal work

(C) use fashion to challenge traditional gender roles

(D) teach their children to become informed and responsible citizens

19. Which of the following most shaped the patterns of behavior described in the excerpt?

(A) Cold War anxieties

(B) The Supreme Court decision in *Brown v. Board of Education*

(C) Unprecedented economic prosperity

(D) The ratification of the Equal Rights Amendment (ERA)

Questions 20 to 22 refer to the excerpt below.

I know it may not be fashionable to speak of patriotism or national destiny these days. But I feel it is appropriate to do so on this occasion. . . .

Let historians not record that when America was the most powerful nation in the world we passed on the other side of the road and allowed the last hopes for peace and freedom of millions of people to be suffocated by the forces of totalitarianism. And so tonight to you, the great silent majority of my fellow Americans, I ask for your support. . . . Let us be united for peace. Let us also be united against defeat. Because let us understand: North Vietnam cannot defeat or humiliate the United States. Only Americans can do that.

— Richard Nixon, Address to the Nation, November 3, 1969

20. Nixon's primary purpose in the excerpt was to

(A) rally public support for his policy of détente

(B) rally public support for his policy of Vietnamization

(C) rally public support for his policy of bombing Cambodia

(D) rally public support for his policy of executive privilege

21. Which of the following ideas most directly contributed to America's involvement in the conflict with North Vietnam?

(A) The strategy of brinksmanship

(B) The concept of mutually assured destruction

(C) The growing fear of nationalist movements in Africa

(D) The belief in the domino theory

22. Nixon's address was delivered in response to

(A) the emergence of the black power movement

(B) the increasing radicalization of the feminist movement

(C) a growing public debate over the rationale for the Vietnam War

(D) Cold War tensions in Berlin

Questions 23 to 25 refer to the excerpt below.

"It was in suburbs such as Garden Grove, Orange County, [California] . . . that small groups of middle-class men and women met in their new tract homes, seeking to turn the tide of liberal dominance. Recruiting the like-minded, they organized study groups, opened 'Freedom Forum' bookstores, filled the rolls of the John Birch Society, entered school board races, and worked within the Republican Party, all in an urgent struggle to safeguard their particular vision of freedom and the American heritage.

— Lisa McGirr, historian, *Suburban Warriors: The Origins of the New American Right*, 2015

23. The "middle-class men and women" referenced in the excerpt were part of which broader historical movement?

(A) The emergence of a counterculture

(B) The rise of radical feminists

(C) The protests of the Civil Rights movement

(D) The growth of the conservative movement

24. The "tide of liberal dominance" refers to all of the following EXCEPT

(A) Great Society programs

(B) The emergence of environmental activism

(C) The increasing participation of women in the labor force during the Second World War

(D) Supreme Court decisions prohibiting officially sponsored prayer and Bible readings in the public schools

25. Which of the following ultimately became political allies of the Orange County men and women described in this excerpt?

    (A) Discontented blue-collar workers in the North

    (B) Environmental activists in the Pacific Northwest

    (C) Black Power protestors in urban ghettos

    (D) Native American activists in South Dakota

ANSWERS AND EXPLANATIONS

1. (A) The Columbian Exchange refers to the exchange of plants, animals, and diseases between the New World and Europe following the discovery of America in 1492. The excerpt discusses examples of how the Columbian Exchange affected New World peoples.

2. (C) Smallpox and other contagious European diseases decimated New World societies. Demographers estimate that the Native American population plummeted by as much as 90 percent in the first century of contact with Europeans.

3. (D) Bacon charges that the "men in authority" are "sponges" and "parasites" whose fortunes have been supported by "the public charge." Tax records from 1650 to 1675 would provide evidence to substantiate Bacon's charges.

4. (B) Bacon's Rebellion exposed tensions between impoverished former indentured servants and the privileged gentry. As planters became more wary of their former indentured servants, they turned to enslaved Africans as a more reliable and cost-effective source of labor.

5. (A) As the leader of a rebellion, Bacon wrote his "Manifesto" to justify his actions and explain his opposition to colonial policies.

6. (D) The massacre at Hamburg, South Carolina, and violence in Mississippi and Louisiana provide examples of determined Southern resistance. Grant's failure to back up his words of

support with forceful actions illustrate the North's waning resolve. The Supreme Court decision in *Plessy v. Ferguson* occurred in 1896, two decades after Grant's letter.

7. (C) Radical Republicans would endorse Grant's condemnation of the violence in South Carolina. Southern Redeemers and Southern Democrats supported the end of Radical Reconstruction. West Coast nativists were focused on the status of Chinese immigrants in California.

8. (D) Redeemer governments used poll taxes, literacy tests, and white primaries to disenfranchise African American voters. Loyalty oaths were part of the McCarthy-era Red Scare. They were never used to disenfranchise African American voters.

9. (A) Columbia is a poetic alternative name for America. The cartoonist portrays Columbia as a female figure proudly adjusting an Easter bonnet, which is actually a battleship labeled "World Power." The battleship bonnet is spewing thick black smoke labeled "Expansion." The cartoonist uses this image to convey his support for America's growing world power.

10. (D) Created in 1901, the image celebrates America's victory in the Spanish-American War and the nation's emergence as a world power.

11. (A) The Treaty of Paris ceded the Philippines to the United States. The agreement aroused a powerful anti-imperialist movement to block ratification. The cartoonist clearly endorsed the treaty. After a heated debate, the Senate approved the Treaty of Paris. The United States was soon forced to use overwhelming military power to crush a Philippine independence movement.

12. (B) Du Bois wrote this essay less than 10 years after the Supreme Court decision in *Plessy v. Ferguson* legalized the doctrine of "separate but equal." Du Bois called for "ceaseless agitation" to expose the accepted belief that segregated public facilities were appropriate.

13. (C) Both Du Bois and the women's rights movement focused on fighting to end unjust discrimination directed against a specific group of people.

14. (B) In 1895, Booker T. Washington delivered his famous Atlanta Compromise speech, urging African Americans to accept segregation and focus on programs of economic self-help. Du Bois forcefully rejected this policy of gradualism and accommodation.

15. (C) The sit-in demonstrations provide a powerful example of the use of "ceaseless agitation" to expose injustice.

16. (D) During the 1950s, Beat Generation writers such as Jack Kerouac scorned middle-class suburban life. Gilded Age "luck and pluck" novels such as the Horatio Alger stories celebrated America as the land of opportunity.

17. (D) The endless rows of identical box homes embodied the conformity and materialism that dominated American culture during the 1950s.

18. (A) The 1950s witnessed a revival of the cult of domesticity. It glorified American women performing their "natural" roles as wives and mothers.

19. (C) America's unprecedented economic prosperity supported a suburban lifestyle that consigned educated women such as Betty Friedan to a monotonous routine of household chores.

20. (B) After taking office, President Nixon began to implement a gradual policy known as Vietnamization whereby South Vietnamese troops replaced American combat forces. His address attempted to rally public support for this policy. Nixon did not initiate his policy of détente until his famous 1972 trips to China and Russia.

21. (D) First articulated by President Eisenhower, the domino theory predicted that if one country fell to communism, its neighbors would become susceptible to communist influence and control. Cold War hawks predicted that the fall of South Vietnam would inevitably lead to the fall of Southeast Asia.

22. (C) During the fall of 1969, huge antiwar demonstrations protested Nixon's gradual approach to ending the Vietnam War. Nixon called upon "the great silent majority" to support his policies and allow him to stay the course and achieve "peace with honor."

23. (D) Middle-class men and women living in Sun Belt communities such as Garden Grove formed a key part of the conservative movement that helped elect Ronald Reagan president in 1980.

24. (C) The Great Society, environmental activism, and Supreme Court decisions banning school prayer were all part of the "tide of liberal dominance" that prevailed during most of the 1960s. The patriotic participation of women in the labor force during World War II preceded the period of liberal dominance during the 1960s.

25. (A) The conservative coalition ultimately included discontented blue-collar workers known as "Reagan Democrats." Environmental activists, Black Power protesters, and Native American activists did not support the conservative agenda pioneered by the Orange County conservatives described in this excerpt.

Chapter 34

STRATEGIES FOR THE SHORT-ANSWER QUESTIONS

Your APUSH exam will continue with a 40-minute section containing four short-answer questions covering topics from Native Americans before Columbus's voyages to events and trends in the early twenty-first century. You are required to answer the first two questions. They will both cover material from Periods 3 to 8 (1754–1980). You will then answer the third OR the fourth question. Question 3 will cover Periods 1 to 5 (1491–1877), while Question 4 will cover Periods 6 to 9 (1865–2010).

Question 1 features a pair of passages by dueling historians or contrasting contemporaries. Question 2 will ask you to analyze a political cartoon or historical poster. Both prompts are followed by a set of three very focused sub-questions. Questions 3 and 4 ask you to compare the similarities and differences between two major intellectual movements, geographic regions, political movements, or legislative programs. Each question includes three specific sub-questions.

The three short-answer questions are worth 28 points, or 20 percent of your total exam score. Each of the three sub-questions is worth 3.1 points.

STRATEGY 1

Use complete sentences to answer each sub-question. You will *not* be awarded points for using an outline or a bulleted list of points.

STRATEGY 2

Write succinct answers. You will be given one page for each of the three questions you choose to answer. Each page contains just 23 lines. Answers that exceed these limitations will not be scored.

STRATEGY 3

Each of the three sub-parts of a short-answer question is an all-or-nothing proposition. That is, you will either receive full credit for your answer or you will receive a zero. Remember, there is no guessing penalty. Since a blank space will receive a zero, always try to write a plausible answer.

STRATEGY 4

Most of the sub-questions can be answered in a variety of ways. Your goal is therefore not to find *the* answer. Instead, your goal is to find and write about *an* answer.

SHORT-ANSWER QUESTION 1: DUELING HISTORIANS

Betraying the hopes of the world, breaking treaties and commitments, the Soviet government after World War II embarked on a new course of forcible expansion and aggression. In 1945 and 1946, Russia's neighbors in Europe and the Far East, their territory occupied by the Red Army at the end of the fighting, were transformed into a new kind of dependencies, so-called satellites, with the Communist Party in power. Although the United States and her Western allies protested this course, Moscow remained adamant, fully aware of the inability of the Western allies to prevent this process of expansion.

— David J. Dallin, historian, *Dubious Victory*, 1973

It is pointless to try to place all the blame for the Cold War on either the Communist World or the so-called Free World. Can we blame dogs for being hostile to cats, or water for being incompatible with oil, or fire for reacting violently to gasoline?

Communism, by the very nature of its closed society, has a built-in hostility to open-door capitalism—a hostility that existed from the beginning and will always exist as long as the two systems keep their basic identity and ideology. In this sense the Cold War has existed since 1917, when the Communists took over in Russia and proclaimed their undying hostility to the capitalist world. Basic frictions and suspicions were temporarily ignored during the anti-Hitler war, but they were always present; and circumstances in the postwar years increased the friction as each side sought to promote its ideologically directed aims. If the West feared Communist world revolution, the Soviet leaders feared, or professed to fear, capitalist encirclement. The Cold War came so naturally that its avoidance would have been more remarkable than its occurrence."

— Thomas A. Bailey, historian, Probing America's Past, 1973

Using the excerpts above, answer (A), (B), and (C).

(A) Briefly describe ONE major difference between Dallin's and Bailey's historical interpretations of the causes of the Cold War.

(B) Briefly explain how ONE event or development from the period 1945–1953 that is not explicitly mentioned in the excerpts could be used to support Dallin's argument.

(C) Briefly explain how ONE event or development from the period 1945–1953 that is not explicitly mentioned in the excerpts could be used to support Bailey's argument.

ANSWERS:

(A) Dallin argues that the Soviet Union caused the Cold War by following a "new course of forcible expansion" and by deliberately "breaking treaties and commitments." In contrast, Bailey argues that the Cold War was the inevitable result of irreconcilable differences between the United States and the Soviet Union.

(B) Soviet policy in Poland supports Dallin's argument. Joseph Stalin broke his Yalta pledges by forbidding free elections in Poland and by installing a puppet or satellite communist regime. This intrusion into Eastern and Central Europe violated the principle of national self-determination and posed a real threat to Western Europe. As the leader of the Free World, the United States had to implement a policy of containment to block Soviet expansion.

(C) The United States formed NATO to block Soviet expansion into Western Europe. The alliance provided American forces with strategic military bases that posed a deterrence to the Soviet Union. Russian leaders responded by forming the Warsaw Pact to defend their sphere of influence in Eastern Europe. The two rival alliances support Bailey's argument that the Cold War was an inevitable result of rivalry between the opposing political and economic systems.

SHORT-ANSWER QUESTION 2: ANALYZING AN IMAGE

National Archives, 1943

The image above was created in 1943 by the Office of War Information. It depicts workers at an integrated aircraft plant. Using the image, answer (A), (B), and (C).

(A) Briefly describe ONE specific event or development that led to the historical situation depicted in the image.

(B) Briefly describe how the image depicts the government's point of view about the role of African American workers during the Second World War.

(C) Briefly explain ONE specific effect in the period from 1943 to 1953 of the development referenced by the image.

ANSWERS:

(A) In 1941, A. Philip Randolph and other African American leaders planned a march on Washington, D.C., to protest racial discrimination in defense industries. President Roosevelt avoided the march by issuing Executive Order 8802, prohibiting ethnic or racial discrimination in the nation's defense industry. The order marked the first time since Reconstruction that the federal government committed itself to opposing racial discrimination.

(B) The image depicts a white and black worker working together to build an aircraft that will be used to defend America's way of life. The image underscores the important role African American workers are playing in the war effort.

(C) The image was part of the African American "Double V" campaign to achieve victory over fascism abroad and over racism at home. In the decades following the Second World War, the Double V campaign led to notable successes in the campaign to fight racial discrimination. For example, in 1947 Jackie Robinson became the first African American Major League Baseball player. The following year President Truman issued an executive order abolishing racial discrimination in the U.S. Armed Forces.

SHORT-ANSWER QUESTION 3: MAKING COMPARISONS

Answer (A), (B), and (C). Confine your response to the period from 1607 to 1776.

(A) Briefly describe ONE specific difference between the British West Indies colonies and the Chesapeake colonies in the years between 1607 and 1776.

(B) Briefly describe ONE specific similarity between the British West Indies colonies and the Chesapeake colonies in the years between 1607 and 1776.

(C) Briefly describe ONE specific historical effect of the difference between the British West Indies colonies and the Chesapeake colonies in the years between 1607 and 1776.

ANSWERS:

(A) The British West Indian sugar plantations created a society consisting of a fabulously wealthy planter elite, a vast population of enslaved Africans, and a small number of white foremen and managers. The Chesapeake tobacco plantations also produced a society dominated by a wealthy planter elite. However, the Chesapeake colonies had a much larger number of yeoman white farmers than did the British West Indies colonies.

(B) Plantations devoted to producing cash crops dominated the economies of both the British West Indies and the Chesapeake colonies. Plantations in the British West Indies produced sugar, while those in the Chesapeake produced tobacco. Planters in both regions relied upon a large body of enslaved Africans.

(C) The tobacco planters and white yeoman farmers in Virginia and Maryland supported the growing movement to declare independence from Great Britain. In contrast, the wealthy sugar planters in the West Indies remained loyal to the British Crown.

SHORT-ANSWER QUESTION 4: MAKING COMPARISONS

Answer (A), (B), and (C).

(A) Briefly describe ONE similarity between New Deal and Great Society objectives and programs.

(B) Briefly describe ONE difference between New Deal and Great Society objectives and programs.

(C) Briefly explain ONE reason for a difference between New Deal and Great Society objectives and programs.

ANSWERS:

(A) Both the New Deal and the Great Society addressed the needs of America's senior citizens. For example, the New Deal's Social Security Act created a federal pension system funded by taxes on a worker's wages and by an equivalent contribution by employers. The Great Society created the Medicare and Medicaid programs to address the pressing health care needs of America's senior citizens.

(B) The New Deal did not directly confront racial injustice. For example, Civilian Conservation Corps camps were often racially segregated. In contrast, the Great Society directly addressed the legacy of Jim Crow segregation. For example, the landmark Civil Rights Act of 1964 banned discrimination in public facilities, while the Voting Rights Act of 1965 ended literacy tests and other devices used to prevent African Americans from voting.

(C) FDR and his "brain trust" advisors designed the New Deal to confront a grave economic crisis. As a result, the New Deal focused on programs designed to provide economic relief, recovery, and reform. In contrast, LBJ conceived the Great Society during a period of unprecedented economic prosperity. As a result, the Great Society did not have to address a severe banking crisis and instead focused on an "unconditional War on Poverty."

STRATEGIES FOR THE DOCUMENT-BASED ESSAY QUESTION

Chapter 35

After completing the short-answer questions, you will have a well-deserved 10-minute break. When you return to your desk, your exam will resume with the document-based essay question (DBQ).

The DBQ is an essay question requiring you to interpret and analyze seven brief primary source documents. The documents are typically excerpts from letters, newspapers, speeches, diaries, official decrees, and even songs. In addition, the DBQ often includes a statistical table, map, political cartoon, or a work of art.

The College Board recommends that you devote 60 minutes to the DBQ. It typically requires about 15 minutes to read the documents, organize your thoughts, determine a thesis, and create an outline for your essay. You will then have about 45 minutes to write your DBQ essay.

Your DBQ can earn up to seven rubric points. Each rubric point is worth 5 exam points. So a perfect score of 7 is worth 35 points, or 25 percent of your total exam score. It is important to remember that earning five of the seven possible rubric points will keep you on pace to earn an overall score of 5 on your APUSH exam.

THE DBQ SCORING RUBRIC

The APUSH DBQ scoring rubric is divided into the following four categories:

1. **THESIS—1 POINT**
   - Responds to the prompt with a historically defensible thesis/claim that establishes your basic argument.
   - Consists of one or more sentences located in one place; can be written as part of the introduction or the conclusion.
2. **CONTEXTUALIZATION—1 POINT**
   - Describes a broader historic context relevant to the prompt.
   - Places the prompt in its proper historic setting.

- Connects the prompt to broader historical events or trends occurring before or during the prompt's time frame.

3. EVIDENCE: DOCUMENT CONTENT—1 OR 2 POINTS

- Uses the content of at least THREE documents to address the topic of the prompt (1 point).

OR

- Supports an argument using at least SIX documents. Response must provide an accurate description and not just quotes from the documents (2 points).

3A. EVIDENCE: BEYOND THE DOCUMENTS—1 POINT

- Uses at least one additional piece of specific and relevant historical evidence beyond what is found in the documents or in the contextualization paragraph.
- Explains, supports, or helps prove the thesis argument.

4. ANALYSIS AND REASONING: SOURCING—1 POINT

- Explains the significance of the author's point of view, the author's purpose, historic context, or audience for at least THREE of the documents.
- Applies just one of these criteria to each document. For example, you can describe the point of view of one document and the intended audience of a second document.

4A. ANALYSIS AND REASONING: COMPLEXITY—1 POINT

- Demonstrates a *complex understanding* of the historical development that is the focus of the prompt using evidence to corroborate (reinforce), qualify, or modify an argument that addresses the question.
- Complex understanding can be accomplished in a variety of ways including:
  - — explaining both similarities and differences, or explaining both continuity and change, or explaining multiple causes, or explaining both causes and effects;
  - — explaining relevant and insightful connections within and across periods;
  - — confirming the validity of an argument by corroborating multiple perspectives across themes;
  - — qualifying or modifying an argument by considering diverse or alternative viewpoints or evidence.

A SAMPLE DBQ AND ANNOTATED ESSAY

Practice is the key to performing well on the DBQ. The following sample DBQ is designed to illustrate how to use a guided set of seven strategies that can be applied to any DBQ.

1. BEGIN BY CAREFULLY READING THE ASSIGNMENT.

Begin by carefully reading the assignment. Here is a sample assignment that asks you to use the historical reasoning process of describing and evaluating patterns of change and continuity over time.

Analyze major changes and continuities in the lives of African Americans who migrated from the rural South to urban areas in the North during the period 1900 to 1930.

2. CAREFULLY EXAMINE EACH OF THE SEVEN DOCUMENTS.

Your next step is to read, analyze, and organize the following seven documents:

Document 1: Editorial by the editor of the *Richmond Times*, 1900

> It is necessary that this principle [racial segregation] be applied in every relation of Southern life. God Almighty drew the color line and it cannot be obliterated. The Negro must stay on his side of the line and the white man must stay on his side, and the sooner both races recognize this fact and accept it, the better it will be for both.

Document 2: Southern African American folk saying, 1910s

> De white man he got ha'f de crop
> Boll-Weevil took de res'.
> Ain't got no home,
> Ain't got no home.

Document 3: Originally published by the white-owned *Athens Daily Banner* in Georgia on September 7, 1917. Reprinted by the black-owned *Chicago Defender* on September 15, 1917, under the headline, "Read This, Then Laugh."

> Investigation by state and federal officials into the Negro exodus situation has brought to the conclusion that the greatest disturbing element which has yet entered Georgia is the circulation of the Negro newspaper known as *The Chicago Defender* which has agitated the Negroes to leave the South on the word picture of equality with the whites, the freedom of hotels, theaters and other places of public amusement on an

equal basis with the white people and "equality of citizenship" in the North and East.

Document 4: Dwight Thompson Farnham, Northern white efficiency expert, article titled "Negroes as a Source of Industrial Labor," Industrial Management, August 1918

> A certain amount of segregation is necessary at times to preserve the peace. This is especially true when Negroes are first introduced into a plant. It is a question if it is not always best to have separate wash rooms and the like. In places where different races necessarily come into close contact and in places where inherited characteristics are especially accentuated, it is better to keep their respective folkways from clashing wherever possible.

Document 5: Lizzie Miles, African American singer, lyrics to the song "Cotton Belt Blues," 1923

> Look at me. Look at me.
> And you see a gal.
> With a heart bogged down with woe.
> Because I'm all alone,
> Far from my Southern home.
> Dixie Dan. That's the man.
> Took me from the Land of Cotton
> To that cold, cold minded North.
> Threw me down. Hit the town.
> And I've never seen him henceforth.
> Just cause I trusted. I'm broke and disgusted.
> I got the Cotton Belt Blues.

Document 6: U.S. Bureau of the Census, "Population of the 100 Largest Cities and Other Urban Places in the U.S.: 1790–1990."

AFRICAN AMERICANS AS A PERCENTAGE OF THE POPULATION OF SELECTED U.S. CITIES, 1900–1970

CITY	1900	1910	1920	1930	1940	1950	1960	1970
Chicago	1.8	2.0	4.1	6.9	8.2	13.6	22.9	32.7
Detroit	1.4	1.2	4.1	7.7	9.2	16.2	28.9	43.7
Los Angeles	2.1	2.4	2.7	3.1	4.2	8.7	13.5	17.9
New York City	1.8	1.9	2.7	4.7	6.1	9.5	14.0	21.1
Philadelphia	4.8	5.5	7.4	11.3	13.0	18.2	26.4	33.6
St. Louis	6.2	6.4	9.0	11.4	13.3	17.9	28.6	40.9

Document 7: Alain LeRoy Locke, *The New Negro*, 1925

> If we were to offer a symbol of what Harlem has come to mean in the short span of twenty years it would be another statue of liberty on the landward side of New York. It stands for a folk-movement which in human significance can be compared only with the pushing back of the Western frontier in the first half of the last century, or the waves of immigration which have swept in from overseas in the last half. Numerically far smaller than either of these movements, the volume of migration is such nonetheless that Harlem has become the greatest Negro community the world has known—without counterpart in the South or in Africa. But beyond this, Harlem represents the Negro's latest thrust toward Democracy. . . . In Harlem, Negro life is seizing upon its first chances for group expression and self-determination.

3. CREATE AN ORGANIZATIONAL CHART.

Many students find it very helpful to organize the documents by placing them into a chart. Your first column should always be labeled Point of View. For this assignment your next two columns should focus on Continuity and Change. Here is an example of what your chart could look like:

	Point of View	Continuity	Change
Document 1	White segregationist newspaper editor	Defends the color line and white supremacy	
Document 2	Expresses sharecropper woes	Cycle of poverty and debt continues	
Document 3	White-owned Southern newspaper and the black-owned *Chicago Defender*		North offers new opportunity and new civic equality
Document 4	White efficiency expert in the North	Limited segregation in the workplace	
Document 5	African American singer	Broke and disgusted in the North	
Document 6	US Bureau of the Census		Major increase in the percentage of blacks living in selected Northern cities
Document 7	Major Harlem Renaissance writer		Harlem represents a new "thrust towards Democracy."

4. **WRITE AN OPENING PARAGRAPH THAT ESTABLISHES THE HISTORIC *CONTEXT* OF THE EVENT.**

Your opening paragraph is an excellent place to establish the historic context for the event specified in your DBQ assignment. Remember that the contextualization point will contribute almost 5 points to your total exam score. Here is a sample introductory paragraph that establishes the context for the Great Migration:

Between 1900 and 1930, over 1.5 million African Americans migrated from the rural South to urban centers in the North. Known as the Great Migration, this mass movement of people did not occur in isolation. During the same period migrants from American farms and immigrants from villages in Southern and Eastern Europe also poured into Northern cities. By 1920, the federal census reported that for the first time a majority of Americans lived in urban areas.

5. **WRITE A THESIS STATEMENT THAT DIRECTLY ADDRESSES YOUR DBQ ASSIGNMENT.**

A thesis is your position or historic claim about the assigned topic. Having a clearly defined and focused thesis is absolutely essential. Your organizational chart reveals that African Americans experienced BOTH continuity and change during the Great Migration. Your thesis should acknowledge the existence of these two historical processes. However, your job is not to be a neutral observer. Which process—continuity or change—was the most important? There is evidence to support both processes. Your job is to make a JUDGMENT and incorporate that judgment into your thesis. Note how the following sample thesis acknowledges the importance of continuity but concludes that changes played the most significant role in the lives of African Americans who migrated to the North.

The Great Migration produced both significant changes and continuities in the social and economic experience of African Americans living in the urban areas in the North. Although the migrants continued to experience poverty, discrimination, and segregation, these conditions were not as rigid as those in the Jim Crow South. At the same time, the Great Migration produced changes in Black identity and aspirations that left an irrevocable mark on the African American experience.

6. CAREFULLY DEVELOP YOUR THESIS IN A SERIES OF BODY PARAGRAPHS.

Now that you have written a strong thesis, your next step is to develop it in a series of body paragraphs. These vital paragraphs are where you can earn 4 additional rubric points by analyzing the content of at least 6 documents, evaluating the purpose, point of view, audience, or historic setting of at least 3 documents, and providing evidence beyond the documents to further develop your argument.

Our sample DBQ provides clear sourcing material for Documents 3, 4, and 7. The short but important paragraph on the Harlem Renaissance provides specific and relevant information that is not found in the seven documents.

> *Documents 1 and 2 describe the "push" factors that explain why many African Americans wanted to leave the South. About 90 percent of African Americans lived in the South in 1900. Most were concentrated in rural areas where they worked as sharecroppers on cotton farms. Sharecropping forced African Americans into a cycle of poverty and debt in which "De white man he got ha'f the crop" (Doc. 2). At that same time an infestation of boll weevils swept across the Deep South devastating the cotton industry (Doc. 2). Jim Crow laws sanctioned by the* Plessy v. Ferguson *"separate but equal" decision created a rigid "color line" that white supremacists insisted could not be "obliterated" (Doc. 1). Racial violence that included lynchings terrorized black communities.*
>
> *Document 3 provides a persuasive explanation of the "pull" factors that prompted many African Americans to seek better lives outside the South. First published in a white-owned newspaper in Athens, Georgia,* The Chicago Defender *gleefully reprinted the article. The black-owned newspaper played an important role in condemning Jim Crow laws and in encouraging African Americans to migrate to Chicago and to other Northern cities. The article from the* Athens Daily Banner *unintentionally substantiated* The Defender's *numerous articles describing Chicago as an attractive destination offering good jobs, public entertainment, a chance for economic success, and most of all "equality in citizenship."*
>
> *African Americans did find new jobs in the North. But the "equality with whites" promised by* The Chicago Defender *proved to be elusive. In Document 4, a Northern white efficiency expert offers his fellow industrial managers advice on how "to preserve the peace" between white and African American workers. According to his matter-of-fact report, prudent managers should "create separate wash rooms" and other segregated facilities.*

This policy would, he believes, help employees avoid unwanted cultural clashes. Although not as systematic as Jim Crow segregation, this "certain amount of segregation" represents an important example of continuity in the social and economic experience of African Americans in Northern cities.

The problems experienced by African American migrants were not limited to workplace discrimination. The optimism encouraged by The Chicago Defender *soon encountered the harsh realities of trying to establish a new life in the North. The lyrics of the song "Cotton Belt Blues" (Doc. 5) express the disillusionment felt by many African Americans who left "the land of cotton" only to become "broke and disgusted" in crowded and callous cities. Document 5 thus provides lyrics that corroborate the same economic plight expressed by the African American folk saying in Document 2.*

Job discrimination and economic setbacks did not deter African Americans from leaving the South. Document 6 provides statistical data documenting the percentage growth of African Americans in six major cities. The chart reveals that the promise of war-related jobs and the possibility of escaping Jim Crow segregation caused a surge in black migration between 1910 and 1920. The end of World War I did not stop the Great Migration. Instead, it accelerated during the 1920s as the black population of Northern cities continued to increase (Doc. 6).

New York City proved to be a particularly important destination. (Doc. 6). Harlem is a large neighborhood in the northern section of the New York City borough of Manhattan. During the 1920s, Harlem became the vibrant center of an outpouring of African American literary, artistic, and political expression known as the Harlem Renaissance.

In Document 7, Alain LeRoy Locke equates the symbolic importance of Harlem to "another statue of liberty." He proudly describes Harlem as "the greatest Negro community the world has known." Harlem's greatness is not based upon its size; it is based upon its importance as the creative nerve center of the "Negro's latest thrust toward democracy." Locke's emphasis upon "group expression and self-determination" reinforce the message of equality in Document 3.

7. WRITE A CONCLUDING PARAGRAPH THAT RESTATES YOUR THESIS AND DEMONSTRATES COMPLEXITY.

Now that you have written a convincing series of analytical body paragraphs, your final task is to write a succinct paragraph restating your thesis. Here is a sample concluding paragraph:

> *The Great Migration produced far-reaching changes in the African American experience. When the migration began in 1900, African Americans lived impoverished lives as sharecroppers in the rural South (Doc. 2). When it ended in 1930, African Americans were rapidly becoming an urbanized population (Doc. 6) that escaped the worst abuses of racial segregation in the South. Although poverty and some forms of discrimination continued in the North, African American migrants who left "the land of cotton" proudly crossed the "color line" (Doc. 1) by asserting a more confident identity as "New Negroes."*

Chapter 36

STRATEGIES FOR THE LONG-ESSAY QUESTION

After completing the DBQ, you will yearn for a break to rest your tired writing hand. Unfortunately, there is no break. Instead, you must be resolute and focus on the next and final APUSH challenge: the long-essay question.

The long-essay section will ask you to examine three questions focusing on the same historical thinking skill. Fortunately, you only have to answer ONE of the questions. You will have 40 minutes to write your essay.

Your long essay can earn up to 6 rubric points. Each point is worth 3.5 exam points. So a perfect score of 6 is worth 21 points or 15 percent of your total exam score. It is important to remember that earning 4 of the 6 possible rubric points will keep you on pace to earn an overall score of 5 on your APUSH exam.

THE LONG-ESSAY SCORING RUBRIC

The APUSH long-essay scoring rubric is divided into the following four categories:

1. **THESIS—1 POINT**
   - Responds to the prompt with a historically defensible thesis/claim that establishes your basic argument.
   - Consists of one or more sentences located in one place, either the introduction or the conclusion.

2. **CONTEXTUALIZATION—1 POINT**
   - Describes a broader historical context relevant to the prompt.
   - Places the prompt in its proper historic setting.
   - Connects the prompt to broader historical events or trends occurring before or during the prompt's time frame.

3. **EVIDENCE—2 POINTS**

- Provides specific examples of evidence relevant to the topic of the prompt (1 point).

OR

- Supports the argument with specific and relevant examples of evidence (2 points).

4. **ANALYSIS AND REASONING: HISTORICAL REASONING—1 POINT**

- Uses historical reasoning to frame or structure an argument by addressing one of the following targeted historical thinking skills: comparison, causation, or continuity and change over time (1 point).
  - — For the skill of *comparison* you can earn one point by describing similarities and differences among historic individuals, developments, or processes.
  - — For the skill of *causation* you can earn one point for describing the causes and/or effects of a historical event, development, or process.
  - — For the skill of *continuity and change over time* you can earn one point for describing historical continuity and/or historic change over time.

OR

4A. **ANALYSIS AND REASONING: COMPLEXITY—2 POINTS**

- Demonstrates a *complex understanding* of the historical development that is the focus of the prompt using evidence to corroborate (reinforce), qualify, or modify an argument that addresses the question (2 points).
- Complex understanding can be accomplished in a variety of ways including:
  - — explaining both similarities and differences, or explaining both continuity and change, or explaining multiple causes, or explaining both causes and effects;
  - — explaining relevant and insightful connections within and across periods;
  - — confirming the validity of an argument by corroborating multiple perspectives across themes;
  - — qualifying or modifying an argument by considering diverse or alternative viewpoints or evidence.

THREE QUESTIONS COVERING THREE DIFFERENT TIME PERIODS

The long-essay section will provide you with three long-essay questions. DON'T PANIC! You will only be asked to select and answer ONE of the questions.

Your exam will contain one question dealing with periods 1–3, one question dealing with periods 4–6, and one question dealing with periods 7–9. The three questions will all address the same theme and reasoning skill (i.e., comparison, causation, or continuity and change over time).

A SAMPLE ANNOTATED LONG ESSAY

Practice is the key to performing well on the long essay. The following sample long essay is designed to illustrate how to use a guided set of five strategies that can be applied to any long-essay question.

1. BEGIN BY CAREFULLY ANALYZING THE ASSIGNMENT AND MAKING A PRAGMATIC CHOICE.

Your first task is to select which one of the three long answer questions you want to write about. Here are three long-essay questions that test the historical thinking skill continuity and change over time:

- Evaluate the extent to which the Constitution fostered political and social change in the United States from 1783 to 1800.
- Evaluate the extent to which the Mexican-American War fostered political and social change in the United States from 1840 to 1860.
- Evaluate the extent to which the Supreme Court decision in *Brown v. Board of Education of Topeka, Kansas* fostered political and social change in the United States from 1954 to 1965.

Begin by taking about five minutes to evaluate the three questions. Above all, make a pragmatic choice. A common mistake many students make is to choose the question they find the most challenging. Avoid this pitfall. Always choose the question that you know the most about.

2. BEGIN YOUR ESSAY WITH A CLEAR, WELL-DEVELOPED THESIS (1 POINT).

Remember, a thesis statement is your position on the question. Writing a clear, well-developed thesis statement is essential to earning a high score on the long-essay question. Make sure that your thesis fully addresses the entire question.

Here is a clear and fully developed thesis statement for the first question: Evaluate the extent to which the Constitution fostered political and social change in the United States from 1783 to 1800.

> *The Constitution created a new national government based upon the principle that sovereignty rests with the people not the states. This marked a momentous change in American political history. However, the changes in America's political institutions were not matched by equally significant political and social changes for women, Native Americans, and enslaved Africans.*

This thesis statement provides what APUSH scoring commentaries call "a sophisticated thesis." A "sophisticated thesis" is clear, defensible, and also nuanced. A *nuance* is a shade of difference. A one-dimensional thesis would simply state that political change dominated the period between 1783 and 1800. Our sample thesis is nuanced because it notes that *both* political changes and social continuities existed in this period. A nuanced thesis will enable you to present a complex understanding of the historic development that is the focus of the prompt.

3. WRITE A CONTEXTUAL PARAGRAPH (1 POINT).

Now that you have written a sophisticated thesis, your next step is to write a contextualization paragraph. *Contextualization* is a long word for a simple concept—it means describing key historic trends and events taking place just before or at the beginning of the time frame of the question.

> *America's victory in the Revolutionary War created a new nation with vast territory, a diverse and growing population, and a flawed national government. Ratified in 1781, the Articles of Confederation created a loose union among sovereign states. Designed to be a "firm league of friendship," the government lacked a chief executive to enforce its laws and a judiciary to interpret them. The Articles did call for a unicameral Congress. However, it lacked the power to levy taxes, regulate commerce, and enforce unified economic policies. These weaknesses became glaringly apparent when Congress proved unable to raise a militia to suppress Shays' Rebellion.*

4. PROVIDE RELEVANT SUPPORTING EVIDENCE (2 POINTS).

Your opening paragraph asserted a thesis and your second paragraph established its historic context. Your next step is to provide at least two examples of specific historic evidence that support your argument that political changes dominated the period from 1783 to 1800.

The nation's chaotic economy and Shays' Rebellion fueled dissatisfaction with the Articles of Confederation. On May 25, 1787, fifty-five delegates from twelve states gathered in Philadelphia to revive the Articles. However, the delegates quickly abandoned this limited objective and instead created a new national government.

The Framers successfully seized control of America's political destiny. In a bold decision, they transformed sovereignty from the states to the people. For example, their decision to hold popular elections to select members of the House of Representatives marked an unprecedented expansion of democracy.

The new Constitution provided America with a flexible and enduring government that included an amendment process and a division of power among executive, legislative, and judicial branches. The new national government fostered a series of impressive political changes including Washington's successful assertion of federal authority to quell the Whiskey Rebellion and the first peaceful transfer of power following the presidential election of 1800.

5. DEMONSTRATE A COMPLEX UNDERSTANDING (2 POINTS).

Your final task is to demonstrate a complex understanding of the historical developments that are the focus of the prompt. Complexity can be demonstrated in a number of ways. The following section begins by pointing out continuities in the status of women, Native Americans, and enslaved Africans. It concludes by asserting a sophisticated thesis and by providing insightful connections across American history.

Although the Constitution marked the beginning of momentous political changes, it did not initiate the beginning of equally significant social changes. The Constitution's opening words, "We the People," did not extend the revolutionary rhetoric about equality to women, Native Americans, and enslaved Africans. Women did not obtain new rights as the Framers failed to "Remember the Ladies." Native Americans were denied citizenship and continued to lose their lands and their autonomy. Enslaved Africans did benefit from emancipation laws in the North. However, over 90 percent of the slaves lived in the South where conditions did not change.

The continued discrimination against women, Native Americans, and enslaved Africans did not overshadow the historic changes launched by the new Constitution. The Framers successfully altered America's political history. Although women, Native Americans, and enslaved Africans were initially excluded from the American political community, the institutions created by the Framers permitted long-term changes. The Fifteenth Amendment gave African Americans the right to vote and the Nineteenth Amendment extended the suffrage to women. The Indian Citizenship Act of 1924 granted citizenship to all Native Americans. Although belated, these actions demonstrate the Constitution's ability to successfully foster political and social change.